Talk and Social Structure

Talk and Social Structure

Studies in Ethnomethodology and
Conversation Analysis

Edited by
DEIRDRE BODEN AND DON H. ZIMMERMAN

Polity Press

Copyright © this collection Polity Press 1991
Each chapter © the contributor 1991

First published 1991 by Polity Press
in association with Blackwell Publishers

First published in paperback 1993

Editorial office:
Polity Press, 65 Bridge Street,
Cambridge CB2 1UR, UK

Marketing and production:
Blackwell Publishers
108 Cowley Road, Oxford, OX4 1JF, UK

ISBN 0 7456 0446 3
ISBN 0 7456 1240 7

British Library Cataloguing in Publication Data

A CIP catalogue record for this book is available from the British Library.

Typeset in 10 on 12pt Garamond
by Hope Services (Abingdon) Ltd
Printed and bound in Great Britain by
Biddles Ltd, Guildford and King's Lynn

Contents

medical

Contributors

Deirdre Boden, Lecturer in Sociology, Lancaster University

Graham Button, Lecturer in Sociology, Lancaster University

David Greatbatch, University Research Fellow, School of Social Studies, University of Nottingham

Paul ten Have, Associate Professor, Department of Sociology, University of Amsterdam, The Netherlands

John Heritage, Professor, Department of Sociology, University of California, Los Angeles, USA

Robert Hopper, Charles Sapp Centennial Professor of Communication, University of Texas, Austin, USA

Hanneke Houtkoop-Steenstra, Assistant Professor, Department of Dutch, State University, Utrecht, The Netherlands

Douglas W. Maynard, Professor of Sociology, Indiana University, USA

Hugh Mehan, Professor, Department of Sociology, University of California, San Diego, USA

George Psathas, Professor, Department of Sociology, Boston University, Boston, USA

Emanuel A. Schegloff, Professor, Department of Sociology, University of California, Los Angeles, USA

Thomas P. Wilson, Professor, Department of Sociology, University of California, Santa Barbara, USA

Don H. Zimmerman, Professor, Department of Sociology, University of California, Santa Barbara, USA

Preface

This collection presents the work of authors whose lives and work revolve around locations as far apart as Amsterdam in Holland and Austin, York and Madison, Boston and San Diego in the United States. Yet, daily and across these distances, their scholarly activities are animated by shared interest in talk. The debate that provides the focal point for this collection started some years ago at a conference held at the University of California at Santa Barbara in March, 1986. It was a rather special conference, one of those almost inevitably sunny Santa Barbara affairs that took place with the speakers standing against the backdrop of the sparkling Pacific. Several days of lively discussion of the basic issues of "talk and social structure" took both the theme and the participants in many directions, elaborated first in that interactive setting and later with the development of these selected papers. As editors, we have particularly encouraged and appreciated the ways in which the authors presented here have shared their growing and, at times, divergent, discussions with each other, and with us. We feel honored to be able to present the results of this quite intensely and genuinely explored set of issues.

These chapters represent but a small selection of the many fine papers presented at the Talk and Social Structure Conference. We would like therefore to also thank all the participants in the conference for it is their ideas and interest in the general theme and in studies in ethnomethodology and conversation analysis that brings books like this one to fruition, in the fullest sense.

The conference itself was the accomplishment of people working together with the generous support of several organizations. We should like to acknowlege funding support from the Office of the Chancellor, the Office of Research Development and Administration, and the Department of Sociology at UCSB, and a grant from the American Sociological Association.

Particular thanks are due to Harvey Molotch, then Chair of the Department, for his unfailing support and boundless enthusiasm which lent us the energy and instilled the confidence to pursue the conference through to its successful conclusion. Chris Allen, Management Services Office for the Department, provided the indispensable administrative know-how to pull all the threads together, with willing help from Ellie Hyder, Kristin Loft and Rita Schumaker. Thanks are also due to Wayne Mellinger as Conference Coordinator. Steven Clayman and Bill Shay helped where help was needed.

The volume has come together mostly in St Louis, where Stephen Humes was a most willing Editorial Assistant, and the staff of the Department of Sociology at Washington University have provided gracious help and frequent support. We have benefited, too, from the good cheer and editorial precision provided by Polity Press, especially Debbie Seymour and Ann Bone.

Tom P. Wilson, friend, colleague, and co-conspirator, was in at the beginning, and went the distance with us – both with the conference and on the book. Doug Maynard, Jack Whalen and John Heritage have also aided and abetted in all the right ways. Siu Zimmerman lived the conference and the book with us, and was there to make sure it was worth it.

It is possible that detailed study of small phenomena may give an enormous understanding of the way humans do things and the kinds of objects they use to construct and order their affairs. It may well be that things are very finely ordered; that there are collections of social objects . . . that persons assemble to do their activities; that the way they assemble them is describable with respect to any one of the activities they happen to do, and has to be seen by attempting to analyze particular objects.

Harvey Sacks, *"Notes on Methodology"*

It is in talk alone that we can learn our period and ourselves. In short, the first duty of a man is to speak; that is his chief business in this world; and talk, which is the harmonious speech of two or more, is by far the most accessible of pleasures. It costs nothing in money; it completes our education, founds and fosters our friendships, and can be enjoyed at any age and in almost any state of health.

Robert Louis Stevenson, *"Talk and the Talkers"*

PART I

Current Debates

Talk is @ heart of daily life, yet its evanescence has led social scientists to treat it as epiphenomenal to social structure. This book – CA – holds that "talk-in-interaction" provides the fundamental framework of social interaction & social institutions.

Focus: talk-in-interaction & social structure's relationship.

A central task: discover & describe the organization of conversational interaction. How do people use talk to accomplish activities in society? Want to fundamentally rethink concepts such as social structure (Sa.Str).

Social structure central to sociologists, helps them frame res. Qs. One RQ is how talk relates to social structure in the form of age, class, gender. But this may imply that talk is only an indicator of the structure, not part of how it is constructed. Talk does construct social structure, too. Claims sociolx see talk as a product of social forces (e.g. Labov). Much of sociology assumes that structures are bigger than actions & that lg structures such as institutions thus determine individual action. This volume presents alternative: talk helps shape (but does not determine) actions. Defines structure, social pg 5-6.

Ethnomethodology says we need to look at members' methodical practices to see how they produce & make sense of actions. The char. of social structure is thus found in local & particular detail of practical actions. This the focus of empirical study in ethnomethodology.

Talk is social interaction hence term t-in-interaction. The organization of talk allows us to do interactional tasks. Talk is both:
1) context-free – allowing for contextual variations such as changing identities of speakers & #s of spkers, content, etc
2) contextually-sensitive – relates to the local circumstances of particular turns in particular conversations

The "resources for mutual understdg are found in the fundmtl nature of sequencing." p18

mutual understdg is a methodical achievement.

Agency arises as spkers design their talk for specific audiences & hearers interpret talk as such. Spkers can avoid the expected response (say Q-A), but are held accountable as a result & their actions set up expectations of future sequential actions.

Social structure is a member's notion related to external states of affairs to which members are oriented (Wilson, p 11). Schegloff says the machinery of talk is invariant to historical progression & cultural variation. [! Reisman? Tannen?]

To the extent that talk's organization is general, modifications to unique forms for different institutional settings should be rare. The in sistr factors work to modify the default mechanisms of everyday talk.

Talk in institutional settings notable for systematic patterns & systematic absences of patterns (e.g. set order of who can talk & what content in courtroom; lack of acknowledgement token by interviewers). Need to note 1) machinery of talk, 2) discourse identities of participants, & 3) recurrent pattern of normatively oriented to strated identities (p.13). Examine the talk to find what is normative & oriented to.

Claims that multiparty groups tend to break into dyadic talk constraints (as in courtrooms) that work to keep 'shared attentiveness' to one line of talk. Provides a few example (pp 14-16) incl. 'perspective-display series' Maynard

look at Drew's section for comments on institutional talk

Overviews 3 parts book
Structure-in-action articulates the agency/structure relationship. Talk sequentially & locally reproduces social structure. Action & structure are essentially reflexive, making available, via talk, structure-in-action.

1

Structure-in-Action: An Introduction

Don H. Zimmerman and Deirdre Boden

Talk is at the heart of everyday existence. It is pervasive and central to human history, in every setting of human affairs, at all levels of society, in virtually every social context. Yet the evanescence of speech has led social scientists to treat it almost always as epiphenomenal to the affairs, actions, and even accidents of human actors, and, across time, to social structure. In the chapters that follow, in a variety of voices, a different view is offered, one that holds that talk – more precisely, talk-in-interaction (Schegloff 1987a) – provides the fundamental framework of social interaction and social institutions.

The guiding concern of this collection is thus the relationship between talk-in-interaction and social structure. The chapters that make up this volume trace this relationship in part as an elaboration of the tension between action and structure as debated within sociology and beyond, and even more directly as part of an active set of issues current within ethnomethodology and conversation analysis.

As will be evident throughout the pages of this book, practitioners of these approaches entertain some conceptual and methodological reservations concerning the issue of the connection between conversational interaction and the so-called "larger contexts" of social action. One tack has been to put aside such questions as premature and unprofitable diversions from the central task of discovering and describing the organization of conversational interaction as such (Schegloff 1987a, and chapter 3 below). Much of the sensitivity on this issue derives from a wariness toward conventional understandings of sociology in which, as we suggest below, questions of "social structure" are assumed to have priority over the detailed investigation of the organization of talk-in-interaction as an object of study (see Button, chapter 11 below; cf. Coser 1975a; Zimmerman 1976).

The issue need not however be framed in this fashion. Schegloff (1987a:208) has suggested that the organization of conversational activities such as turn-taking functions to "enable" a broad range of social activities (cf. also Goffman 1971, 1983a:4; and Giddens 1984). In this formulation, the question of how actors deploy the mechanisms of talk-in-interaction to accomplish institutionally oriented activities (see below, Wilson, chapter 2, Heritage and Greatbatch, chapter 5, ten Have, chapter 6, Maynard, chapter 7) is important if, for example, we are to specify the extent to which these interactional mechanisms enable the production and reproduction of the varieties of social formations found in society.

Moreover, a concern for understanding the enabling character of the mechanisms of talk-in-interaction does not deny the importance of the study of mundane conversation in its own right. Quite to the contrary, the role talk plays in accomplishing the structural or institutional features of activities and settings cannot be properly understood without reference to more basic mechanisms of mundane or everyday conversation, as Wilson emphasizes in chapter 2 and Heritage and Greatbatch explore in some detail in chapter 5. On this view, then, study of the organization of mundane conversation is central for understanding social interaction as well as for elucidating social structure as an everyday, practical accomplishment (cf. Garfinkel and Sacks 1970).

The authors in this volume all share common ground in arguing for a fundamental rethinking of the constituent issues attending the question of talk and social structure. These constituent elements include, for example, how to conceive of the notion of social structure itself (see especially Wilson, chapter 2, Mehan, chapter 4, Psathas, chapter 8, Hopper, chapter 9); how to appropriately demonstrate the relationship of external, "large scale" structural constraints to the detailed local achievement of orderly patterns of talk-in-interaction (for instance, Wilson, chapter 2, Schegloff, chapter 3, Mehan, chapter 4, Heritage and Greatbatch, chapter 5); and how the organization of talk-in-interaction itself "enables" or constitutes the structures of social action which characterize both mundane and institutional settings (see Heritage and Greatbatch, chapter 5, ten Have, chapter 6, Maynard, chapter 7). All of these studies address finely ordered "small phenomena"[1] in order to understand "the way humans do things" (Sacks 1984:24). Indeed, a central argument that is woven through this collection, in a variety of ways, is that social structure is something humans do (see for instance Hopper, chapter 9).

Our purpose here is to provide a context for these discussions within a framework that illuminates key characteristics of the chapters that follow, both as they inform a broad range of social scientific issues and as they develop quite important specific elements of the joint enterprise of ethnomethodology and conversation analysis. We will be thus less interested in providing an exposition of particular chapters than with presenting the conceptual and analytic concerns that animate the work represented in this volume.

"Social structure" is obviously one of these concerns. Accordingly, we begin with a brief discussion of the concept.

The Concept of Social Structure

The concept of social structure is central to the way sociologists view social phenomena and frame their research questions. One such question is that of the connection between social structure, for example in the form of age, sex, or class categories, and the features of everyday language use. Posed in this fashion, situated activities like talk are, in Goffman's words, treated as "effects", that is, as indicators, expressions or symptoms of social structures such as relationships, informal groups, age grades, gender, ethnic minorities, social classes and the like, with no great concern to treat these effects as data in their own terms (1983a:2).

Social structure, in this conventional view, is taken to condition or "cause" social conduct, and social interaction itself can be treated as the intersection between structurally located actors and events (for example, Blau 1977; Burt 1982; Hechter 1983). Within this received view, to speak of the relation between talk and social structure presumes that observed forms of talk-in-interaction are dependent on and determined by structural arrangements. In such a framework, talk and, indeed, all interaction of actual actors in social situations is seen as a *product* of those social forces. Sociolinguists, for instance, routinely accept such a premise in their studies of social structure in relation to variation in linguistic features (Labov 1972; Hudson 1980). Culture can similarly function as an explanatory context for verbal interaction (Gumperz 1982).

Rather obviously, the term "social structure" is composed of two elements. One element, "structure," refers to some domain of orderly relationships among specified units, that is, the site of regular, repetitive, nonrandom events that stand in a systematic relationship to one another (Smelser 1988:103). The concept of structure is undeniably central to and enormously useful for sociological inquiry in general; the problem becomes one of not allowing it to take on an analytic life of its own. All too easily, in sociology, "social structure" assumes the properties of what

Merleau-Ponty has called the "retrospective illusion" (1968), namely that
having conceptualized, for example, a web of patterned social relations
external to and prior to ourselves we then *retrospectively* assume its
predominance "over" us.[2]

The other element – the "social" – specifies the nature of the domain of
orderly phenomenon, a task Durkheim self-consciously undertook when
he attempted to demonstrate the social (as opposed, for example, to
psychological or biological) causation of phenomena such as suicide
(Durkheim 1952). The social, in Durkheimian terms, implicates a
collective (as opposed to individual) phenomenon, and an emergent level
of analysis (Durkheim 1938; Lukes 1972:16–22; cf. Parsons 1937:378–86;
Giddens 1971:86–91). It is also understood to refer to arrangements that
vary across time and space and between different groups of people.

The term thus locates the phenomena of sociological interest in societal
arrangements that shape everyday experience and conduct in often
unrecognized ways (see Parsons 1937; cf. Giddens 1984:5–14). Similarly,
institutions and organizations are thought to exercise related causal
influence. Thus, the notion *builds in* a metaphor of scale – for example,
Tilly's (1984) "big structures" and "large processes" – as well as a
standard for assessing sociological significance: since social structure
forms the presumptive context of activities of lesser scale, such as social
interaction, it is ultimately the fundamental explanatory resource and
hence the arbiter of which research questions are interesting and
important, and which are not (Coser 1975b; cf. Collins 1981, 1987).

Implicitly or explicitly, the contributors to this volume challenge this
conception of social structure, and the consequences that flow from it (its
determinism, for example), which trivializes questions of human agency
and practical reasoning; and the fact that it narrowly circumscribes the
very notion of social structure itself by equating it with "large scale"
arrangements. This challenge needs to be understood against the
backdrop of ethnomethodology and conversation analysis.

Ethnomethodology

A fundamental insight of ethnomethodology is that the primordial site of
social order is found in members' use of methodical practices to produce,
make sense of, and thereby render accountable, features of their local
circumstances. In so doing, they constitute these circumstances as a real-
world setting of practical action. As an alternative to the assumption that
social order is ultimately found only at the aggregate level of social life –
expressed in differential rates and distributions of social activities, in

statistical associations between such variables, or in social formations that lie behind observed large-scale regularities – ethnomethodology turns instead to the detailed study of how the features of social life are recurrently accomplished on singular occasions through these incarnate practices (Garfinkel 1988). Indeed, Garfinkel elsewhere persuasively argues that even the grand enterprise of the natural or "discovering sciences" is analyzable as the practical management of the contingencies of everyday, *in situ*, laboratory specific, workbench activities[3] (Garfinkel 1988; Garfinkel et al. 1986). The socially structured character of the sciences or of *any* enterprise undertaken by members is thus not exterior or extrinsic to their everyday workings, but interior and intrinsic, residing in the local and particular detail of practical actions undertaken by members uniquely competent to do so.

This focus on situated activities has transformed what is ordinarily taken for granted by members and social scientists alike into ethnomethodology's problematic. Thus, the methodical ways in which members produce, recognize, and render accountable actions-in-context here become the focus of empirical study. Obviously, this is not to say that all ethnomethodologists would agree with the central role accorded to talk-in-interaction in the investigation of situated action emphasized in this introduction, and in the chapters that comprise this volume. See, for example, Garfinkel et al. (1986), and a number of related studies such as those by Lynch (1985), Livingston (1986), and Liberman (1986), as well as the work of Coulter (1979, 1989), Pollner (1988), and others (cf. Sharrock and Anderson 1986; Maynard and Clayman 1991).

Accountability should not be thought of as simply the provision of descriptions, stories, excuses, or the like (Scott and Lyman 1968). Instead, stress should be placed on the practices that secure the *accountability* of actions-in-context, that is, the detailed, collaborative ways in which members manage their conduct and their circumstances to achieve the observably orderly features of their activities. As Garfinkel has noted:

> any social setting [should] be viewed as self-organizing with respect to the intelligible character of its own appearances . . . Any setting organizes its activities to make its properties as an organized environment of practical activities detectable, countable, recordable, reportable, tell-a-story-aboutable, analyzable – in short, *accountable*. (1967:33)

In making activities accountable, members produce and reproduce the features of social structure, in particular its cohort independence, facticity, and constraining character (cf. Garfinkel and Sacks 1970; Cicourel 1981a). And, as we shall suggest shortly, it is in the accomplishment of accountable activities that *agency* emerges not as a metaphysical principle or a members' illusion but as an essential feature of the organization of social interaction. The detailed workings of this organization are the subject matter both of ethnomethodology and conversation analysis, to which we turn next.

Talk-in-Interaction

The term "talk-in-interaction" (Schegloff 1987a) reminds us that talking with one another is social interaction, and that talk is ubiquitous in social life. Furthermore, it has become increasingly clear over two decades of research in conversation analysis that talk is very orderly indeed. It is, moreover, organized by use of machinery deployed in and adapted to local contingencies of interaction across an immense variety of social settings and participants (Heritage 1984a, 1985a; Schegloff 1987a, 1987b; Zimmerman 1988). For example, whenever, wherever, and by whomever, turns have to be taken, encounters have to be opened and closed, questions asked and answered, requests made and granted or denied, assessments offered and seconded, and so forth. The organization of talk provides the formal resources to accomplish these interactional tasks, and deploys these resources in a manner that is sensitive to just what circumstances and participants happen to be at hand – which is to say *locally*. The shape of talk found in a specific site thus reflects the context-sensitive (and thus particularized) application of a more general, context-free (and thus anonymous) interactional mechanism.

This understanding of the organization of talk-in-interaction has emerged from an approach in which information concerning the setting or occasion, the identity and relationship of the participants, and other "contextual" materials do not figure systematically in the analysis, except insofar as such features are oriented to by the participants[4] (Schegloff chapter 3 below). As an analytic strategy, this tack has yielded impressive results (cf. Heritage 1984a, 1985a). The treatment of conversation as a virtually autonomous domain emerges from a methodological strategy which directs that conversational data be examined for what they will reveal in their own terms. That is, data are not selected for their relevance to some standard sociological problem, but instead are examined for the questions they might raise or the discoveries they might permit (Sacks 1984).

Viewed as activities in their own right, conversational structures are therefore examined in their own terms as specimens of concrete social interaction. Since the primary object of investigation is elucidation of the

organization of talk-in-interaction as such, the presumptive relevance
of standard sociological concerns such as the nature of the setting or
the social identities of participants is suspended (cf. Zimmerman 1988:
408).

This "analytic isolation" (Sharrock and Anderson 1987:316) or
"autonomy principle" (Zimmerman 1988:416–17) should not be construed
to imply that conversational interaction is a realm of activity empirically
disconnected from societal and institutional formations, much less from
other, more proximate contexts (cf. Goffman 1983a; Zimmerman
1984:210; Boden forthcoming). Indeed, the contributors to this collection
have variously considered how conversational mechanisms (including
turn-taking) act to "enable" the local achievement and reproduction of
institutional and organizational patterns in society (see, for instance,
below, Psathas, chapter 8, Hopper, chapter 9 and Houtkoop, chapter 10;
see also Schegloff 1987a:208). We will return shortly to a more extended
discussion of the sense in which institutions are "talked" into being
(Heritage 1984a:290; see also Heritage and Greatbatch, chapter 5 below,
and Maynard, chapter 7). At this juncture, however, it is appropriate to
consider the way conversation analysis focuses on sequential organization,
particularly as it influences the issue of the relationship between talk and
social structure.

Sequential organization

Conversation analysis has focused on the organization of conversational
interaction as such, and in particular on the analysis of its endogenously
generated sequential opportunities and constraints as these are observed
to operate turn by turn within conversations across diverse occasions,
different participants, and distinct languages (Boden 1983; Ren 1989).
Thus, for conversation analysis, the varieties of sequential organization –
the turn-taking system for managing the construction, allocation turns at
talk, sequences for entry into and exit from conversation, and for the
repair of trouble or for doing invitations, requests, assessments, and the
like – provide the structure for conversational encounters, and talk-in-
interaction more generally. As a consequence, the sequential environment
of talk provides the primary context for participants' understanding,
appreciation and use of what is being said, meant and, most importantly,
done in and through the talk (Schegloff and Sacks 1973).

Heritage provides a convenient account of this "architecture of
intersubjectivity" furnished by sequential organization (1984a:254ff.):

conversational interaction is structured by an organization of action which is implemented on a turn-by-turn basis. By means of this organization, *a context of publically displayed and continuously updated intersubjective understandings is systematically sustained*. It is through this "turn by turn" character of talk that the participants display their understandings of the state of "the talk for one another" . . . Mutual understanding is thus displayed, to use Garfinkel's term, "incarnately" in the sequentially organized details of conversational interaction. Moreover, because these understandings are publically produced, they are available as a resource for social scientific analysis. (p. 259)[5]

It bears repeating that what is at issue for the achievement of mutual understanding and coordinated action is not resolved by reference to shared symbol systems which encode and decode the meaning and import of the talk. Instead, the resources for mutual understanding are found in the fundamental nature of sequencing – that the elements of interaction are not merely serially realized as "once and for all" objects but are rather *actions* that are *shaped* and *reshaped* over the course of the talk. The initiation of an action and the response to it create the immediate sequential context of these events, and occasions as well as exhibits the participants' analysis and understanding of the unfolding course of the interaction. Mutual understanding is thus a methodical *achievement* employing the resources provided by the mechanisms of conversational interaction (Garfinkel 1967:38–42; Heritage 1984a:259).

Agency

The sequential organization of participants' talk-in-interaction does not, however, imply that members are judgmental dopes (Garfinkel 1984) programmed to enact the requirements of sequential structure in lock-step fashion. To take an elementary example, the occurrence of a question strongly projects an answer as a next positioned action, but questions can be evaded, ignored, challenged, or otherwise operated on and transformed by the recipient. Such moves may themselves initiate new sequences (for repairing, blaming, accusing, arguing, etc.; see, for instance, Whalen, Zimmerman and Whalen 1988) through which participants' motives, intentions, goodwill or its opposite, etc., are displayed and disputed through the orderly operation of the sequential machinery of talk. In short, participants can (and do) evade, bend, or violate the constraints established by the current sequential environment of their talk. But such work is itself accountable and also constitutive of a sequential context for further actions.

Note that sequential organization shapes conduct through the locally administered, turn-by-turn architecture of intersubjectivity sketched above. This endogenous process of turn-by-turn understanding depends on the presumption by all parties to the interaction that any particular turn was intended – and accordingly shaped – for the specific audience at hand (recipient design). Current speaker is held accountable for so designing her or his action, and hearers are likewise accountable for understanding current speaker's action *as* so designed. Consequently, what a participant *does* in talking or in responding to another's talk is warrantably used as information concerning his or her intentions, motives, character, and the like (Heritage 1984a:245–64, 1989).

From the viewpoint of Wilson (1989), what we have just described is *human agency*, understood to be intrinsic to the machinery that organizes social interaction. He suggests that there can be no social interaction without participants *acting* on the assumption that they as well as their co-participants are autonomous, morally responsible agents whose actions are neither determined nor random. The organization of interaction builds in such an assumption as a fundamental principle.

Viewed this way, agency must be understood as a basic *members'* notion (as, it turns out, is *social structure* – see below). Wilson argues: "From a scientific point of view, agency cannot be explained, since it cannot be reduced to either determinism (hard or soft) or randomness without destroying the essential quality of agency (just as miracles cannot be explained without destroying their quality as miracles)" (1989). By recognizing that agency is a members' notion, the reality of agency *for* the member is preserved. For the analyst, the reality of agency is bracketed, and it instead becomes a topic for non-ironic inquiry. As noted above, a fundamental sense of agency characterizes the workings of sequential organization in everyday interaction.

Structure-in-Action

We have just argued that agency is a members' notion. And we alluded to Wilson (chapter 2 below) as suggesting that social structure is also a members' notion pertaining to external states of affairs to which members are oriented. "Orientation to social structure" refers to the fact that members recognize, respond to, and render accountable such conventional objects as "categories of institutional identity, [and] the activities associated with those categories" (see p. 26).

By treating social structure as an object that members attend to as a condition and resource for organizing various occasions of interaction for particular kinds of action and inference, Wilson provides an alternative way to conceive of the talk/social structure linkage. He proposes that social structures, institutions, organizations, and like social formations are conventional, culturally variable, and historically contingent whereas, as Sacks, Schegloff and Jefferson (1974:724–7) note, the machinery of conversation is both context sensitive and context-free. In short, Schegloff's "enabling institution," that is, the machinery of talk-in-interaction, is not subject to negotiation (unlike those social formations based on convention) and, strictly speaking, should not be referred to as an institution at all. This machinery is assumed to underlie the construction of conventions of all sorts, and to be invariant to historical progression and cultural variation. The organization of talk-in-interaction is thus basic or primordial[6] (cf. Sacks, Schegloff and Jefferson 1974; Schegloff 1987a:208).

From this perspective, the mechanisms of mundane conversation organize the basic forms of social action and interaction out of which patterns of repetitive activity taken to be evidence of social structure are built. Consideration of the contribution of talk-in-interaction to the constitution of institutional settings (and the production of social structure) will show how this fundamental organization operates as an "enabling" mechanism for institutional modes of conduct. Extending the study of talk-in-interaction to those occasions of talk demonstrably oriented to institutional or organizational aspects of settings is a first approximation to understanding how forms of talk-in-interaction are selected, adapted and combined – in a word, configured – to reflexively produce and reproduce social structure.

In these terms, then, the pertinent question becomes: how to move from the analysis of conversational organization as it operates in everyday life to its specification or modification in diverse settings to build and animate a variety of social formations. As noted earlier, this is not a matter of the institutional setting "causing" or creating some distinctive verbal format.[7] To the extent that conversational organization is general, forms of talk unique to institutional settings should be rare. Instead, we should expect to find mundane forms selected and shaped to address the interactional contingencies of a given setting. It is the constellation of *in situ* contingencies and the configuration of conversational machinery assembled to deal with them that generate the structures of social action in and of a particular site.

Talk oriented to institutional settings

Talk oriented to institutional settings involves repetitive episodes that, within a constrained range of variation, exhibit a similar structure.[8] Relative to the wide range of mundane conversations and the diversity of conversationalists, occasions of "institutional talk" appear to involve recurrent and relatively specialized sets of situated identities[9] as well as a concentration and modification of particular machinery (Heritage 1984a; Whalen and Zimmerman 1987). In addition, certain tokens or sequences may not occur in the environments they ordinarily inhabit in everyday talk (see below).

Accordingly, the structure of institutional talk minimally consists of the recurrent pattern of normatively oriented-to,[10] situated identities along with the corresponding discourse identities and the conversational machinery through which the work allotted to participants assuming such identities is done. In the case of television news interviews, for example, interviewer–interviewee are the oriented-to identities which allocate (and constrain) certain discourse activities, for example, asking questions and giving answers (see Heritage and Greatbatch, chapter 5 below).

We should note, however, that this formulation does not assert that only "institutional identities" are assumed in formal settings, or that they are continuously relevant (Schegloff 1987a:214–20). Obviously, any workplace will yield numerous instances of "informal" or "conversational" interaction, either within the phases or interstices of task activity or interwoven with the work itself (see ten Have, chapter 6 below; see also Whalen and Zimmerman 1987:176–8). In the analysis of institutional interaction, care must be taken to demonstrate, in the details of conduct, the "normatively oriented-to" or interactionally relevant identities (see Schegloff, chapter 3 below).

Conventional constraints on turn-taking

Consider as an example the case of a "procedurally consequential" (see Schegloff, p. 52 below) connection between talk and social structure: the conventional configuration of speech exchange systems characteristic of a variety of "formal settings" involving multiple participants – meetings of various kinds, legal settings such as courtrooms and official hearings, classrooms, press conferences, etc. (Atkinson 1982: Atkinson and Drew 1979; McHoul 1978; Mehan 1979; Schegloff 1987a; Greatbatch 1988;

Boden, forthcoming). In Atkinson's terms, mundane conversational practices may not appropriately address one of the basic requirements of settings of this sort, namely "achieving and sustaining the shared attentiveness of co-present parties to a single sequence of actions" (Atkinson 1982:97). In multiparty situations, the conversational turn-taking system exhibits a bias toward a "breakdown" into two-party talk. Without some constraint on turn-taking, the parties present could divide into a number of smaller conversational groupings rather than attend to a single focus of attention.

Other "problems" for formal interaction posed by the conversational turn-taking system is the lack of systematic constraint on the type of turn that particular participants may take, or on who may attempt to speak next.[11] In ordinary conversation, turn size, turn content and type, and turn order are free to vary, that is, they are locally and interactionally determined (see Sacks, Schegloff and Jefferson 1974). In courtrooms, meetings, media interviews, press conferences and other occasions when a number of people gather to conduct business of some sort, various conventionally specified, systematic modifications of the turn system for mundane conversation can be found. These (usually explicit) modifications may involve pre-allocation of turn – who may speak in what order; pre-allocation of turn type – what kind of turn a particular participant may produce and turn mediation – the conferral of special rights (for instance, to a judge or moderator) to determine who may speak when, what they may say, when they must stop, and the like (Atkinson 1982:102–3; Atkinson and Drew 1979; Heritage and Greatbatch 1986 and chapter 5 below; Schegloff 1987a; Clayman 1988, 1989; Clayman and Whalen 1989; Boden forthcoming).

Such conventional constraints on turn-taking transform the speech exchange of ordinary conversation to provide both for the organization of activity requisite for the kind of task addressed, and for the recognizability of the activity as a form of institutional interaction (Atkinson 1982; Levinson 1979; cf. Schegloff 1988a). It is worthwhile noting here that ordinary conversation and its turn-taking system remains the "default" option when, for whatever reason, participants move away from an alternative turn-taking system (see Clayman and Whalen 1989; Schegloff 1989). The speech exchange system constituting mundane conversation is the base from which other systems depart.

The implication is clear: the general mechanisms of conversation – in this case, the speech exchange system – can be made responsive to a set of contingencies that are posed by particular tasks, the accomplishment of which relies (in whole or in part) on talk-in-interaction. These contingencies can reasonably be expected to vary across tasks (and settings); hence, the particular configuration of talk will also vary, although within limits imposed by the stable, underlying mechanisms of conversational interaction.

Situated adaptation and modification

Conventional constraints on the character of speech exchange systems are not the only way conversational interaction might be marshalled to enable the enactment of a particular setting or social occasion. As Heritage (1984a:239–41) has suggested, such mechanisms may be adapted and differentially deployed in specialized or modified form to constitute distinctive patterns of talk in particular settings.

For example, many calls to emergency numbers (police, fire, paramedics) are, like other service encounters over the telephone, organized via an adjacency-pair insertion/expansion sequence. A complaint or request for assistance (a first pair part) is followed by a series of question/answer pairs which elicit information relevant to servicing the request. When the insertion sequence is concluded, the delayed second pair part, the response to the request is provided (Zimmerman 1984; Whalen and Zimmerman 1987; Whalen, Zimmerman and Whalen 1988).[12]

The mechanisms involved – particularly the insertion sequence – are plainly part of the organization of mundane conversation, and similar extended interrogations can be observed in casual encounters (see Schegloff 1987a). What is distinctive about the case of emergency calls is the configuration of these mechanisms, not only, for example, what devices are routinely present and in what form, but which are routinely absent in environments in which they might ordinarily occur.[13]

In the case of emergency calls, the parties are aligned as anonymous seeker of service and provider of service in a specialized and reduced opening sequence[14] prior to the initiation of the insertion sequence (Whalen and Zimmerman 1987; Zimmerman, forthcoming). The turns involved in the insertion sequence are relatively "austere," that is, they are tightly focused and generally contain, respectively, only a question and only an answer, these being addressed to a relatively narrow range of standard issues, such as the nature of the problem, its location, and other items relevant to police work. Further, calls of this type have a single piece of business to accomplish – they are "monotopical" in this sense – and the completion of that business (marked by the delivery of a response to the initial request) provides the relevance of closing. Where other components are found in the turns comprising the insertion sequence, such components are usually the source of, or directed to the repair of, some trouble in the interaction (Whalen, Zimmerman and Whalen 1988).

While many of the mechanisms of conversational organization have been subjected to fine-grained description and analysis, the actual distribution of particular mechanisms or sequences has received less attention. It should be noted that the import of such distributional facts, like the density (or the sparseness) with which some mechanism is deployed across occasions of a given type (as in the case of insertion/ expansion sequences in emergency calls discussed just above), rests on a prior description and analysis of the mechanism and its functions. It is not simply the systematic presence (or absence) of a mechanism that is of interest, but rather what that systematic presence (or absence) is *doing on and for* such occasions.

For example, Maynard's contribution to this volume describes a "perspective-display series" which physicians in a clinic dealing with developmental disabilities employ to elicit parents' assessment of their child's "problem." This mode of delivery is an alternative to a "straightforward" delivery which does not seek prior assessment by the parents. Tactically, the perspective-display series appears to be deployed when the physician has some basis to assume that the parents' assessment can be brought in line with the clinical results. This means the distressing diagnostic news occurs in an environment of agreement, that is, an environment prepared by the solicited parents' assessment followed by the physician's report of the clinical findings which aligns a professional opinion with a lay perception of the problem.

This type of sequence is not unique to lay–professional interactions in medical settings. Nor is it targeted to specifically medical issues, for it addresses the interactional issue of accomplishing agreement or alignment between the parties. Maynard (1989c) reports that the perspective-display series can be observed in ordinary conversation, where (in the data Maynard consulted) it is deployed in manner which may be characterized as "cautious" or even "delicate." For example, the sequence was observed in initial encounters between unacquainted parties who faced the task of "getting to know one another," which entailed, among other things, the sometimes delicate task of discovering each other's views on an array of topics (Maynard and Zimmerman 1984). Thus, a procedure usable for cautious probing in everyday talk is adapted to (and becomes a stable feature of) the interactionally delicate circumstances of a particular kind of medical encounter. In the case of diagnostic news delivery, achieving an alignment is relevant to the receptivity of parents to the diagnosis as a medical characterization of the child's developmental status and future prospects.

The point to be stressed is that while there are persistent, widespread contingencies of interaction that must be respected for talk as talk to proceed, the response to these contingencies may be achieved through the adaptation of general mechanisms to their management in specific circumstances in which local requirements pose additional issues. Whatever structures can be demonstrated "generally" (that is, across many and various mundane conversations) may also be shown to have repetitive, particular, specialized configurations, and the shape of these configurations as they are deployed both prepare and shape the setting "in" which they occur as well as having consequences for the concerted, connected activities of the setting in question. The "fitting" of these mechanisms to the work of constituting institutional settings locates the intersection of general contingencies of talk-in-interaction with the specific requirements of particular situated activity systems.

Conclusion

Structure, as defined throughout this discussion, is accomplished in and through the moment-to-moment turn-taking procedures of everyday talk in both mundane and momentous settings of human intercourse (see Whalen, Zimmerman and Whalen 1988; Boden 1990). The instantiation of structure is, moreover, a local and contingent matter, one that is endogenous to interaction and shaped by it. The enabling mechanisms of everyday talk thus practically and accountably accomplish structure-in-action.

The chapters that follow are organized to provide three areas of exploration of this general topic of talk and social structure. Part I continues with the writings of Wilson, Schegloff and Mehan to provide the range of this debate. These authors, as noted above, disagree in certain important and analytically consequential ways about *how* the relation between talk and structure is to be addressed. Their differences form an important base on which the materials in part II and part III may be assessed. They share, moreover, much common ground in arguing the need to redefine and respecify conventional sociological notions of action and structure.

These concerns are picked up, rather explicitly yet highly ethnomethodologically, in part II where what Heritage and Greatbatch call "the institutional character of institutional talk" (chapter 5) is developed in several distinct ways: in the context of television news interviews, in medical interactions (ten Have, chapter 6) and in clinical settings (Maynard, chapter 7). These chapters explore, in different ways, central and currently debated issues by extending basic agendas of ethnomethodology and conversation analysis into broader institutional domains

[margin annotation: Part I]

[margin annotation: Part II]

while, at the same time, retaining an essential focus on interactional settings. The data addressed by each of these authors consists of conversational materials recorded in and specifically organized in relation to their institutional domains, whether television broadcasting, clinical settings or health care delivery environments.

Part III

Finally, in part III, the theme returns to what Heritage has appropriately termed the "primacy of mundane conversation" (1984a:238–40), namely to the ordinary, everyday conversational settings out of which social life is constituted, turn by turn. A central position of conversation analysis is, as noted, that the basic mechanisms – or structures – of naturally occurring conversation is a kind of "bedrock" out of which all other forms of interaction are built, whether the formal mechanisms of courtrooms and classrooms and tribunals, or the institutionally mediated settings described above. At the heart of all verbal interaction, it is argued, are the "structures of social action" (Atkinson and Heritage 1984) through which all manner of human intercourse is achieved. In chapter 8, for example, Psathas shows that the everyday activity of giving and receiving directions is an interactionally structured activity in which actors collaborate in the ongoing production and comprehension of directions. Hopper (chapter 9) looks at the technical innovation of the "call holding" device now available as an everyday, touchtone service which is – quite clearly, as Hopper demonstrates – both an enabling and interactionally constraining condition of modern talk. However, rather than conventionally locating talk as constrained by technology, Hopper shows how the finely tuned and local conversational devices used by interactants to put each other on hold consequentially structure the unfolding interaction. Houtkoop's discussion of the fine-grained specifics of Dutch telephone openings similarly demonstrates the patterned ways in which cultural contingencies are achieved as quite systematic and sequential sorts of social organization. In chapter 11, Button develops an elegant argument for the ways in which interactants blend conversational and interactional commitment and thereby construct, through the ongoing course of their talk, a sense of what he calls conversation-in-a-series, namely that members create *in and through* their talk their shared sense of a "standing" relationship (p. 251 below). Throughout part III, then, the basic turn-taking procedures of everyday talk are seen to be routinely and recurrently available to member and analyst alike as a way of understanding what Goffman (1983a) earlier referred to as the interaction order.

Structure-in-action is thus proposed as a relatively new way of articulating the agency/structure intersection. The work of the ethnomethodologists and conversation analysts throughout these chapters repeatedly attests the essentially and unavoidably *sequential* and *local* coherence of social interaction and social organization. Social structure, on this view, is not something "out there" independent of members' activities, nor are the structures of social action located at the unobservable level of Durkheim's collective. Rather, they are the practical accomplishment of members of society. Members can and must make their actions available and reasonable to each other and, in so doing, the everyday organization of experience *produces* and *reproduces* the patterned and patterning qualities we have come to call social structure. The organization of talk displays the essential reflexivity of action and structure and, in so doing, makes available what we are calling structure-in-action.

Notes

1 The issue of scale is important to what follows since much sociological convention massively assumes, as noted below, that structure is somehow *bigger* than action, and that a central concern of sociology is (and should be) on how large-scale structures are *determinative* of individual action (see Parsons 1937; Durkheim 1938) and on how such social forces shape the "human-size" (Collins 1988) events of everyday life. An alternative to this view is presented in this volume, namely, of talk-in-interaction (and social interaction more generally) as a social institution which pervasively organizes and shapes, but does not determine actions or their outcomes.

2 See, in this regard, Garfinkel's (1967:66–75) discussion of the "judgmental dope."

3 The rational achievements of the sciences remain unchanged under this treatment, that is, their objectivity, generality, and so on. What is changed is the recognition that these properties are the ongoing accomplishment of the worksite-specific, endogenous structures of practical action (Garfinkel 1988).

4 The commitment of conversation analysis to formal, sequential analysis has been subject to criticism, the gist of which is that such an approach is unsociological. Schegloff (1988a:96) notes Goffman's suggestions that the requirements and constraints of sequential structures of concern to conversation analysis are "what would appear to be the sheer physical constraints of any communication system" and that conversation analysis deals "with talk as a communications engineer might, someone optimistic about the possibility of culture-free formulations" (Goffman 1981:14–15). Schegloff goes on to comment, "Many [conversation analysis] concerns are included here, concerns with the distribution of turns, with evidence that messages are getting through, devices for attracting, retaining and displaying attention, for participant identification, forms for dealing with trouble in the talk – all these are described in a dismissive idiom as of no special interest, and as the subject matter for some other discipline than sociology or anthropology" (1988a:96). Schegloff further notes Goffman's (1983b) claim that the concerns of

conversation analysis are peripheral to sociological ones, and he suggests that Goffman does not recognize "that the constitution of some form of talk as some recognizable action can involve its sequential placement, its selection of words by reference to recipient design considerations or its correction mid-course . . . *What could be more social than the constitution of social action, and its implementation in interaction*" (1988a:99, emphasis added).

5 The "architecture" described here does not merely organize responses of second utterances to a first. It also applies to "first" utterances, for the initiation of some sequence itself displays an analysis "that 'then and there' is an appropriate place for that to occur" (Heritage 1984a:259).

6 One sense of "primordial" is that the machinery of conversation addresses fundamental issues which must be dealt with in order for interaction to proceed. Schegloff, commenting on the treatment of turn-taking as merely a "politeness" issue, proposes the following *gedankenexperiment* which posits "a society with *no* turn-taking system . . . [I]t would not be one that was especially impolite or uncivil. It would be one in which *the very possibility – the assured possibility of coordinated action through talk had been lost*, for example, the sense of one action as *responsive* to another" (1988a:98, emphasis in original). See also Sacks, Schegloff and Jefferson 1974; Heritage, 1984a:245–53.

7 It is essential to emphasize that we do not view talk-in-interaction that does "institutional" work to be in some sense "dependent on" institutional setting. Such imagery is natural in the received view of social structure discussed earlier, but it is seriously misleading for it wrongly supposes that institutional settings are some how constituted and can be recognized entirely independently of the actions occurring within them. Instead, measurement of "institutional setting" as the "independent" variable is irremediably confounded with measurement of "configuration of talk" as the dependent variable. Consequently, the relationship between the two is, from a structural-equation point of view, entirely circular, and any model involving it is hopelessly underidentified. From an ethnomethodological perspective, the relation is essentially *reflexive*, where such reflexive relations are not a methodological nuisance but an essential property of social action.

8 The observed structure is an interactional accomplishment. As such, it reflects participants' "coming to terms" with the actual situation in which they act (including each others' actions) rather than a mere enactment of some institutional "script." Occasionally, participants cannot or do not deal with the emergent features of the situation, in which case the routine structure of the presumptively institutional encounter becomes transformed into a rather different type of interaction, as in the case of the notorious Bush–Rather interview (see Clayman and Whalen 1989; Schegloff 1989; see also Whalen, Zimmerman and Whalen 1988 for the interactional transformation of a call for medical assistance into a virtual character contest).

9 A situated identity, as the term implies, is one which is closely linked to particular occasions or situations. Occupational identities constitute one class of situated identities (cf. Sacks 1972a).

10 The term "normatively oriented-to" is used here to note that such identities form an accounting scheme for participants in assessing and explaining their own and others' conduct under the auspices of a given set of identities (cf. Heritage 1984a, 1988; Wilson 1989).

11 Constraint on who may speak next does occur locally in mundane conversation when current speaker employs a next-speaker selection technique (see Sacks, Schegloff and Jefferson 1974).

12 Not every call is characterized by the deployment of insertion/expansion sequence (dubbed an "interrogative series"); some callers are able to produce an extended first turn which provides the information needed for the service provider to process the request (see Zimmerman 1984; Whalen and Zimmerman 1987:176).

13 We take it as understood that to speak of absences, it must be shown that the "missing" element was one which, in mundane conversation, ordinarily occurs in some specifiable class of sequential locations and achieves thereby some feature or features of the interaction. Its systematic absence in particular institutional settings presumably permits participants to achieve some other interactional feature. For example, withholding of response and acknowledgment tokens or news receipts at turn boundaries in multi-unit turns by interviewees allows interviewers to avoid the role of primary addressee and achieve the feature of news interviews as addressed to an overhearing audience, just as extended "report" turns in business meetings are typically unmonitored and thus provide for a "shared attentiveness" and general transmission of information to the meeting as a whole (Heritage and Greatbatch, chapter 5 below, and see also Jefferson and Lee 1981; Boden, forthcoming).

14 The alignment is usually accomplished by the answerer's specialized opening, a categorical self-identification, for instance, "911 Emergency" and the caller's acknowledging "Yes." Given that identification, not recognition, is the relevant issue for this type of transaction, the opening sequence is reduced relative to openings in mundane telephone calls by the routine absence of the "greeting" and "howareyou" sequences (Whalen and Zimmerman 1987: 175–6; cf. Schegloff 1986c).

2

Social Structure and the Sequential Organization of Interaction

Thomas P. Wilson

This paper is concerned with the connections between the sequential organization of social interaction, on the one hand, and participants' orientation to the social-structural context of their interaction, on the other. By the former I mean the way participants organize their interaction turn by turn over its course, and by the latter, the participants' orientation to what their interaction is about and their relevant biographies and institutional identities in that particular situation. Problems related to the connections between orientation to social-structural context and the sequential organization of interaction have arisen in various ways at the periphery of conversation analysis, but until recently these connections generally have not themselves been the direct focus of analytic attention.[1] However, research has begun to push issues of social structure to the fore, and it is necessary to address them directly.

Over the past two decades conversation analysis has developed into a strongly cumulative field of sociological research with a clear methodological, conceptual, and theoretical structure.[2] Its central concern is with elucidating the mechanisms of sequential organization of interaction, that is, the way participants construct their interaction turn by turn over its course to accomplish an accountably coherent exchange. This close and restricted attention to sequential organization has produced an impressive accumulation of knowledge concerning the mechanisms through which people organize and construct mundane conversation, that is, interaction in which the order, length, and contents of turns are not controlled by prior arrangements.[3] These mechanisms include procedures for turn-taking, repair of interactional troubles, adjacency-pair organization, and the like. The general result from this research is that social interaction proceeds through members using mechanisms that are extremely general, and in this sense context-free, but which also are context sensitive in that parties to an interaction must be oriented to the context of their actions to use them competently. Although conversation analysts have focused primarily on mundane conversation, they have also extended their investigations to different types of speech exchange, such as court hearings, news interviews, and classrooms, in which mechanisms such as turn-taking assume different forms, principally through specialization and restriction of the mechanisms employed in mundane conversation. For this reason we regard the mechanisms of sequential organization of mundane conversation as the fundamental mechanisms of interaction (Sacks, Schegloff and Jefferson 1974:730–1; Schegloff 1987b:101).

Because of this emphasis on sequential organization *per se*, conversation analysts have for the most part restricted explicit attention to purely sequential phenomena. As Schegloff (1987b) has noted, the principal research strategy has been to identify a collection of instances of a particular phenomenon across different conversations in order to examine the general features of interactional mechanisms. Consequently, until recently conversation analysts have generally left the relation between sequential organization and social-structural context more or less implicit. This informal handling of social-structural context is unsatisfactory, however, for it obscures matters that should be brought under explicit analytic control. Thus, while much remains to be discovered concerning the sequential organization of social interaction, it is now essential also to direct explicit attention to the relation between social structure and sequential organization. Schegloff (1987a, 1987b, 1987c) has raised some of the broad methodological issues in treating social structure explicitly in conversation analysis. Moreover, social-structural issues figure in a growing body of empirical studies, particularly of settings characterized by alternative speech exchange systems (for instance, Atkinson and Drew 1979; Molotch and Boden 1985; Button 1987; Clayman 1987; Greatbatch 1988) and of institutional talk (Jefferson and Lee 1981; Atkinson 1982; Maynard 1984; West 1984; Heritage 1985a; Heath 1986; Boden, forthcoming). Several recent papers have also focused specifically on the manner in which the fundamental mechanisms of interaction are configured in various ways to reflexively constitute particular settings (for instance, Zimmerman 1984; Whalen and Zimmerman 1987; cf. Heritage 1984a).

In addition, I shall argue, orientation to social structure is interwoven with the sequential organization of interaction in a second and equally fundamental way, namely through constitution of the particular objects to which the mechanisms of a speech exchange system apply, whether that be mundane conversation or some variant. That is, the objects, such as turns, questions, answers, troubles needing repair, and so on, to which participants apply the mechanisms of sequential organization are constituted in part through the participants' orientation to the social-structural context of their interaction (see Wilson 1982).

Conceptual Issues

Several general conceptual issues need to be made explicit as background to this discussion.

Sequential environments and social-structural contexts

The concept of sequential environment is relatively unproblematic: it refers, in the first instance, to the actions immediately preceding and following a particular action, and, relatedly, to environments created through such devices as asking a question, beginning a story, and the like. While the latter environments may be larger than the immediate previous–current–next paradigm, they are still sequential in character, since they are constructed by the participants in the interaction itself through the use, then and there, of particular mechanisms of sequential organization. As Heritage (1984a:242) has summarized the matter, each action is both "context shaped" and "context renewing" in the sense that it is oriented to the current sequential environment and then forms part of the sequential environment for the next action. The major concern in conversation analysis over the past two decades has been to elucidate the role of sequential environment in the organization of social interaction.

Sequential environments do not, however, exhaust the notion of context. An action is not directed to any conceivable audience, but rather is fashioned for just those particular people whom the actor is addressing and the reasons for their being engaged with one another (Sacks 1964–72; Sacks, Schegloff and Jefferson 1974; Schegloff 1972). The fact that action is designed for particular recipients is an essential resource for both speakers and hearers in enabling them to deal with their own and each others' action as coherent and intelligible. That is to say, while people construct their interaction turn by turn, they do so in part through their orientations to their relevant biographies and identities, as well as to what the present occasion is about and its connections to prior occasions and prospective future ones. It is the participants' orientation to these matters that I have termed their orientation to "social-structural context."

The principle of relevance

However, people have many different identities, and the physical setting does not determine which of many possible social-structural contexts is salient on a particular occasion. Consequently, parties to a concrete interaction must address the questions of who they relevantly are and what it is they are about on any given occasion (Sacks 1972a). This is an irremediable circumstance facing the participants, and the analyst cannot settle the issue on their behalf by invoking some theoretical scheme or interpretation of the situation. Instead, the relevance of particular social-structural categories on a given occasion consists in the way the participants in the interaction display to one another their orientations to those categories in a manner that is consequential for their interaction (cf. Schegloff 1987a, 1987b, 1987c). This principle of relevance is fundamental to ethnomethodology and conversation analysis.[4]

Moreover, we must extend this to note that for participants the question of relevance is an ever-present concern, from which there is no "time out." Each action is accountable for displaying understanding of the preceding action and of projected future actions, and hence the context renewing character of action carries with it the presumption that, unless there is reason to suppose otherwise, the already established social-structural context remains in force as the "default" scheme of interpretation. As a consequence, once particular social-structural features have been established in the interaction as relevant, these relevancies stand until further notice as the scheme under which speakers can warrantably expect each other to attempt, at least initially, to understand any next action. Observe, moreover, that one can exploit this to alter the present scheme of relevances by acting in a way that cannot be construed sensibly in terms of what has gone immediately before but nevertheless is intelligible in terms of other things one can warrantably assume are known in common by co-participants. In doing so, one holds them accountable for understanding whatever is said or done as directed specifically and constructed so as to be intelligible to them. Thus, the requirement of displaying understanding turn by turn leads to an initial presumption of continuity of relevancies: the relevant scheme of interpretation need not be renegotiated in each turn, but rather, once established and until altered, is used as a resource and at the same time is reconfirmed in each successive turn.

Conventions versus mechanisms

Plainly the social-structural matters that are the objects of members' recognition and accounting are conventional. The categories of institutional identity, the activities associated with those categories, and the terms of biographical recounting are culturally variable, historically contingent, and negotiable at least in the long run. In contrast, the fundamental mechanisms of interaction are the tools members of society use to construct their interaction. These mechanisms, while context sensitive, are context-free and so are not socially constructed in the same sense. Rather, they are universally available devices employed by members in that work of construction (Sacks, Schegloff and Jefferson 1974; Wilson and Zimmerman 1980:73–5).

These mechanisms, moreover, are not themselves subject to negotiation or change while preserving the interaction as a situation of mundane conversation. For altering the fundamental mechanisms of interaction modifies the parameters of speech exchange and consequently transforms mundane conversation into some other type of conventionally established speech exchange system. But the fundamental mechanisms of interaction remain intact for use in mundane conversation and indeed serve as the final resource for repairing problems in any conventionally arranged alternative speech-exchange system. The fundamental mechanisms of interaction, then, are not conventional but rather underlie the construction of social conventions of all sorts.

Concepts of social structure

Conversation analysis cannot ignore participants' orientation to social-structural context, but neither can it simply import standard sociological conceptions of social structure. Traditionally, sociology seeks to describe and explain social phenomena in terms of notions such as status, role, class, religion, positionally determined interests, attitudes, beliefs, values, and so on. Although these may represent quite different substantive theoretical commitments, they share the fundamental Durkheimian assumption that social structure is exterior to and constraining on individuals and their actions and, consequently, is an independent causal factor that can be adduced to explain social phenomena.

Standard sociological concepts are, however, altogether unworkable for examining the production of social interaction in detail. Although such concepts are, at bottom, analytical abstractions from categories employed by members in organizing their own activities,[5] they are detached from the actual contexts of social interaction. Moreover, standard social-structural concepts depend implicitly if not explicitly on a model of action as generated by some form of literal rule following, whether these rules be institutionalized social norms or internalized psychological dispositions (Wilson 1970), or whether the model be deterministic or probabilistic. That is to say, the actor is portrayed as a judgmental dope whose sense-making activities, if any, are treated as epiphenomenal, since the relations between categories and rules, on the one hand, and their concrete instances, on the other, are assumed for theoretical purposes to be transparent and unproblematic (Garfinkel 1967:68; Wilson 1970:699; Wilson and Zimmerman 1980:55; Heritage 1984a:110–15, 120–9). The consequence is that standard sociological theories cannot describe or account for the detailed orderliness of interaction on particular concrete occasions as they develop over their course (Sacks 1984:21–3; Schegloff 1987b:102).

Nevertheless, the data of conversation analysis will not permit us to abandon social structure as a mere epiphenomenon of social interaction or simply a nominal aggregate of individual actions. Instead, social structure consists of matters that are described and oriented to by members of society on relevant occasions as essential resources for conducting their affairs and, at the same time, reproduced as external and constraining social facts through that same social interaction. Thus, we must abandon any standard Durkheimian conception of social structure that takes externality and constraint for granted as a methodological stipulation. Rather, externality and constraint are members' accomplishments, and social structure and social interaction are reflexively related rather than standing in causal or formal definitional relations to one another.[6]

While a conception of social structure along these lines is clearly at variance with the received sociological tradition,[7] it is required if we are to understand social action in its sequential and social-structural contexts. For ethnomethodological and conversation analytic purposes, social structure is a members' notion, something oriented to by the members of society. What matters for the sequential organization of interaction, then, is not some ostensibly scientific account of social structure but rather the participants' orientations to the social-structural context of their interaction.[8]

The Social-Structural Constitution of Sequential Objects

We observed at the outset that orientation to social-structural context enters into social interaction in two fundamental ways: through alternative speech-exchange systems; and through the constitution of sequential objects such as turns, questions, etc. The first of these has already received attention in the literature, and consequently here I shall focus on the second point: that the objects to which participants apply the mechanisms of sequential organization are constituted through the participants' orientation to the social-structural context of their interaction. I shall argue this in connection with some empirical materials, but first I want to take issue with a way of introducing social-structural concepts that, while very common, is not useful.

A social-structural short circuit

Because sociologists are accustomed to talking about social structure, it is extremely easy simply to invoke standard social-structural concepts in a way that obscures rather than illuminates what is going on. Consider transcript 2.1, which records a sentencing hearing between a public defender (P), a judge (J), a district attorney (D), and a defendant charged with burglary who was present but silent.[9]

2.1		(Mather 1973)
1	P:	Your Honor, we request immediate sentencing
2		and waive the probation report.
3	J:	What's his record?
4	P:	He has a prior drunk and a GTA [Grand Theft Auto].
5		Nothing serious. This is just a shoplifting case.
6		He did enter the K-Mart with the intent to steal.
7		But really all we have here is a petty theft.
8	J:	What do the people have?
9	D:	Nothing either way.
10	J:	How long has he been in?
11	P:	Eighty-three days.
12	J:	I make this a misdemeanor by P.C. Article 17 and
13		sentence you to ninety days in County Jail, with
14		credit for time served

One of the evident features of this interaction is that, following the request at the beginning in lines 1 and 2, the judge controls the allocation of turns. Thus, when the judge asks "What's his record" in line 3, he selects the public defender as the next speaker. Moreover, although the public defender does more in lines 4–7 than simply give a straightforward answer to the judge's query, in the end he does not use his turn to initiate a new course of action or select someone else as next speaker, nor does any other party select himself (Sacks, Schegloff and Jefferson 1974). As a result, the next turn falls again to the judge, who is then in a position to select the next speaker by, for example, asking another question. Another obvious feature of this talk is that, between the initial request and the judge's granting of it in lines 12–14, turn types are severely restricted: the judge asks questions, and the others answer them. We do not find, for example, an attorney responding by first answering the judge in the first part of a turn and then completing the turn with a question addressed to someone else, though such patterns are frequent in other contexts (Maynard and Zimmerman 1984). The question is how we might explain this pattern.

Proceeding along standard sociological lines, one might attribute the judge's control of the interaction to his status and institutional authority in the courtroom (for instance, Wilson 1982). However, such an explanation is inadequate for our purposes because it fails to account for the details of the actual observed course of action. Thus, even if we could agree on some one interpretation of what "authority" means, we would still not have explained how this particular course of action is connected in detail with the authority of the judge on this specific occasion. More importantly, an attempt at explanation along such lines is misdirected, for the phenomena in question result directly from the sequential organization of the interaction *per se*.

As Maynard and Wilson (1980) observed, this interaction has the general structure of an adjacency pair with an insertion sequence.[10] In lines 1–2 we have a request by the public defender to the judge, and in lines 12–14 we find a response by the judge. The intervening talk consists of questions by the judge, answered by the public defender and district attorney, that provide information which warrants the response the judge ultimately gives. Thus, lines 3–11 constitute an insertion sequence in the particular form of an interrogative series. Some important implications follow from this structure.

Recall that an adjacency pair consists of two elements, a first pair part and a second pair part such that a first pair part in one turn projects a second pair part in the next turn. The second pair part is conditionally relevant on the occurrence of the first pair part in the sense that if an appropriate second pair part is not forthcoming in the next turn, its absence is accountable (see Heritage 1984a:106–17, 245–64). For example, a question calls for an answer, and a request calls for a response in the form of granting or denial. However, fashioning an appropriate second pair part may require intervening activity, for example, clarifying a question or gathering information to respond to a request.[11] In such cases, accountability can be maintained through an insertion sequence consisting of intervening actions that, while not the projected second pair part itself, recognizably prepare for it, thus displaying an orientation to the fact that the projected second pair part is still pending.

Next, observe that this structure restricts the distribution of turn types within the insertion sequence. Thus, suppose A issues an initial or "base" first pair part (FPP_b) to B. If B addresses another, "inserted" first pair part (FPP_i) to A, then A's next action is sharply constrained.[12] In effect, the structure thus far is

1	**A:**	FPP_b
2	**B:**	FPP_i
3	**A:**	$\{SPP_i\}$
4	**B:**	$\{SPP_b\}$

where the brackets in lines 3 and 4 indicate that these actions are projected but not completed. A's turn in line 3, then, is constrained by the two pending projected actions. In the simplest case, A can provide an appropriate SPP_i at line 3, but any elaborations, qualifications, or shifts must display an orientation to the fact that SPP_b is still pending and eventually B must regain the turn in order to supply it. A more complex possibility is for A to initiate a nested subinsertion sequence at line 3, but, unless the conditional relevance of the already projected actions is suspended, this must eventually close with A providing an appropriate SPP_i. Finally, note that this permits B to initiate another insertion sequence, perhaps with a different party, or to terminate the matter by providing an appropriate SPP_i. The result is that B is in a position to control the allocation of turns within the sequence.[13]

In other words, the adjacency-pair structure constrains the distribution of turn types within the insertion sequence such that the person to whom the initial first pair part is directed (and who thus is projected to supply a second pair part to it) is able to introduce further inserted first pair parts, but other participants are limited to supplying second pair parts in response to these.[14] Moreover, this restriction of turn types within the insertion sequence leads to turn allocation being controlled by the party projected to supply the second pair part. The result is an interrogative series with the features we have observed in transcript 2.1. Consequently, there is no need to invoke the special status and role of the judge in order to account for these features of the exchange. It reflects not "broader" social factors but instead the sequential organization of an insertion sequence in an adjacency-pair structure.

Generality

The foregoing analysis gives us a parsimonious explanation of the fact that the same phenomena of restricted turn types and control over turn allocation occur in adjacency-pair structures across widely differing social contexts. Consider the second transcript, which is of a call to a metropolitan emergency dispatching center.[15] The caller (C) is a citizen telephoning the local emergency telephone number, and the complaint taker (D) is the person taking the call at the dispatching center. Observe that we have the same general pattern as in the first example. After the exchange of identifications in line 1 and the first part of line 2, the caller makes an explicit request. This is followed by a series of questions, which ends with the complaint taker granting the initial request in line 21.

```
2.2     (MCE:21:21:28)
  1  D:     Midcity emergensee
  2  C:     Yh:es (if ya gotuh) squad car could ya send one
  3            over tuh State Street and Owens Avenue [keyboard]
  4  D:     What's thuh problum there.
  5  C:     Well (.) we jus uh- I jus looked out my window=
  6            =there wuz uh big bang an' looked out- looks like uh
  7            coupluh cars ar'all tangled up out there.
  8  D:     State an' Owens?
  9  C:     Ye:s .hh it's a uh- .hh it's abou:t uh three blo:cks
 10            West of State and High Street there .hh by uh Lake
 11            Gordon? ((background voices))
 12  D:     O:kay uh:=
 13  C:     =Right by that railroad bridge by Basingsto ⌈(   )⌉
 14  D:                                                  ⌊O:h⌋
 15            right I know whatcha talkin about it's over
 16            there ⌈(   )⌉
 17  C:            ⌊(yeah)⌋ they're still milling around
 18            up there but I don' know what happen (t- uh) I know
 19            I know there's some kinduvuh accident but I don'
```

```
20              know if anybody's hurt ur anything.
21   D:         O:kay wull get somebody there=
22   C:         =Ahright fi⌈ne
23   D:               ⌊Thank you ⌈Bye.⌉
24   C:                         ⌊Bye.⌋
```

Again the role of questioner is differentially distributed: in this call, the complaint taker asks the questions and the caller answers them. However, we cannot argue that complaint takers command deference in a way we might be willing to concede for judges. We could, of course, propose that it is the "social role" of complaint takers to ask questions of callers, but this explanatory strategy implies that we must examine each situation separately to locate the social factors in it that lead to the particular pattern of questions and answers we have noted, and, more importantly, fails to account for just how this imputed role actually bears on the current interaction. However, as we have argued, we do not need to do this: the phenomenon arises from the nature of the sequential organization of insertion sequences in general. Thus, by prematurely leaping to a social-structural account, one can miss a considerably deeper understanding of what is going across a range of interaction situations (see also Maynard and Wilson 1980; Maynard 1984; Heritage and Greatbatch, chapter 5 below).

The Constitution of Sequential Objects

The argument thus far has been that certain regularities in social interaction result from members' use of sequential mechanisms rather than through the influence of some supposed supervening social factor. The particular case at hand was the pattern of turn allocation and turn types in insertion sequences. This argument depends, then, on the initial recognizability of an action as a first pair part that can establish the sequential relevance of an insertion sequence. What I want to argue now is that such sequential objects as questions, requests, and so on, are constituted through the participants' orientation to the social-structural context of their interaction. Thus, social structure is involved directly in the turn-by-turn construction of social interaction as an essential resource for competent use of the mechanisms of sequential organization of interaction.

Consider a third example.

2.3   (MCE:21:9:12)

1	**D:**	Mid-City Emergency:
2	**C:**	.hh ((softly)) um: yeah (.) Somebody
3		jus' vandalized my=car,
4	**D:**	.hh What's yer address
5	**C:**	Thirty three twenty two: Elm
6	**D:**	Is this uh house or an apartment
7	**C:**	Ih: tst uh hou:se
8	**D:**	Uh- yur las' name.
9	**C:**	Minsky
10	**D:**	(h) How you spell=it
11	**C:**	M.I.N.S.K.Y.
12	**D:**	Wull sen' someone out=to see you.
13	**C:**	Than' you.=
14	**D:**	=Umhm bye.
15	**C:**	Bye-

This conversation has almost the identical overall structure as the previous example. In line 1 and the first part of 2 we again have a categorical identification and an acknowledgment, and following line 3 there is an interrogative series terminated by a response in line 12.

However, there is a fundamental analytical problem here. In order to treat this as a request–response pair with an insertion sequence, we must understand the last part of the second turn (lines 2 and 3) as a request. But the actual utterance, "somebody jus' vandalized my=car", cannot be construed as a request on the basis of lexical or grammatical considerations alone, nor does its sequential placement *per se* mark it as a request. The problem, then, is how the parties to this conversation hear "somebody jus' vandalized my=car" as a request. One possible argument is retrospective. On the basis of the interrogative series that follows line 2 and the eventual statement by the complaint taker in line 12, "Wull sen' someone out=to see you," one might propose that the second part of line 2 is understood as a request after the fact. However, this fails to account for how the interrogative series and the statement in line 12 are produced in the first place. Notice in transcript 2.2 that the initial request, by projecting a forthcoming response, organizes the ensuing talk between the request and the response. In the present case we have exactly the same kind of structure, and it appears that both the caller and the complaint taker are oriented to a projected response prior to its occurrence.

How, then, can the caller and complaint taker hear "somebody jus' vandalized my=car" as a request? To begin with, in sequential terms, the immediately preceding objects are a categorical self-identification by the complaint taker in line 1, "Mid-City Emergency:", and an acknowledgment by the caller in the first part of line 2, ".hh ((softly)) um: yeah." In this exchange, the complaint taker and caller establish that the caller has reached the emergency dispatching service, and that this was what the caller had intended, at least as the initial phase of some project (Zimmerman 1984; Whalen and Zimmerman 1987). At this point, the relation between the parties has been established in terms of the manifest business of the agency the caller has intentionally reached, namely the dispatching of help in response to requests or reports of trouble. Consequently, as we noted earlier, this is the basis on which interaction will proceed unless someone does something to alter matters.[16]

In sum, caller and answerer have established the potential relevance of a mutual categorization of each other as citizen complainant and complaint taker, where these categorical identities are specifically tied to the particular organization the caller has reached.[17] In Sacks's terms (1972a, 1972b), we have a membership categorization device and category-bound activities established by the institutional arrangements of the emergency dispatching service. In the absence of any work by the parties to modify this, the second part of the second turn is then heard under the auspices of a hearer's maxim to regard it as an action bound to the category of caller to an emergency dispatching service. This, then, provides the warrant for both parties to hear the utterance as a request.

Recall the earlier point that in many cases what may appear to be social-structural phenomena are in fact the products simply of the sequential organization of interaction. In particular, I suggested that the allocation of the discourse identities of questioner and answerer within insertion sequences is a product of the sequential organization of adjacency pairs. However, we cannot have our cake and eat it too. If we are to apply this approach to the present example, we must contrive to understand the second part of line 2 as a request, and this we cannot do without appealing to the co-orientation of the caller and the complaint taker to the institutional context of their interaction. Thus, to avoid inappropriate invocation of social-structural considerations at one level, we must attend to the interweaving of social structure and social interaction in a far deeper and more consequential way.

For another example, let us return once again to the courtroom interaction in the first transcript (p. 28). First, observe that it is the judge to whom the request for sentencing is addressed. The fact that such a request cannot be directed to just anyone is a feature of the institutional structure of the criminal justice system and displays an orientation on the part of the public defender to the location of this event within that institutional system.

Next, consider the interaction in lines 3–9:

3	J:	What's his record?
4	P:	He has a prior drunk and a GTA [Grand Theft Auto].
5		Nothing serious. This is just a shoplifting case.
6		He did enter the K-Mart with the intent to steal.
7		But really all we have here is a petty theft.
8	J:	What do the people have?
9	D:	Nothing either way.

Beginning in line 5 with "this is just a shoplifting case," the public defender offers a reformulation of the original burglary charge, employing devices generally found in disagreement sequences (Pomerantz 1984a): note the "just" in line 5 followed by an acknowledgment of certain facts in line 6, and the contrast foreshadowed by the use of "did enter" rather than simply "entered" in line 6 and made explicit with "but" in line 7. Moreover, in the next turn, line 8, the judge does not reject the public defender's talk as irrelevant to the proceeding but instead solicits a possible difference of opinion by the district attorney; and in line 9 the district attorney indicates there is none, thereby also acknowledging the intelligibility of a possible difference.

The technical issue is how the public defender's talk in lines 5–7 can be heard as a relevant reformulation, rather than, say, as merely quibbling over words or irrelevant details and hence either pointing to or constituting a trouble perhaps needing repair. To begin with, note that the public defender's turn occurs in an insertion sequence, specifically, in answer to the judge's question "what's his record?" in line 3, which is warranted by the original request for sentencing. Thus, the public defender's talk in this turn is to be heard as relevant to that original request. Observe in addition that the request is for sentencing, rather than for something else, such as a continuance, for which the details of the offense would be irrelevant. Moreover, for many purposes, "shoplifting" and "burglary" might be heard as equivalent: for example, they are both nonviolent property crimes. But in the context of a request specifically for sentencing, they contrast sharply: the former is a misdemeanor, the latter a felony. However, the distinction between shoplifting and burglary is not a sequential matter, but rather has to do with the institutional structure of the criminal justice system. Thus, the work that the public defender does in his turn to construct a contrastive formulation is intelligible in terms of the co-orientation of the participants to both the sequential context of the turn itself and the institutional context of the criminal justice system.

Thus, each turn in the insertion sequence displays understanding of two matters: first, what was said in preceding turns, and second, that a request is still pending so that each present turn is to be understood as relevant to providing a response to that request. Moreover, the disagreement is not intelligible given any conceivable request at the beginning of the exchange: instead, it depends on the fact that the request was specifically a request for sentencing, and further, on the institutional features of the criminal justice system involved in such matters as the difference between misdemeanors and felonies.

Finally, consider the judge's last turn in lines 12–14:

```
12  J:     I make this a misdemeanor by P.C. Article 17 and
13         sentence you to ninety days in County Jail, with
14         credit for time served
```

The form of words here is specifically chosen to grant the initial request in a manner that fulfills legal requirements, and failure to adequately adhere to legal forms would result in a possible error, which is to say, the initial request would not have been fulfilled. Thus, the judge is oriented to the relation of this present interaction to subsequent occasions in terms of having performed the act of sentencing in institutionally accountable terms.

Discussion

The fundamental mechanisms of interaction are the foundation of conversation analysis. As we noted earlier, the basic strategy for studying these is to collect a corpus of instances of some phenomenon across an array of mundane conversations. Since, in that case, our concern is with fundamental mechanisms of mundane interaction, the social-structural circumstances of the interactions from which the examples are drawn do not matter in a systematic way. In contrast, when we seek to show how the participants in a particular interaction employ the machinery of interaction on that occasion to produce the sequence of interaction they in fact do, we cannot ignore the participants' orientation to who they are and what they are doing or talking about, even though these orientations may not be the focus of analysis.[18] However, when our attention shifts to the way the fundamental mechanisms of interaction are configured in particular institutional contexts and how institutional contexts are constituted in interaction, we must necessarily make our concern for orientation to social-structural context explicit. As we have seen, orientation to social-structural context is related to sequential organization in two ways. First, a substantial body of research makes clear that the organization of a variant speech-exchange system is reflexively connected with social-structural context. Second, as I have emphasized here, the constitution of the objects to which the mechanisms of sequential organization are applied, be these the mechanisms of mundane conversation or of some variant speech-exchange system, is accomplished through the participants' orientation to the social-structural context of their interaction.

Distributional phenomena

The institutional features of social interaction are closely related to certain distributional phenomena that can be observed within or across different interactions. For example, recall the second transcript, which is from a collection of calls to an emergency telephone number. All of the normal[19] emergency calls in this corpus exhibit the same pattern we observed earlier: turn types are restricted so that, except for nested subinsertion sequences, the person answering the phone asks the questions and the caller answers them, and the caller uniformly gives the turn back to the answerer. In any one of these calls, we can account for why one party to the interaction, let us call him or her "D", is the person who asks the questions and receives the turn back by appealing only to the sequential organization of adjacency pairs within insertion sequences and to the fact that, in this particular call, person D happens to be the one of whom a request was made and so is projected to supply a response. Thus, it is D who initiates the insertion sequence. However, this does not account for the regularity across calls just noted: why is it that uniformly the person answering the phone plays the role of D? In short, how does it happen that the discourse identity of questioner is uniformly associated with the categorical identity of complaint taker?

We can put the matter somewhat more generally by observing that by routinely employing particular conversational mechanisms, participants can transform an initial distribution of events, such as citizen complainants making a request, into a final distribution of other events, such as complaint takers asking questions. The mechanisms themselves, however, are indifferent to the distributional particulars of the initial events. Thus, in the present case, from the point of view of the structure of insertion sequences it is an accident that citizen complainants make requests, and it is equally unimportant that complaint takers ask questions; but the latter fact follows from the former as a result of the nature of insertion sequences. In effect, routine use of the mechanisms of interaction passes an antecedent distribution through to a final distribution. In this sense, then, one can account for the distribution of subsequent events as a product of sequential mechanisms, but only if the distribution of antecedent events is already given.

The problem, then, is to account for the antecedent distribution. Of course, it might in turn be produced in a similar way, which then pushes the problem back another step. Eventually, however, we reach the beginning of the interaction and so must face the issue directly. In the present case the initial distribution of requests, such that these are made by citizen complainants rather than complaint takers, arises from the institutional context that the participants establish as relevant. Thus, ultimately, distributional phenomena in interaction may reflect elements of institutional context, a possibility that in this case can be established directly.

Another form of distributional phenomenon in interaction is found in variations in speech exchange systems. The notion of a variant speech-exchange system originates in the observation that there are regular patterns across interactions in a particular kind of setting, patterns that reflect systematic modifications of the fundamental mechanisms of interaction found in mundane conversation. In the empirical literature, such variant speech-exchange systems are reported in institutionally established contexts: courts, schools, interviews, and so on. Thus, here also, social-structural context is implicated, and in many cases it is apparent from the data that the participants in these interactions are oriented to the named social-structural contexts in the sense discussed here, even if the analysis has not been aimed at establishing that point explicitly.

Nevertheless, it would be a mistake to leap at once from noticing some distribution across a class of interactions to the conclusion that some particular institutional features are relevant. In general, one could construct plausible connections between such an observed distribution and any of an indefinite array of possible institutional features. In short, the principle of relevance applies: any claim to have explained a distributional phenomenon, such as an association between categorical and discourse identities or a regular alteration of the mechanisms of sequential organization, within or across interactions, by reference to features of social structure must be secured by a detailed analysis showing how the distributional phenomenon arises via the orientation of the participants to those social-structural features. In the absence of such a demonstration, institutional "explanations" must be regarded as speculative, no matter how plausible they may seem. For example, West and

Zimmerman (1983) found a differential distribution of interruptions between men and women that has sometimes been regarded as evidence of masculine domination. However, the mechanisms by which this distribution is generated remain obscure, and so any such interpretation, however interesting, is speculative. In some cases, it may be possible to trace out the mechanisms in a fairly straightforward manner, as with the question-asking complaint takers, while in others the process may not be so easily untangled, as with interruptions between men and women.

Equally, however, it would be a mistake to construe this caveat as grounds for dismissing distributional phenomena as having no relevance to conversation analysis. A distributional regularity across a class of interactions poses the problem of how that regularity is produced. In some cases, of course, it may be merely accidental and of no further interest, but in others it may direct attention to locally organized phenomena that otherwise might go unnoticed.

The reproduction of social structure

One of the underlying notions in the preceding discussion is that of a class of interactions that can be treated as homogeneous in some important respects. For example, the corpus of emergency calls mentioned earlier is just such a class, as is a collection of news interviews. The issue is the warrant for such classifications.

The standard sociological procedure is to identify a class of situations either by invoking commonsensically "obvious" criteria or by referring to some conceptual scheme proposed by the observer on the basis of various theoretical and methodological considerations. The difficulty is, of course, that neither of these procedures ensures that there is any but an accidental relation between the criteria according to which the situations are collected together and the phenomena that compose an observed pattern.[20]

Consequently, if a classification is to be used meaningfully as the basis for assembling some sort of distributional regularity, the classification of interactions itself must be shown to be the product of interactional procedures related to the phenomena comprising the observed regularity. Thus, the fundamental justification for a classification of occasions must be that the participants orient to it as a type of situation and, moreover, orient to the present interaction as an instance of that type. We have seen this in the case of emergency calls (see also Zimmerman 1984; Whalen and Zimmerman 1987), and such orientations are also evident in many of the studies reported in the literature. Thus, the issue of relevance once again emerges as central.

There is, finally, another side to the issue of relevance. Insofar as participants establish this present interaction as a citizen calling the police for assistance in an emergency, they reproduce once again another instance of an emergency service call and thereby also reproduce the social-structural context by which that interaction is intelligible for them in the first place.

Conclusion

In this paper I have sought to provide a systematic basis for introducing social-structural concerns into conversation analysis. Orientation to social-structural context is critical to the study of social interaction in two ways. First, social-structural contexts are reflexively tied to the constitution of variant speech-exchange systems. And second, orientation to social-structural context is central to the constitution of the objects to which the mechanisms of interaction are applied. The issue arises most prominently when attention shifts from the fundamental mechanisms of mundane interaction to the organization of variant speech-exchange systems and to interaction in particular institutional contexts. The fundamental principle involved here is that of relevance: because of the recipient design of actions, parties to an interaction hold one another accountable for knowing who they relevantly are and what the current interaction is about over the course of the interaction itself. This creates certain interactional problems for the participants, notably those of arriving at, sustaining, and altering the footing of their interaction. It is in dealing with these matters that participants simultaneously construct their interaction as a meaningful, accountable occurrence and reproduce its social-structural context as something that is, for them, an external and constraining social fact.

Notes

This paper was originally presented at the International Communication Association meetings in Hawaii, 1985, and subsequent revisions were read at the International Conference on Ethnomethodology and Conversation Analysis in Boston, 1985, and the International Conference on Talk and Social Structure in Santa Barbara, 1986. I wish to thank Don Zimmerman, Deirdre Boden, John Heritage, Douglas Maynard, Steven Clayman, Jack Whalen, and Emanuel Schegloff for comments.

1   Explicit concern for this problem in its own right surfaced originally in Maynard and Wilson (1980), Wilson and Zimmerman (1980), and Wilson (1982). However, the question of the connection between talk and social structure was already beginning to emerge in empirical studies of talk in institutional settings (for instance, Atkinson and Drew, 1979).

2   "Conversation" refers to direct social interaction, including nonverbal aspects as well as talk. See Heritage (1984a, especially chapter 8) for an overview of conversation analysis, and for foundational statements and references see Garfinkel (1967), Garfinkel and Sacks (1970), Sacks (1963, 1964–72), Schegloff (1972), Sacks, Schegloff and Jefferson (1974), Wilson and Zimmerman (1980), Atkinson and Heritage (1984), and Heritage (1984a, 1985b).

3   The term "mundane" conversation is from Heritage (1984a). Sacks, Schegloff and Jefferson (1974) appear to use "naturally occurring" in this same sense (see Wilson, Wiemann and Zimmerman 1984). See Boden (1983), Moerman (1977), and Ren (1989) for cross-cultural data.

4   The dominant methodological positions in the social sciences, whether interpretive or positivist, reject this principle. For example, even such a seeming critic of standard sociology as Cicourel (1987) argues instead that the analyst should provide as much ethnographic detail as possible, selected in terms of "stated theoretical goals, methodological strategies employed, and the consistency and convincingness of an argument" (p. 226). This procedure may be appropriate when the analyst's intention is to develop an interpretation commensurate with the participants' own accounts that can be juxtaposed with and used to criticize the members' understandings of their circumstances, what they are about, what is happening, and why. In this case, the theoretical goals, methodological strategy, and thrust of the argument are dictated by the analyst's interests. However, when the purpose is to understand the methods participants themselves employ to construct their interaction over its actual course, the principle of relevance is fundamental.

5   This point has been made repeatedly (Sacks 1963; Garfinkel 1967; Garfinkel and Sacks 1970). For a discussion of methodological implications, see Wilson (1987). Exceptions might be notions derived from biology that are employed, for example, in demography, but only if the sociologist takes care to ensure that research categories are in fact established independently of the social accounting processes with which members of society comprehend biological phenomena. In social research, this qualification is seldom recognized, much less satisfied.

6   The concept of reflexivity as mutual constitution is Garfinkel's (1967); see also Maynard and Wilson (1980), Wilson and Zimmerman (1980), and Wilson (1982). Giddens (1976, 1984), clearly influenced by Garfinkel on this point, refers to it as the "duality" of social structure, while reserving the term "reflexive" to mean self-reflective. Note that Heritage (1984a) uses "reflexive" in each of these senses, depending on the context: specifically, he follows Garfinkel's usage when referring to accounts and Giddens's when referring to Parsons's conception of the actor.

7   For example, Alexander et al. (1987); Schegloff's paper in that collection

(1987a) is anomalous in that it does not share the basic assumptions on which the notion of a "micro–macro" distinction rests. As a consequence, the editors misconstrue his paper, and ethnomethodology and conversation analysis generally, as representing an "individualist" perspective.

8 This does not purport to be an "ethonomethodological theory of social structure." At most, it adumbrates some initial steps toward such a theory, suggesting some facts that any adequate theory will have to accommodate. Giddens is the preeminent contemporary theorist to attempt an elaboration of a concept of social structure that takes the reflexive relation between social structure and social interaction into account, via his notion of the duality of structure. His approach, however, is somewhat more speculative than that underlying the work discussed here.

9 This transcript, unlike the ones to follow, is presented in normalized orthography because we do not have access to the original recording.

10 See Heritage (1984a:245–64) for a lucid discussion of adjacency pairs, conditional relevance, and insertion sequences. The essential ideas can be found in Sacks's lectures (1964–72), Schegloff (1968, 1972), and Schegloff and Sacks (1973).

11 Sometimes the required actions may be not visible or audible by the person initiating the adjacency pair. The present discussion is limited to situations in which such actions can be neglected without affecting the analysis.

12 Recall that the constraint here is not one of law-like inevitability, but rather of normative accountability. If there is a law-like feature to this, it is that of the presence of normative accountability.

13 I am strongly indebted here to Greatbatch (1988). Greatbatch's argument on this point focuses on the way restricting turn types to questions and answers in news interviews leads to interviewer control over the allocation of turns. Here I have placed his argument in the context of an insertion sequence in an adjacency-pair. Note that the mechanism by which turn types are constrained here is sequential in origin and depends crucially on the occurrence of the initial pair part. This contrasts with situations such as news interviews (Greatbatch 1988; Clayman 1987) in which constraints on turn types are pre-established by the institutional conventions of the occasion.

14 In an early formulation, Sacks (1964–72) proposed a "chaining" rule to the effect that a person asking a question had a right to ask another question, on receiving an answer to the first. This, plainly, is not true in general, and he abandoned the conjecture. However, it appears that something like such a pattern does operate in an insertion sequence, though not as a consequence of an independent "rule" but as a result of the constraints imposed by the fact that a second pair part to the original first pair part is still pending.

15 The transcribing conventions are as outlined in the appendix.

16 Note that the slot following an acknowledgment in the caller's turn is in fact available for precisely this use.

17 A categorical identity is one provided for in an institutional membership categorization device (Sacks 1972a, 1972b). In contrast, a discourse identity is one that is intrinsically related to the sequential organization of the

interaction, such as summoner and answerer, or requestor and request recipient.

18 For example, Schegloff (1987b) provides an elegant analysis of the complex ways participants use a variety of interactional mechanisms to produce a single episode. While he does not generally refer directly to the participants' orientations to social-structural context (but see, for instance, pp. 105, 108), his analysis nevertheless depends on them.

19 The warrant for referring to these as "normal" emergency calls is that the openings proceed through a typical identification–acknowledgment sequence in the first turn and a half, this is followed by talk that is oriented to by the participants as a request for assistance, and the closing sequence of the call is initiated by the complaint taker's granting the request for assistance. There are also calls in this corpus in which the caller replaces the identification–acknowledgment sequence to establish some other basis for the call, but each of these calls is marked by explicit activity of some sort to accomplish the changed footing.

20 Note that even if one can fit a sophisticated quantitative model to the data, there is no guarantee that the pattern is meaningful, for the statistical analyses presuppose that the model is correctly specified in the first place.

3

Reflections on Talk and Social Structure

Emanuel A. Schegloff

Published in slightly modified form (different title) in Drew & Heritage, 1992, *Talk @ Work*.

Whether starting from a programmatic address to the structure of face-to-face interaction or from a programmatic concern with the constitutive practices of the mundane world, whether in pursuit of language, culture or action, a range of inquiries in several social science disciplines (most relevantly anthropology, sociology and linguistics) have over the past 25 to 30 years brought special attention to bear on talk-in-interaction. It is not unfair to say that one of the most focused precipitates of this broad interest has been that family of studies grouped under the rubric "conversation analysis." It is, in any case, with such studies of "talk" that I will be concerned in reflecting on "talk and social structure."

Although itself understandable as a sustained exploration of what is entailed in giving an analytic account of "a context" (as in the phrase "in the context of ordinary conversation"), various aspects of inquiry in this tradition of work have prompted an interest in neighboring disciplines in relating features of talk-in-interaction to "contexts" of a more traditional sort – linguistic contexts, cultural contexts, and institutional and social structural contexts. At the same time, investigators working along conversation analytic lines began to deal with talk with properties which were seemingly related to its production by participants oriented to a special "institutional" context; and, wishing to address those distinctive properties rather than ones held in common with other forms of talk (as Sacks had done in some of his earliest work based on group therapy sessions), these investigators faced the analytic problems posed by such an undertaking.

The interest in the theme "talk and social structure" comes, then, from several directions – the most prominent being technical concerns in the analysis of certain forms of talk on the one hand, and an impulse to effectuate a rapprochement with the concerns of classical sociology, and to do so by relating work on talk-in-interaction to those social formations which get referred to as "social structures," or generically as "social structure," on the other hand. My reflections will have this latter impulse as their point of departure, but will quickly seek to engage it by formulating and confronting the analytic problems which it poses.

Of course, a term like "social structure" is used in many different ways. In recent years, to cite but a few cases, Peter Blau (1977) has used the term to refer to the distribution of a population on various parameters asserted to be pertinent to interaction, claiming a derivation from Simmel and his notion of intersecting social circles. Many others have in mind a structure of statuses and/or roles, ordinarily thereby building in an inescapable normative component, of just the sort Blau wishes to avoid. Yet others intend by this term a structured distribution of scarce resources and desirables, such as property, wealth, productive capacity, status, knowledge, privilege, power, the capacity to enforce and preserve privilege, etc. Still others have in mind stably patterned sets of social relations, whether formalized in organizations or more loosely stabilized in networks.

The sense of "social structure" intended in the thematic concern with "talk and social structure" does not range across all these usages. But almost certainly it includes a concern with power and status and its distribution among social formations such as classes, ethnic groups, age grade groups, gender, and professional relations. It is this sense which has animated, for example, the work by West (1979) and Zimmerman and West (1975) on gender and interruption, and West's work (1984) on doctor/patient interaction. And it includes as well a concern with the structured social relations which comprise organizations and occupational practice and the institutional sectors with which they are regularly identified (as, for example, in Atkinson and Drew's treatment of the courts (1979), in the work of Zimmerman and his associates on the police (for instance, Zimmerman 1984; Whalen and Zimmerman 1987), Maynard's work (1984) on the legal system, that of Heritage (1985a) on mass media news, or Boden's (forthcoming) on organizations; see also part II below). Mehan's studies of decision making in the context of educational bureaucracies (Mehan, Hertweck and Meihls 1986; and Mehan, chapter 4 below) touch on both usages (as of course do some of the other studies which I have invoked to exemplify one or the other).

The work which engages with these classical sociological themes and incorporates reference to and treatment of them in studying talk-in-

interaction has revived for me some concerns which were deep preoccupations some 25 years ago when work on the analysis of talk-in-interaction, of the sort now referred to as "conversation analytic," was getting underway. In these reflections, I want among other things to review, restate and update some of those considerations, and ask how contemporary efforts to engage these topics stand with respect to some of these older concerns. Do the old concerns still have the force they once had, or have they faded in felt significance? Are there now solutions to the problems as once formulated? Or can the results of current work at the interface of conversation and social structure be usefully enriched or constrained by engaging these issues?

Whatever answers we arrive at to these questions, there is one point I want to make before taking them up. Whatever substantive gains there are to be had from focusing on the relationship between talk and social structure in the traditional sense, this focus is not needed in order to supply conversation analysis with its sociological credentials. The work which is focused on the organization of talk-in-interaction in its own right – work on the organization of turn-taking, or on the organization of sequences, work addressed to the actions being done in turns and the formats through which they are done, work on the organization of repair, and work directed to the many discrete practices of talking and acting through talk which do not converge into domains of organization – this work is itself dealing with social organization and social structures, albeit of a different sort than in the received uses of those terms, and is no less sociological in impulse and relevance (Schegloff 1987b).

For some, the fact that conversation analysis (henceforth, CA) concerns itself with the details of talking has meant that it is a form of linguistics. Perhaps so, but certainly not exclusively so. If it is not a distinctive discipline of its own (which it may well turn out to be), CA is at a point where linguistics and sociology (and several other disciplines, anthropology and psychology among them) meet. For the target of its inquiries stands where talk amounts to action, where action projects consequences in a structure and texture of interaction which the talk is itself progressively embodying and realizing, and where the particulars of the talk inform what actions are being done and what sort of social scene is being constituted. Now, from the start, one central preoccupation of sociology and social theory has been with the character of social action and what drives it (reason, passion, interest, utility) – this is familiar enough. Another concern has been with the character of interaction in which action is embedded, for it is observations about some aspects of the character of interaction that motivated such hoary old distinctions as those between *Gemeinschaft* and *Gesellschaft*, between status and contract, and the like. "Action in interaction" is, then, a longstanding theme of social analysis.

CA's enterprise, concerned as it is with (among other things) the detailed analysis of how talk-in-interaction is conducted as an activity in its own right and as the instrument for the full range of social action and practice, is then addressed to one of the classic themes of sociology, although to be sure in a distinctive way. Of the several ways in which CA shows its deep preoccupation with root themes of social science and sociology in particular, these standing conversation analytic preoccupations resonate more with the title of the recent Atkinson/Heritage collection (1984): they are concerned with "structures of social action" – structures of single actions and of series and sequences of them. Atkinson and Heritage's title is, of course, a thoroughly unveiled allusion to the title of Talcott Parsons's first major work, *The Structure of Social Action* (1937), the work which launched the enterprise of Parsonian action theory. The difference between Parsons's title and the Atkinson/Heritage allusion, "*The Structure* of Social Action" versus "*Structures* of Social Action," may suggest some of the distinctiveness.

Parsons's tack was conceptual and global. For him there was "*the* structure," and it was arrived at by theoretic stipulation of the necessary components of an analytical unit – the "unit act," components such as "ends," "means," "conditions." This was a thoroughly conceptual enterprise on a thoroughly analytic object. The Atkinson/Heritage "structures of" suggests not only multiplicity of structures, but the empirical nature of the enterprise. The units are concrete activities, and the search for their "components" involves examination and description of empirical instances.

But with all the differences in conception, mode of working, etc., there is a common enterprise here, and it has long been a central one for sociology and the social sciences more generally – to try to get at the character of social action and social interaction. In CA's addressing of this theme and the varied problems and analytic tasks to which it gives rise, it is itself engaged in "*echt*" sociology, even without the introduction of traditional sociological concerns such as "social structure." But the claim that the problems which have preoccupied conversation analysis *are* sociological in impulse and import is without prejudice to our engagement with the work which tries to relate talk to more traditional conceptions of social structure. That engagement is already underway.

The reasons for thinking about the relationships of talk and social structure are ready to hand. Both our casual and our studied examination of interaction and talk-in-interaction provide a lively sense of the occasions on which who the parties are relative to one another seems to matter, and matter to *them*. And these include senses of "who they are" that connect directly to what is ordinarily meant by "social structure" – their relative status, the power they differentially can command, the group affiliations they display or can readily have attributed to them such as their racial or ethnic memberships, their gender and age-grade status, their occupational status and its general standing and immediate interactional significance, and the other categories of membership in the society which can matter to the participants and which fall under the traditional sociological rubric "social structure."

The issue I mean to address is not: is there such a thing as gender/class/ power/status/organization/etc.? Or: does it affect anything in the world? Rather, the question is: whatever observations we initially make about how such features of social organization as these work and bear on interaction, how do we translate them into defensible, empirically based analyses that help us to get access to previously unnoticed particular details of talk-in-interaction, and appreciate their significance. For the lively sense we may all share of the relevance of social structure along the lines I have mentioned needs to be converted into the hard currency (if you'll pardon the cash nexus) of defensible analysis – analysis which departs from, and can always be referred to and grounded in, the details of actual occurrences of conduct in interaction.

Again, I do not mean to be addressing myself to two apparently neighboring stances, although there may well be implications for them. I am not centrally concerned with those investigators whose primary analytic commitment is to social structure in the received senses of that term, and who mean to incorporate examination of talk into their inquiries because of the role attributable to it in the "production" of social structure – although I do later comment on them (see pp. 64–5). And I do not take up the position (apparently embraced in Goffman 1983a) in which the prima facie relevance of social structure to the organization of interaction is in principle to be disputed (although I do suggest that some received notions may not be sustainable when required to come to terms with the details of actual occurrences). Rather, I mean to formulate and explore the challenges faced by those attracted to the interaction/social structure nexus. A solution must be found to the analytic problems which obstruct the conversion of intuition, casual (however well-informed) observation, or theoretically motivated observation into demonstrable analysis. For without solutions to these problems, we are left with "a *sense* of how the world works," but without its detailed explication.

So what *were* those problems? Or, rather: what *are* those problems? My discussion will be organized around three issues: the problem of relevance, the issue of "procedural consequentiality," and a concern for the competing attentional and analytic claims of conversational structures and "social structure" respectively in the analysis of the data of talk-in-interaction.[1]

The Problem of Relevance

First, *relevance*. Here I draw directly from among the earliest contributions to conversation analysis, the first systematically developed work of Harvey Sacks, now over 20 years old (1972a, 1972b, but the arguments were developing as early as the lectures in Sacks 1964–5). Let me remind you of some issues he raised with respect to how "members" characterize, identify, describe, refer to, indeed "conceive of" persons, in talking to others.

The original focus of the work by Sacks which I mean to recall was the way in which persons engaged in talk-in-interaction did their talk, specifically with respect to reference to persons. Sacks noted that members refer to persons by various category terms – as man/woman, protestant/catholic/jew, doctor/patient, white/black/chicano, first baseman/second baseman/shortstop, and the like. He remarked that these category terms come in collections. In presenting them above, they are inscribed in groups: [man/woman], [protestant/catholic/jew], and so on; and that is the correct way to present them. It is not [man/woman/protestant], [catholic/jew]. This is what is being noted in the observation that the category terms are organized in *collections*.

Some of these collections Sacks called "Pn adequate;" they were adequate to characterize or categorize any member of any population, however specified, whether or not it had been specified (for example, counted, characterized or bounded) in some fashion (1972a:32–3). Other collections were not Pn adequate. [Male/female] *is* Pn adequate; [first baseman/second baseman/shortstop . . .] is *not* Pn adequate, because the latter is only usable on populations already specified or characterized as "baseball teams," whereas the former is not subject to such restrictions.

One of Sacks's main points was that there demonstrably are many Pn-adequate category collections. The collection of category terms for gender/sex and age are the most obvious ones, and these two alone serve to allow the posing of the problem of relevance. The point is that since everyone who is an instance of some category in one of those collections is necessarily (for that is the import of Pn adequacy) also an instance of some category in the other, or *an* other, the fact that someone *is* male, or *is* middle aged, or *is* white, or *is* Jewish is, by itself, no warrant for so referring to them, for the warrant of "correctness" would provide for use of any of the other reference forms as well. Some principle of relevance must underlie use of a reference form, and has to be adduced in order to provide for one rather than another of those ways of characterizing or categorizing some member. That is the problem of relevance: not just the descriptive adequacy of the terms used to characterize the objects being referred to, but the relevance that one has to provide if one means to account for the use of some term – the relevance of that term relative to the alternative terms that are demonstrably available.

Now, this problem was developed by Sacks initially in describing how members talk about members. It showed the inadequacy of an account of a conversationalist's reference to another as a "cousin" by reference to the other "actually being a cousin." But, once raised, the point is directly relevant to the enterprise of *professional* analysts as well. Once we recognize that whoever can be characterized as "male" or as "protestant," or as "president" or whatever, can be characterized or categorized in other ways as well, our scholarly/professional/scientific account cannot "naively" rely on such characterizations, that is, cannot rely on them with no justification or warrant of their relevance.

Roughly speaking, there are two types of solution to this problem in the methodology of professional analysis. One type of solution can be characterized as the "positivist" stance, in one of the many senses in which that term is currently used. In this view, the way to warrant one, as compared to another, characterization of the participants (for example, in interaction) is the "success" of that way of characterizing them in producing a professionally acceptable account of the data being addressed. "Success" is measured by some "technology" – by statistical significance, a preponderance of historical evidence, and so forth. Sometimes there is an additional requirement that the characterization which produces "successful" analysis be theoretically interpretable; that is, that the selection of descriptive terms for the participants converge with the terms of a professional/scientific theory relevant to the object of description. In this type of solution, which I am calling "positivistic," it does not matter whether or not the terms that are used to characterize the participants in some domain of action, and which have yielded "significant" results, are otherwise demonstrably oriented to or not by the participants being described. That is what makes this solution of the problem "positivist."

The alternative type of solution insists on something else, and that is that professional characterizations of the participants be grounded in aspects of what is going on that are demonstrably relevant *to* the participants, and at that moment – at the moment that whatever we are trying to provide an account of occurs. Not, then, just that we see them to be characterizeable as "president/assistant," as "chicano/black," as "professor/student," etc. But that for them, at that moment, those are terms relevant for producing and interpreting conduct in the interaction.

This issue should be of concern when we try to bring the kind of traditional sociological analysis that is implied by the term "social structure" to bear on talk-in-interaction. Much of what is meant by "social structure" in the traditional sense directly implicates such characterizations or categorizations of the participants as Sacks was examining. If the sense of social structure we are dealing with is the one that turns on the differential distribution of valued resources in society, whether status or power or money or any of the other "goods" whose distribution can be used to characterize social structure, then that implies a characterization or categorization of the participants on that occasion as one relevantly to be selected from that set of terms. But then the problem presents itself of the relevance of those terms to the participants for what they are doing. Without a show of that warrant, we are back to a "positivistic" stance, even though the animating concerns may be drawn from quite anti-positivistic theoretical sources or commitments.

Now let us be clear about what *is* and what is *not* being said here. The point is not that persons are somehow *not* male or female, upper or lower class, with or without power, professors and/or students. They may be, on some occasion, demonstrably members of one or another of those categories. Nor is the issue that those aspects of the society do not matter, or did not matter on that occasion. We may share a lively sense that indeed they do matter, and that they mattered on that occasion, and mattered for just that aspect of some interaction on which we are focusing. There is still the problem of *showing from the details of the talk or other conduct in the materials* that we are analyzing that those aspects of the scene are what the *parties* are oriented to. *For that is to show how the parties are embodying for one another the relevancies of the interaction and are thereby producing the social structure.*

The point here is not only methodological but substantive. It is not just to add a methodological apparatus supporting analyses already in hand. It is rather to add to, and potentially to transform, the analysis of the talk and other conduct itself by enriching our account of it with additional detail; and to show that, and how, "social structure" in the traditional sense enters into the production and interpretation of determinate facets of conduct, and is thereby confirmed, reproduced, modulated, neutralized or incrementally transformed in that actual conduct to which it must finally be referred.

This is not, to my mind, an issue of preferring or rejecting some line of analysis, some research program or agenda. It is a problem of analysis to be worked at: how to examine the data so as to be able to show that the parties were, with and for one another, demonstrably oriented to those aspects of who they are, and those aspects of their context, which are respectively implicated in the "social structures" which we may wish to relate to the talk. If we treat this as a problem of analytic craft, we can use it as leverage to enhance the possibility of learning something about how talk-in-interaction is done, for it requires us to return again to the details of the talk to make the demonstration.

So, one issue posed by the theme "talk and social structure" is relevance.

The Issue of Procedural Consequentiality

The issue just discussed with respect to the characterization of the participants in some talk-in-interaction also is relevant to a characterization of "the context" in which they talk and interact. "Context" can be as much a part of what traditionally has been meant by "social structure" as attributes of the participants are. So, for example, remarking that some talk is being conducted "in the context of a bureaucracy," "in a classroom," "on a city street," etc. is part of what is sometimes intended by incorporating the relevance of social structure.

Such characterizations invoke particular aspects of the setting and not others. They involve selections among alternatives, and among subalternatives. For example, one type of formulation of context characterizes it by "place," and this is an alternative to various other sorts of context characterization. But within that context type, various forms of place formulation are available, all of which can be correct (Schegloff 1972). So, although the details of the argument have not been fully and formally worked out for the characterization of context or setting in the way that Sacks worked them out for the characterization of participants, it appears likely that the issue of relevance can be posed in much the same way for context as it has been for person reference.

What I want to do here is add something to this relevance problem for contexts. It concerns what I am calling the "procedural consequentiality" of contexts.

Even if we can show by analysis of the details of the interaction that some characterization of the context or the setting in which the talk is going on (such as "in the hospital") is relevant for the parties, that they are oriented to the setting so characterized, there remains another problem, and that is to show how the context or the setting (the local social structure), *in that aspect*, is procedurally consequential to the talk.

How does the fact that the talk is being conducted in some setting (say, "the hospital") issue in any consequences for the shape, form, trajectory, content, or character of the interaction that the parties conduct? And *what is the mechanism by which the context-so-understood has determinate consequences for the talk?*

This is a real problem, it seems to me, because without a specification of such a linkage we can end up with characterizations of context or setting which, however demonstrably relevant to the parties, do little in helping us to analyze, to explain, to understand, to give an account of how the interaction proceeded in the way in which it did, how it came to have the trajectory, the direction, the shape that it ended up having.[2] When a formulation of the context is proposed, it is *ipso facto* taken to be somehow relevant and consequential for what occurs in the context. It is the analyst's responsibility either to deliver analytic specifics of that consequentiality or to abjure that characterization of the context. Otherwise, the analysis exploits a tacit feature of its own discursive format, but evades the corresponding analytic onus. A sense of understanding and grasp is conveyed to, and elicited from, the reader, but is not earned by the elucidation of new observations about the talk.[3]

So, this is an open question, somewhat less formally stated than the other: how shall we find formulations of context or setting that will allow us (a) to connect to the theme that many want to connect to – social structure in the traditional sense, but (b) that will do so in a way that takes into account not only the demonstrable orientation of the participants, but, further, (c) that will allow us to make a direct "procedural" connection between the context so formulated and what actually happens in the talk. Otherwise we have a characterization that "hovers around" the interaction, so to speak, but is not shown actually to inform the production and grasp of the details of its conduct.

As with the issue of "relevance," I am here putting forward not principled objections to the invocation of social structure as context, but jobs to be taken on by those concerned with the intersection of talk and familiar senses of social structure. They challenge us to be alert to possible ways of showing such connections. I will just mention a few possible directions here.

Some formulations of setting do the sort of job I have in mind because they capture features of the setting that fall under the general rubric of "speech exchange systems" (Sacks, Schegloff and Jefferson 1974:729ff.). They satisfy this concern because they characterize a setting or context both in ways that connect to our general notions of social structure and in ways which directly refer to aspects of the practices by which the participants organize their talk. Some such settings carry with them as well a set of relevant identifications for the participants.

Consider, for example, the case of the courtroom in session (cf. Atkinson and Drew 1979; my remarks here rest on a much looser, vernacular and unstudied sense of the setting). To focus just on the turn-taking organization, it *is* the "courtroom-ness" of courtrooms in session which seems in fact to organize the way in which the talk is distributed among the persons present, among the *categories* of persons present, in the physical setting. So, for example, onlookers (members of the "audience") are not potential next speakers, as the official proceedings go on. And among the others who *are* potential next speakers at various points – the judge, the attorneys, the witness and the like, there are socially organized procedures for determining when they can talk, what they can do in their talk, and the like. It could be argued, then, that to characterize some setting of talk-in-interaction as in "a court-in-session" characterizes it with a formulation of context which can not only be claimed to connect to the general concern for "social structure" (for it certainly relates to institutional context), but can be shown to be procedurally consequential as well. Insofar as members of the audience sitting behind the bar never get up and talk but rather whisper to one another in asides, whereas the ones in front of the bar talk in defined and regular ways, by the very form of their conduct they show themselves to be oriented to the particular identities that are legally provided by that setting and show themselves to be oriented to "the-court-in-session" as a context.[4]

We have to be careful here to see what sorts of characterizations of context will satisfy these requirements. It is clear to me that vernacular accounts or formulations of context, even if informed by social scientific considerations, will not necessarily do it, if they do not specify how the talk is organized. One example, one not uncommon kind of proposed context description of talk-in-interaction is "an experiment" or "in a laboratory setting." Those terms sound like an adequate formulation of a kind of setting, and for some concerns perhaps they are. But these characterizations do not satisfy the concerns we have been discussing; under the rubrics "laboratory" or "experiment" very different sorts of organization of talk-in-interaction can be conducted.

Consider, for example, a study of repair recently published by the Dutch psycholinguist Willem Levelt (1983). Levelt had conducted an experiment on the so-called "linearization problem" (organizing a mass of simultaneously presented information into a temporally organized, hence linearized, format in talk). He asked a number of subjects to look at a screen on which were projected different shapes – circles, triangles, and the like, which were connected by lines of various sorts. Their job was to describe these figures so that someone else (not present) would be able to retrieve the figure from the description. The descriptions were all tape recorded. Levelt noticed that in the course of producing the descriptions, people regularly "mispoke;" they started to say one thing, cut themselves off and went back and "fixed" it. Levelt recognized these as self-repairs (Schegloff, Jefferson and Sacks 1977), and he wrote up a separate paper on various aspects of the placement and organization of self-repair and the evidence it gives about processes of self-monitoring by speakers.

But it seems to me that the findings of this work, at least with respect to the organization of repair, have an equivocal status at the present time. Why? Not simply because the talk was produced in a laboratory or experimental context. That the data come from laboratory-produced protocols does not tell us what consequences for the character of the talk are entailed. For example, it does not tell us what the speech exchange system was in which this talk was produced. As it happens, this *was* consequential, and has a bearing on the topic of the research report.

The speech exchange system in which this talk was produced was one whose turn-taking organization denied anyone else the right to talk besides the experimental subject. That is to say, within the boundaries of "the experiment," there was no possibility of a sequence in which current speaker's turn (that is, the subject's) is followed by a next turn in which some recipient (that is, the experimenter or a lab assistant) could have initiated repair. That is, this speech exchange system's turn-taking organization transforms the familiar organization by which opportunities to initiate repair are ordered (Schegloff, Jefferson and Sacks 1977). In fact, one of the classical rationales for the insistence on the methodology of experiments, *formal* experiments, is precisely to exclude the talk or other "extraneous" conduct of the experimenter. The whole point was to hold everything (except the variables of interest) constant. And one part of holding everything constant is to keep the experimenter or the experimenter's agent from talking in potentially varying ways to the different subjects, thereby introducing extraneous, and unmeasured, effects into the experimental results. So the whole point of this sort of experimental format *requires* the denial of the possibility of a next turn in which recipient/experimenter could talk.

We have then a very different turn-taking organization that seems to be subsumed by the formulation of context that we call "laboratory" or "experiment," with various sorts of consequences for the organization of repair. Aside from general organizational considerations that relate next-turn repair to same-turn repair (Schegloff 1979b), more specific analytic issues are implicated, only one of which can be mentioned in passing here.

It is that the sequential possibility of a next turn by another participant, and orientation to such a possibility, adds a wholly different *sort* of position for initiating repair to the ones incorporated into Levelt's account. He describes the positions in which repair is initiated *within* a turn in terms of their relationship to that which is being repaired (as do Schegloff, Jefferson and Sacks 1977 with respect to the initiation of repair *across* turns). However, he does not (and with his materials he *can* not) formulate the placement of the initiation of repair relative to the structure of the turn in which it occurs. For example, the initiation of repair cannot be formulated relative to possible completion of the ongoing turn by current speaker and possible start of a next turn by another (the relevance of which is analytically instantiated in Schegloff 1987b:111), a matter we would expect to be strategic if there is a "preference for self-correction."[5]

Until someone does a parallel analysis on talk from ordinary interaction, and sees whether the findings about same-turn repair come out the same way or not, we will not know the status of Levelt's findings about how same-turn repair is organized (where repair is initiated relative to the trouble source, how far back people go when they are going to reframe the trouble source and the like) – how substantial a contribution to our understanding of repair it can be.

In this case, I think the notion of "the laboratory as context" raises some serious concerns about particular research that was conducted under its auspices. But this is by virtue of the particular speech exchange system which composed it on that occasion, which provides the link of procedural consequentiality to the particular features of the talk being focused on in the research.

Compare with this the data addressed in such work as that reported in Zimmerman and West (1975) and Maynard and Zimmerman (1984). These data are also referred to as occurring in a "laboratory" context. But the speech exchange system involved here is a wholly different one. That speech exchange system provided for the parties (in this case, two "subjects") to talk to each other. The organization of the talk did not render any speaker free of the contingency of someone talking next (with the opportunity, in principle, of initiating repair). Were one to use those tapes to study self-repair, I do not think the results would be subject to the concerns raised above about Levelt's results, even though both of those settings can be characterized by a single context descriptor: "laboratory." The vernacular terms do not do the work. In one case "laboratory" is, and in the other case it is not, procedurally consequential *for the particular phenomena being studied.*[6]

In the search, then, for characterizations of context which will link talk to social structure, we cannot necessarily rely on the social-structural terms we have inherited from the past. Some of them will be procedurally consequential, and some of them will not, just as some will be demonstrably relevant to the participants and some will not. We have to find those terms for formulating context which are both demonstrably relevant to the participants and are procedurally consequential for the aspects of the conduct being treated, *on any given occasion.*

But it is not necessarily our *loss* that we cannot just appropriate terms from the traditional lexicon of "social structure" to understand talk. For we come thereby to use our data as a test of the relevance and viability of our sociological inheritance. We should be prepared to find that some of what we have received from the past, however cherished theoretically, culturally, politically, or ideologically, will not pass this test, and must therefore not be incorporated in our analysis. Rather, we should exercise our capacity to address the details of conduct, and exploit our data as challenges to our theoretical and analytic acumen, to enhance and expand our understanding of what "social structure" could consist of, as a robust and expanding tool of analysis rather than as an inheritance from the disciplinary past.

Social Structure or Conversational Structure?

The third concern mobilized by the present theme is for the balance between the focus on social structure and the focus on conversational structure in studying talk-in-interaction. These two thematic focuses (we would like to think) are potentially complementary. But are they really? We must figure out how to make them complementary, because they can also be alternatives in a more competitive sense. Each makes its own claims in organizing observation and analysis of the data, and one can preempt the other. In particular, the more familiar concerns with social structure can preempt new findings about conversational phenomena.

Let me offer some illustrations of this tension, and exemplify them from a recent paper of Zimmerman's, "Talk and its occasion" (1984), whose object of interest is "calls to the police" (an object with which I have also had some experience, cf. Schegloff 1967). The paper's enterprise appears directed specifically to attending both to the concerns of social structure and to the concerns of conversational structure. It offers a full account of this type of talk-in-interaction, and it does so with a sensitivity not only to the social structure involved, but also to the conversational structure of these occurrences. For example, the paper begins with an account of the kind of overall structural organization of the calls, and then focuses on the particular sequence type that makes up most of the calls, namely, an extended request or complaint sequence.[7]

Despite this commitment to both concerns, it seems to me, there is a tendency for the formulated social-structural context to "absorb" and "naturalize" various details of the talk. These features of the talk are thereby made unavailable, in practice if not in principle, for notice and analysis as accountable details of the talk. Their character as aspects of the talk produced by reference to some conversational or interactional organization is vulnerable to being slighted, in favor of assimilation to some social-structural, institutional, or vernacularly contextual source. How to balance these competing claims on our attention, when the competition takes this form, will be a matter to which analysts who are concerned with the thematics of talk-and-social structure will have to remain sensitive. Let me mention just three instances of the tension of which I speak which come up in Zimmerman's paper, and their consequences, to alert investigators to some of the forms which the issue can take.

One form which this issue takes concerns the proper analytic locus of some observed conversational phenomenon. There is, for example, the treatment of requests by organizations, and service agencies in particular. The police are clearly a service agency, and Zimmerman provides data on animal control services, emergency services, and an airline company, to support the claim that it is the "service agency organization" aspect of the setting which matters. Zimmerman's point is that the requests that callers introduce can involve contingencies, and specifically *organizational* contingencies, that are unknown to the caller. "Social structure" is thus doubly oriented to here, first in the institutional locus of "the police," and second in the fact that one of the parties to the conversation can be characterized as "an organization."

Zimmerman points out that in many of these calls a fair amount of talk intervenes between the request or complaint and its remedy. Regularly this takes the form of a series of question–answer sequences, which Zimmerman terms an "interrogative series." He notes that, sequentially speaking, it is a form of "insertion sequence" (Schegloff 1972), but stresses another aspect of this talk, namely that a number of inquiries get made by the recipient-of-the-request which reflect on the *organizational* contingencies and considerations which the request has occasioned. For example, the police have to decide whether the request is something actionable by the police, and that is not something the caller can be supposed to have the technical information to assess. Zimmerman's discussion (1984:220–2) links the occurrence of extensive insertion sequences or interrogative series to the contingencies generated by the fact that one of the parties to the request sequence is an *organization*.[8] If this were so, this might be a type case in which we would *have* to invoke the social-structural characteristics of one party to the conversation in order adequately to understand features of the talk (Levinson 1979).

But there are many occurrences in which non-organizational, non-service agency recipients of a request go through a quite similar insertion sequence before responding. One example with which I am familiar in detail is a telephone call involving a 15-year-old boy who has been asked by his 14-year-old "sometimes girlfriend" whether she can borrow his "gun." The request sequence itself goes on for four pages of transcript, and he takes her through a series of considerations – an "interrogative series," if you will: what do you want it for? what kind of gun? why that kind? etc. It turns out that there are considerations that apparently never entered her mind in making this request – should it be the longest one? the best one? the best looking one? the best shooting one? Indeed, when he asks "which gun," it is unclear that she knows the "right" terms with which to characterize which one she wants. (The sequence is discussed in Schegloff 1990).

The point is that we have here a long insertion between request and response. Neither participant is an organization or a service agency. The insertion is addressed to such matters as the warrant for the request and its consequent "actionability" by its recipient. It is not clear, then, what distinctively turns on the participation of *organizations* in request or complaint sequences. We seem to have here a regular expansion property of request/complaint sequences (including, perhaps, some recurrent insert types, such as warrant seeking). Perhaps there are particular features of the conduct of insert expansions which are distinctive when organizations are parties to the talk, but this needs to be shown by analysis which juxtaposes request sequences from organizational settings with request sequences (or their cognates) from other settings: that is, what is distinctive to this talk must be spelled out, and it needs to be shown that for the parties it has to do with "doing organizational talk," or with adapting the talk to their organizational exigencies.[9]

The problem to which I am trying to call attention is the cooptation or preemption of a sequential feature of the talk by a social-structural formulation of its context. In this case, if expansions of the sort here illustrated are endemic to request or complaint sequences, if they are part of the methodic practices for doing *sequences of that sort*, then there is no warrant for introducing *social structures of that sort* into the account. They are not "needed." Further, to introduce the social-structural specification of context is to risk missing the potentially general relevance of insertions to sequences of this type. The attributions to social structure, then, can be *at the expense of* increments to our understanding of conversational organization.[10]

A second issue concerning the tension between the social-structural and the conversation-specific is its persistence within a particular analysis. An illustration is provided by the discussion of a call to the police in which, after the police clerk opens the call with a self-identification as police, the caller says, "Yes, I'd like tuh report a loud party." Zimmerman writes:

> What is being made focally relevant in the opening segment of the call is the division of labor in our society with regard to matters of social control. In Sharrock and Turner's terms . . . a socially organized resource – police power – is being mobilized to deal with a problem that others cannot or choose not to deal with by other means. This mobilization raises certain issues, i.e., the policeable nature of the problem and its urgency . . . *The point to be noted here is that the hearability of an utterance as a "complaint" draws on its location within an institutional framework – that of policing – which touches the interactional realm through the organization of the call.* That organization provides a place, just after the alignment of identities in the opening sequence, the "first topic" slot . . . which is where the reason for the call is ordinarily provided. (1984:213, emphasis added)

There is an intended mutual resonance and grounding between the point of this paragraph and the cited instance – that is, between the caller's utterance being a complaint and having been said in what is "in fact" a call to the police. Again, then, institutional context seems criterial to conversational outcome. Indeed, this seems to be an almost ideal case in point, where the articulation of different components of social structure (via the division of labor with respect to police power) is localized and specified in conversation-structural terms – first-topic position after the opening section.

But how is the bearing of the institutional context – its relevance and procedural consequentiality – provided for here as a resource for analyzing the talk? Well, the police have self-identified as police; that appears to certify the relevance of the institutional context, at least for the police participant. But how about the caller? In a corpus of calls to the police with which I worked some years ago, some callers were not "controlled" by the self-identification by the answerer as "Police," but in the very next turn initiated a transformation of the relevant identities of the participants into personal acquaintances (Schegloff 1967:ch. 5; this happens in Zimmerman's corpus as well, cf. Whalen and Zimmerman 1987:177). The fact that the call is on the "police line," and has been answered by a "police" self-identification, does not *ipso facto* guarantee that is the orientation relevant to the caller.

This issue does not remain unaddressed. Zimmerman points out that callers/complainants ordinarily begin their first turns with a response token ("yes" or "yeah") which registers the police self-identification and reconciles it "with the caller's sense of who the recipient of the upcoming complaint or report should properly be" (1984:218). When the initial response by the police (or other service agency) presents some problem in this regard, the caller's first turn does not begin with such a token. Thus, Zimmerman concludes that these initial bits of utterance, "in aligning their situated identities, provide a working framework which commits participants to the nature of the occasion summoned up by the initiation of the call and thereby *provides for the presumptive hearability of utterances as relevant to the purposes of that occasion of talk*" (1984:219, emphasis added). This is the basis for the earlier cited claim that "the hearability of an utterance as a 'complaint' draws on its location within an institutional framework." The opening utterances establish that framework, on which the subsequent talk may then "draw."[11]

It is, however, in point to observe that the understanding of the caller's initial utterance as a request or complaint is not provided for solely by the institutional context which the opening may have shown to be mutually relevant. The caller, in the call whose examination is at issue here, has constructed the talk in his/her first turn ("Yes, I'd like tuh report a loud party") not only to *be* "calling the police," but to *do* "calling the police." The format employed for the turn, "I'd like to report . . ." appears to be a format for "reporting to the authorities," and perhaps even for "reporting to the police" specifically.[12] A complaint to the landlord is not, I think, done in this way. In this case, it could be argued, the hearability of the utterance as a complaint most proximately draws on *its conversational construction* as "a complaint to the police." Invoking its "factual" institutional location distracts from the method of its conversational accomplishment.[13]

Here again, the social-structural formulation masks the practices of the talk, in this case as *conversationally constituting* the context for the interaction. Once the identification talk in the opening has been invoked to establish the relevance of the institution for the participants, that institutional locus serves to "naturalize" the mode of talk, to provide a tacit covering principle that normalizes the particular way the participants construct the talk. The vernacular characterization "absorbs" the details of the talk as an unnoticed "of course" in such a "formulated-as-institutional" setting, and does not prompt one to note and explicate how the talk enacts "doing being in that setting". There is a mutually grounding relationship between the details of the talk (here, the "I'd like to report . . ." format) and the global provision that this is a "call to the police," with the former having not been explicitly noted at all, and with the latter shown to be relevant by the police opening self-identification. Relevance having been shown by that, concern for the issue is relaxed. The question is not pressed: how is the next (and *any* next) utterance constructed so as to show/do "calling the police"?

A methodological canon is suggested: establishing relevance and establishing procedural consequentiality should not be "threshold" issues, in the sense that once you have done "enough" to show it, you are finished. Rather they are questions for continuing analysis. And not necessarily in the "loaded" form of "how are they now doing 'calling the police'?", but in "open" form – "what does the form of the talk show about recipient design considerations and about orientation to context (institutional, social-structural, sequential, or whatever)." Because we "know" that not everything said *in* some context (institutional or other) is relevantly oriented to that context.

If the focus of inquiry is the organization of conduct, the details of action, the practices of talk, then every opportunity should be pressed to enhance our understanding of any available detail about those topics. Invoking social structure at the outset can systematically distract from, even blind us to, details of those domains of event in the world.

If the goal of inquiry is the elucidation of *social structure*, one might think that quite a different stance would be warranted, and one would want to give freer play to the effective scope of social structure, and to do so free of the constraints I have been discussing. Though this stance has much to recommend it, it could as well be argued that one does not best serve the understanding of social structure by attributing to it properties which are better understood as the products of other aspects of organized social life, such as interactional structure, or by failing to explicate how social structure is accomplished *in* the conduct. In any case, the understanding of social structure will be enhanced if we explicate how its embodiment in particular contexts on particular occasions permeates the "membrane" (Goffman 1961) surrounding episodes of interaction to register its stamp within them.

A third expression of the tension between social-structural and conversation structural interests in talk data concerns the direction in which analysis is pursued; it can distract pursuit of otherwise inviting analytic tacks on the structure of the talk. For example, Zimmerman reports (1984:219–20) that most of his data accord with the Sharrock and Turner finding that callers package their complaints in a "single utterance format" (Sharrock and Turner 1978), but he displays as well an instance in which the complaint is presented in a multiple utterance format. It appears that this multiple utterance format (or multiple "turn – constructional unit" turn, Sacks, Schegloff and Jefferson 1974) is a structural alternative to the insertion sequence (the "interrogative series") which occurs in the more common cases. For example, the response to the request which ordinarily follows only after an interrogative series here follows directly after completion of the multi-unit request/complaint turn itself.

This relationship (as possible structural alternatives) between [single-utterance request + interrogative series + response] on the one hand, and [multi-unit request + no interrogative series + response] on the other hand, presents some attractive possibilities for analysis. What varies regularly between organization of a story in a multi-unit, single-turn format as compared to a sequence (that is, multi-turn) format? What are the consequences of the contrasting divisions of labor involved in the two formats, especially the differing "steering" potentials? What is added to or subtracted from or modified in the talk by the imposition of sequence structure on it, or by its preemption by single speaker organization? These questions may be put while "holding constant" that the callers are soliciting police action by the telling.[14]

Of course, such questions may remain unaddressed because inquiry is addressed to other matters, equally conversation relevant, and because one cannot do everything in a single paper. But it is possible that the focus on showing how conversations are articulated with, and shaped by, social and institutional structure diverts attention from the questions about conversation structures which particular details of the talk might otherwise prompt.

What then shall be the balance between the claims of conversational structure, with its stress on the methodic ways of talking in which turns and sequences have ways of developing anonymously, whoever the parties are, as aspects of particular structures of action, sometimes shaped by the participants for the particular co-participants with whom they are engaged – what shall be the balance between those claims on the one hand, and on the other hand those of social structure, with their implication of the constitutive relevance for action and interaction of differentiation, both of participants and of institutional contexts? Clearly there are observations here about the nature of organizations, and perhaps of organizations as participants on one end of the conversation. But how shall we assess their relative claims? When shall we attribute some feature we have noticed about the organization of talk to "internal," conversation structural concerns, and when to "external," social-structural or organizational ones?

Let me introduce here what I will call the "paradox of proximateness," a consideration prompted by various efforts to argue the indispensability of social or legal context for understanding talk.[15] If it is to be argued that some legal, organizational or social environment underlies the participants' organizing some occasion of talk-in-interaction in some particular way, then either one *can* show the *details in the talk* which that argument allows us to notice, and which in return supply the demonstrable warrant for the claim by showing the relevant presence of the sociolegal context in the talk; or one *cannot* point to such detail. If the detail *is* available, then it is the participants' demonstrable orientations *in* the interaction which are the effective agents for the relevant aspects of the interaction (though the parties may also talk in a way which attributes their orientation to some legal constraint, etc.). If the detail *is not* demonstrable, then for the task of explicating the organization and practices of the *talk*, it is not clear what warrant there is for invoking the relevance of the legal and social context or environment which the analyst may want to claim. That is, either there is a proximate, conversationally represented indication of the relevance of context, in which case invocations of more remote context are unnecessary; or there is no conversationally represented indication of the relevance of the aspects of context which have been invoked, in which case the warrant for invoking it has not been established.

An analyst may feel the need to invoke such contexts for the distributional and institutional concerns which animate an inquiry. But if the inquiry is animated by distributional, institutional, or traditional social-structural concerns, why should the character of inquiry into the nature of talk-in-interaction be shaped by considerations extrinsic to *that* enterprise, but felt necessary to another? Indeed, one might argue that the study of talk should be allowed to proceed under its own imperatives, with the hope that its results will provide more effective tools for the analysis of distributional, institutional, and social-structural problems later on than would be the case if the analysis of talk had, from the outset, to be made answerable to problems extrinsic to it.

It may, of course, be the case that talk (or *some* talk) is not analyzable *for its own problematics* without reference to social and institutional contexts of the traditional sort. But that has to be shown. That is, it has to be shown that it is necessary to invoke such contexts in order to understand aspects of the talk itself, rather than aspects of the context in which the talk occurs, or distributional or institutional aspects of that context. (It is, of course, quite a different claim to say that the context is necessary in order to understand the context.) Once it has been shown that some particular spate of talk cannot be adequately analyzed without reference to its "context," it will be necessary to elucidate what in its claimed context is needed to understand the talk, and how to articulate and blend such analysis of context with analysis of the talk. Such a blend will need to adapt, but nonetheless incorporate, such previously discussed constraints on analysis as relevance and procedural consequentiality.

In considering the respective concerns for conversational structure and social structure, then, we must first be clear about the overall commitments and preoccupations of inquiry. It is one thing to be addressed to the understanding of talk-in-interaction as the object of inquiry, and to ask how references to social structure bear on it and might need or permit incorporation in it. It is quite another to be addressed to understanding distributional or institutional or social-structural features of social life, and to ask how talk-in-interaction figures in their social production. I have taken the former of these enterprises as the premise of my discussion. I think the latter enterprise would benefit from analyzing talk by methods appropriate for the analysis of talk in its own right. But the latter enterprise *can* be understood as a development quite independent of the one concerned with the fundamental organization of talk-in-interaction – as a kind of extension of mainstream institutional sociology. In that regard, it could be quite free of the analytic constraints under which conversation analysis has developed. On the other hand, that enterprise, too, might find a quite fresh turning were it to respect the constraints on the study of talk-in-interaction in its own right.

Conclusion

These then are three sorts of issues mobilized, or remobilized, for me when the talk turns to "talk and social structure." However lively our intuitions, in general or with respect to specific details, that it matters that some participants in data we are examining are police, or female, or deciding matters which are specifically constrained by the law or by economic or organizational contingencies, however insistent our sense of the reality and decisive bearing of such features of "social structure" in the traditional sense, the challenge posed is to find a way to show these claims, and show them from the data in three respects:

1 that what is so loomingly relevant for us (as competent members of the society or as professional social scientists) was relevant for the parties to the interaction we are examining, and thereby arguably implicated in their production of the details of that interaction;
2 that what seems inescapably relevant, both to us and to the participants, about the "context" of the interaction is demonstrably consequential for some specifiable aspect of that interaction; and

3   that an adequate account for some specifiable features of the interaction cannot be fashioned from the details of the talk and other conduct of the participants as the vehicle by which *they* display the relevance of social-structural context for the character of the talk, but rather that this must be otherwise invoked by the analyst, who furthermore has developed defensible arguments for doing so.

In brief, the issue is how to convert insistent intuition, however correct, into empirically detailed analysis.

This is a heavy burden to impose. Meeting it may well lead to exciting new results. But if it is not to be met in one or more respects, arguments will have to be put forward that the concerns I have discussed are no longer in point, are superseded by other considerations, or must yield to the new sorts of findings that are possible if one holds them in abeyance. Simple invocation of the burden of the sociological past will not suffice.

With respect to social structure, then, as with respect to other notions from social science's past such as "intention," the stance we might well consider is treating them as programmatically relevant for the parties, and hence for us. In principle, some one or more aspects of who the parties are and where/when they are talking may be indispensably relevant for producing and grasping the talk, but these are not decisively knowable a priori. It is not for us to *know* what about context is crucial, but to *discover* it, and to discover *new sorts* of such things. Not, then, to privilege sociology's concerns under the rubric "social structure," but to discover them in the members' worlds, if they are there.

Otherwise, we risk volunteering for a path which has led close inquiry into social life astray in the past, but which we now have an opportunity to avoid. In the past, one has needed a special warrant or license to examine closely the details of ordinary life and conduct. Whether it was the "defectiveness" of the people involved as with the mentally ill or retarded or physically handicapped, their moral taint as with criminals, delinquents or other versions of "evil," or the possibilities of enhanced efficacy, as in the improvement of production processes or bureaucratic administration, or enhanced justice or fairness, there was always a "good reason" for looking closely at the details of conduct.

With the license came a shaped focus, either on a target population, a target set of behaviors, or a target aspect of conduct which one examined. What was found was then generally attributed to the license under which one found it. Thus, early investigations into the language of schizophrenics (see Kasanin 1944) came upon the phenomenon of a spate of talk being touched off by the sound of some word in a prior utterance (so-called "clang association"), a phenomenon which students of conversation will recognize as not uncommon in ordinary talk. But having found it through the close examination of schizophrenic talk (talk which could be so closely examined by virtue of its speakers' diagnoses), it was taken as specially characteristic of such talk. So also with children's talk, etc.

If the study of conversation and talk-in-interaction is once again required to be "licensed," whether by practical concerns or by the institutionalized interests of traditional disciplines, then we may well find ourselves attributing – now to "social structure" – what are the indigenous features of talk-in-interaction. Should we not give the latter a chance to be recognized in their own right, especially since they constitute their own sociology in any case?

Notes

These reflections were prepared to serve as the opening presentation of the Talk and Social Structure Conference. In some places they address once again matters taken up in an earlier paper (Schegloff 1987a), but different facets of those matters or in a more detailed fashion. My thanks to Jennifer Mandelbaum for contributions of tact and clarity in the preparation of this written version. I am also indebted to Deirdre Boden, Paul Drew, Douglas Maynard and especially Jack Whalen, whose reactions to an earlier draft, or to the reactions of others to the earlier draft, helped in my efforts to arrive at a text which might be understood as I meant it.

1 Of course, these need not be *competing* claims; the aim must be to make them complementary. For a penetrating treatment of many of the issues taken up here, cf. Heritage 1984a:280–90.
2 A similar argument is made in Schegloff 1987c for explicating how cultural/ linguistic context has the consequences attributed to it. Aspects of prosody may well have consequences for misunderstanding in cross-cultural interaction (e.g., Gumperz 1982), but understanding how they issue in the particular misunderstandings which ensue will require explicating what in the structure of talk-in-interaction converts that prosody into that *type* of misunderstanding.
3 Reasons both of relevance and of procedural consequentiality motivated a decision not to characterize the "Opening up closings" paper (Schegloff and Sacks 1973) as contextually specific to American culture, as had been requested by an anthropologically oriented referee (cf. p. 291, note 4, and also Sacks, Schegloff and Jefferson 1974, p. 700, note 10, on the same issue). That request invoked on behalf of anthropology a cultural sense of "context," parallel to the invocation by sociologists of social-structural senses of "context."
4 A penetrating account along these lines of the constituting of a speech exchange system through practices of talking, in this case of "the job

interview," may be found in Button 1987, see also Heritage and Greatbatch, chapter 5 below.

5 I leave aside here the exclusion of interactional considerations (Jefferson 1974) which can bear on where and how repair is initiated, an exclusion which allows the depiction of the initiation of repair in strictly grammatical terms.

6 One could harbor a concern that the setting of the Zimmerman/Maynard data *is* procedurally consequential for the organization of topic talk which is their focus, since the participants in their experiment were asked to talk while knowing they were to be interrupted for the start of an experiment in a "few minutes" (Maynard and Zimmerman 1984), a prospect which may well constrain the sort of topic talk participants undertake. There are naturalistic settings which are in many respects similar (such as medical waiting rooms, though there is no injunction to talk there) in which the seriousness of this concern might be assessed.

7 In addition, as several readers of an earlier version of this chapter have pointed out, Zimmerman has in various other writings (both general, as in Wilson and Zimmerman 1980, and other reports of the project on the police, such as Whalen and Zimmerman 1987, 1990) aligned himself with the principles of analysis with which the text here is preoccupied. What is at issue in the ensuing discussion is, then, not a difference over principle, but a concern about how general theoretical and analytic principles are embodied in the *practice* of analysis and its reports. It is a concern with the vulnerability of a newer and technical stance toward the materials of talk-in-interaction in the face of an older stance and idiom, one which furthermore mobilizes our vernacular intuitions despite our contrary resolve.

8 For example, he writes: "Of particular interest here is the fact that making a request engages an organization rather than simply an individual, and thus, varying with the circumstances of the call, encounters contingencies of response which are evident to the organizational personnel receiving the request, but are perhaps unknown or only vaguely perceived by the caller. Thus, a complaint or request routinely involves some processing, that is, some course in which its features – many of which have yet to be made evident – are fit to the requirements of organizational response" (p. 220).

9 One candidate is suggested in another report from the same project (Whalen and Zimmerman 1990). There they suggest that when the call to the police comes from another organization, the police do not undertake to test out the robustness of the report by the caller, as they do when the caller is a "private party," apparently taking it that an "organizational caller" would already have established the actionability of the reported state of affairs. Here the bearing of "organizations" is not the fact that the police *are* an organization, but is rather what they do by virtue of their *interlocutor* being an organization. And what is critical for the way the police complaint-taker proceeds is not just that the complainant actually *is* an organization, but the complaint-takers' *orientation* to its being an organization, and inferences occasioned by that orientation. Still, the argument is that the police conduct

themselves differently by virtue of the property of their interlocutor that he speaks for an organization.

10   The key here is the juxtaposition of contextually specialized materials with others of canonical form. This sort of tack is taken in the analysis of conversational openings in calls to the police in another report from the same research project (Whalen and Zimmerman 1987), and on other analytic objects in such recent work as Button 1987, Clayman 1989, and Heritage 1985a. Analysis along such lines may prove attractive as well for materials such as those reported on in Maynard's conference paper (chapter 7 below) which concerned parents of retarded children being informed of the retardation by clinic personnel. Such materials might well invite first an account of the structure of announcement sequences in general, then an account of "bad news" announcement sequences in particular, and then the introduction of the particular setting and task under examination, and the ways in which they informed the enactment or realization or modification of such sequences, insofar as they could be shown to be oriented to by the participants (cf. Schegloff 1988b).

On occasion the literature already provides an account of the non-contextually specialized form of the talk (e.g., for the matters taken up in Whalen and Zimmerman 1987) needed for comparative examination. In most cases, however, the investigator of institutionally specialized forms will need to supply the more generic analysis as well (as in Heritage 1985a, for example). In general, the most promising path for research in this area, it seems to me, is for all students of (claimedly) institutionally specialized conduct to work with generic forms as well, if possible.

11   A subsequent paper (Whalen and Zimmerman 1987:178) describes this position as follows (attributing it to Wilson 1985, but not to Zimmerman 1984):

> When callers report or describe events such as crimes, fires or accidents to a representative of the police, fire department or ambulance service, they engage the occupational responsibilities of such a recipient. The force of a description or event as a request is achieved by the alignment of the identities of teller and recipient in a particular way: as a reporting party or complainant speaking to the agent of an organization officially responsible for dealing with such matters. This is accomplished by the completion of the opening identification sequence (categorical self-identification by dispatcher / acknowledgement by caller) occasioned by the telephone summons. This alignment establishes a sequentially realized institutional context for hearing reports/descriptions as requests.

But Whalen and Zimmerman go on to broaden their account of how the openings of these calls work, and to deepen our understanding of the relevance structure which the police bring to the incoming calls. They show convincingly that even silence or "ambient sounds" on the line (without any confirmation by caller of the relevance of the police institutional self-identification) are treated by the police as possible calls for assistance. (This is to my mind the most cogent basis for arguing that "hearability as a complaint" draws on institutional context.) In developing a basis for this, they drive the account backwards in the structure of the occasion – to the orientations of the police participants in the conversations' "pre-beginnings" (Schegloff 1979a:27, 34; Whalen and Zimmerman 1987:180–1) – the moments preceding the first utterance of the conversation itself. What they deepen thereby is our understanding of the orientations which the *police* bring to the talk. What I am concerned with in the text here is, on the other hand, what the *callers* show they bring to the talk, *in* the talk, and after the convergence of identification in the opening.

12   There are other forms of talk in which a caller's first turn displays an orientation to the police, *does* "calling the police," for example, by referring to a car as being "vandalized" (Wilson, chapter 2 above), or, more generally, by use of proto-technical terminology of the criminal law or policing. Jack Whalen (personal communication) reports such forms to be "very frequently employed" in complainants' reports to the police. In a later paper from the same research project (Whalen and Zimmerman 1990), complainants' reports to the police are taken up, but their formulations of "the trouble" are left for treatment in a separate paper.

13   Heritage (1984a:280–90) offers a similar treatment of questions and questioning.

14   These two formats could be examined in concert with a third which might prove instructive. It was Alene Terasaki who suggested several years ago (in work which did not come to written fruition) that "announcements" seem to be prepared by their speakers so as to be deliverable in single sentence formats. This is commonly done through one or more pre-expansions or pre-sequences (in addition to the familiar "pre-announcement"). The prospect is, then, to compare (a) a single, multi-unit turn format, with (b) a single-unit turn followed by insertion sequences, with (c) a single-unit turn "prepared" by pre-sequences. It is unlikely, however, that the third of these possibilities will be found in police call data.

15   The point is occasioned most directly by Mehan's conference presentation (see chapter 4 below). Mehan aims to account for the distribution of a school district's disposition of special education cases, in particular the non-allocation of any cases to one program in particular. The account is built from a description of the organization's ways of processing cases, in which a meeting at which disposition is decided and accepted by the parent figures centrally. Mehan argues that various features of the meeting, including the non-mention of certain program possibilities and the order in which the several phases of the discussion are taken up, are centrally conditioned by various features of the legal and economic context in which the school district finds itself (including various provisions of formal law). This claim is not grounded in overt specifiable details of the talk, however.

4

The School's Work of Sorting Students

Hugh Mehan

In the most general terms, I am interested in common-sense knowledge: the range of procedures by which people make sense of the world and find their way about in the circumstances in which they find themselves. In more specific terms, I am interested in how the sense-making work of schooling gets done. One of the recurrent work activities of the school is the sorting of students into categories or classes for the purposes of educating them. Classification is accomplished by testing, ability grouping, and tracking practices. In order to understand this sorting and classifying work, I study language use in school contexts. This interest forces me to confront the relationship between features of social structure and interactional processes (cf. Molotch and Boden 1985), which some have called the "macro–micro" controversy in sociology (Knorr-Cetina and Cicourel 1981; Alexander et al. 1987). Before I analyze some of the school's sorting work, I will briefly outline some of the dimensions of this controversy.

The Macro–Micro Issue in Sociology

Oversimplifying, the macro–micro issue concerns the relationship between social structure and interaction. The positions taken on the issue range from claims that there are no connections between macro and micro to proposals that there is no distinction between them.

The separation of social structure and social interaction

For some sociologists (for instance, Blau 1987) the solution to the macro–micro issue is simple: there is no connection, hence there is no problem. Macro and micro sociology are fundamentally incommensurate because individual and interactional phenomena exist at a level which is separate and distinct from collective and aggregate phenomena. This position results in a neat division of labor. Macro sociologists are responsible for studying the organization of the world system, stratification, the division of labor and the like at the level of large-scale political and economic institutions. Micro sociologists are allocated the responsibility of studying individual motivation, socialization, small group coalitions, or the exchange of significant symbols.

For other sociologists, the solution to the macro–micro problem is technical or methodological. Coleman (1987), for example, proposes a technical connection between macro structures and micro processes. An observed or hypothesized relation between two or more variables – structures or processes – typically is explained by translating the independent macro variable into an individual or micro level counterpart variable, linking the micro counterpart by psychological processes in a second micro variable, then aggregating the latter to arrive at the micro effect identified in the dependent variable.

Locating social structure in social interaction

A second position on macro–micro relationships denies that the phenomenal aspects of society are merely reflections of large-scale institutional and historical forces. Instead, they are contingent outcomes of people's practical activity (Giddens 1979). Researchers in this constructionist tradition attempt to locate social structure in social interaction.

Such seemingly fixed characteristics as one's gender (Garfinkel 1967), social identity (Goffman 1959), mental health (Edgerton 1967), and personal experiences such as religion (Jules-Rosette 1976) have been analyzed as social collaborations. Some of the "social facts" of the legal, medical and educational institutional orders have been analyzed as social accomplishments. Crime, deviance and normality have been shown to be a consequence of the practices by which police on the beat, judges and lawyers in the courtroom engage in interaction with suspects (Bittner 1967a, 1967b; Cicourel 1967; R. Emerson 1969; Pollner 1975, 1988;

Atkinson and Drew 1979; Maroules 1985). Physical disease, mental illness and medical treatment have been shown to be a collaborative construction involving patients with various health officials (Cicourel 1981a, 1981b; Fisher 1983; Coulter 1979; Scheff 1966; Frankel 1983; Mishler 1984; Tannen and Wallet 1983; Sudnow 1967; Todd 1983; West 1984). Students' intelligence, their educational identities as mentally gifted or pariahs, as mentally retarded (Mercer 1974) or learning disabled (Mehan, Hertweck and Meihls 1986; Hood, McDermott and Cole 1980; Cole and Traupmann 1980; Maynard, chapter 7 below) are produced in concerted interaction.

So, too, the facts of scientific observation emerge from a social nexus, one in which observations become findings through arguments and rhetoric, not through simple measurement and discovery (Latour and Woolgar 1986; Knorr-Cetina 1981; Knorr-Cetina and Mulkay 1983; Gusfield 1981; Garfinkel et al. 1986). Pollner and McDonald Wikler (1985), examining the routine transactions of a family with their severely mentally retarded child, found that the family employed practices which sustained its belief in the competence of the child in the face of overwhelming evidence to the contrary, that is, the child had been diagnosed as severely mentally retarded. Family members prestructured the child's environment to maximize the likelihood that whatever the child did could be seen as meaningful, intentional activity. The child's family would establish a definition of the situation and use it as a frame of reference for interpreting and describing any and all of the child's subsequent behavior or track the child's ongoing behavior and develop physical or verbal contexts that could render the behavior intelligent and interactionally responsive.

The social constructionist position I am outlining must not be confused with those readings of Goffman and Garfinkel which infer that the social world is made up anew on each occasion of interaction. Social actors cannot make up meanings in any old way. The construction of meanings is constrained by the structure of language, historical precedents, conventions and institutional histories. Constructionists do not dismiss "mental illness" and "crime" and "intelligence" as merely romantic fictions; they examine how the factual status of such phenomena are assembled in social settings. This conception of macro–micro relationships requires an examination of institutional arrangements, public policies, history and biography. It should be clear, then, that this sense of construction is *social* in nature. Social structures are accomplished by situated collaborative work of people within institutional, cultural and historical context, not the interior mental work of a solitary problem solver or decision maker.

Unfortunately, Garfinkel and his colleagues contribute to this confusion, this equation of constructionism with radical situationalism. Consider, for example, their description of the discovery of the independent Galilean pulsar (IGP). In a line of research consistent with the formulation laid out in Garfinkel (1967), Garfinkel, Lynch and Livingston (1981) asked: how was the IGP discovered? They propose that the answer to that question is to be found in the activities of the scientists on the night of the discovery. Through the routine work that these scientists engage in each and every night – watching screen displays, reading printouts – they made the pulsar visible. Explicit in this formulation is a significant statement about scientific inquiry: scientific objects are not simply on computer screens or in computer printouts waiting to be discovered; scientific objects are extracted from materials through scientists' interactive work. Cocke and Disney worked together that night, as other nights, and through that work transformed a set of markings on a computer printout into a cultural object – the pulsar.

In suggesting that this is the work of scientific discovery, Garfinkel, Lynch and Livingston are adopting a radical position: they are insisting that scientific discovery can only be apprehended sociologically through the study of local practices of work at the benchsite, for it is there that cultural objects are composed. Scientific discovery is composed of the situationally achieved, temporally unfolding scientists' laboratory work. The IGP is not separate from that work; the IGP *is* that work. It is the goal of ethnomethodology to explicate those benchsite practices which make objects visible, recognizable and objective. To be sure, these practices are completely social in nature: "from the local historicity of the embodied night's work, they [Cocke and Disney] extracted a cultural object, the independent Galilean pulsar. The IGP retains the material contents of astronomical *things* in their entirety. The IGP is a *cultural* object, *not* a 'physical' or a 'natural' object" (Garfinkel, Lynch and Livingston 1981:141).

But we may ask: isn't the work of science more than the night's work? Doesn't the work of science also comprise the transformation of a "discovery" into a "cultural object" by its inscription as scholarly reports (Latour and Woolgar 1986)? Doesn't science have a history, cultural conventions, institutional demands which impinge upon "the night's work" (Knorr-Cetina 1981)? Weren't Cocke and Disney trained in a tradition of investigation that enabled them to "see" in the computer runs the cultural object that ordinary citizens or even other scientists could not see (Kuhn 1970)?

Garfinkel, Lynch and Livingston seem ambiguous on this point. If we read them as saying that the IGP *is* the benchsite work and nothing else but the benchsite work, then they have reduced science to local practices and ethnomethodology remains the study of practices divorced from the historical and cultural dimensions of social context (cf. Garfinkel 1987 for a formulation which reinforces this conception of ethnomethodology). If we read them as having investigated one among many events in a long line from discovery to publicity, then we have (yet another) incomplete albeit insightful suggestion of how to go about a culturally and historically contextualized enterprise.

The constructionist line of investigation, as I see it, studies the situated artful practices of people and the ways in which these are employed to create an objectified everyday world without losing sight of institutional and cultural context. In this line of work, everyday practices are examined for the way in which they exhibit, indeed, generate, social structures. Structures are taken here in a strict Durkheimian sense, that is, as "social facts." In addition to being "external and constraining" upon the social situation, social structures are not subject to change as an act of will or volition by individuals (Garfinkel and Sacks 1970). The practices which generate the social structures are treated as endogenous to the work domains in which they occur and which they constitute (Heritage 1984a). Furthermore, the practices are not simply an analytic device of the researcher. They are "members' phenomena." Participants in the settings recognize the practices and orient to them during the course of interaction (Garfinkel and Sacks 1970: cf. McDermott, Gospodinoff and Aron 1978).

Conversational structure *is* social structure

Some conversation analysts, many of whom are represented in this volume, take a much more radical stance on the macro–micro issue. They say that when the analysis of ordinary conversation is completed, there will be no difference between macro and micro. We will discover that conversational structure *is* social structure. This position, in effect, collapses the distinction between macro and micro, equating the one with the other.

Conversation analysts ask: how much of human action is sequentially organized – and only sequentially organized? To answer this question, they become agnostic concerning social structure; they make no a priori assumptions concerning its importance. Instead, the relevance of social-structural considerations must be shown in the sequential organization of conversation. This position is motivated by the fact that social situations can be described in multiple ways. Sacks (1963) points out that any person's identity can be formulated differently (male, student, lover, etc.).

This poses a problem for both participants and analysts of interaction: which identity is relevant for this occasion of interaction? The multiplicity of identities poses an additional problem for analysts: how is the relevance of any identity revealed in the interaction?

Schegloff (1987a) says contexts, like identities, can be described in many ways. Contexts are commonly referred to: (1) in organizational terms – bureaucratic, medical, legal, classroom and the like; (2) in activity terms – getting acquainted, conducting lessons; or (3) in relational terms – doctor–patient interaction, teacher–student interaction, etc. Because any setting can be described in many ways, the members' label for the context, in and of itself, is not an adequate warrant for its use (cf. Frake 1983; McDermott, Gospodinoff and Aron 1978). Just because a conversation is taking place in a hospital, for example, does not automatically make medical language technically relevant for participants in a conversation that is occurring there. Nor does the fact that the topic of the talk is "medical" render the "hospital setting" as relevant for the talk at a given moment.

To counter the problem of multiple, vernacular descriptions, Schegloff proposes that the analyst must determine which of many possible descriptions is relevant in the ongoing course of interaction. The canons of conversation analysis require that investigators be able to warrant any description by showing that it is relevant to the participants and is relevant for the participants *at the time of its occurrence in the interaction* (see also chapter 3 above, at p. 51). And because the definition of the situation can change moment to moment, the analyst's relevance procedure must be sensitive to changes in the flow of conversation that can occur as often as turn by turn. Those "internal to the setting" relevancies serve as constraints on the investigator's characterization of the setting (cf. McDermott, Gospodinoff and Aron 1978). Schegloff (1987a) says this approach challenges us to replace vernacular formulations of macro considerations (for example, identity and context) with technical descriptions (that is, those located in the sequential structure of conversation). This substitution is recommended because a technical description will capture what is relevant for participants better than vernacular descriptions.

One concern of conversation analysis is to identify and describe procedures of talk that are not dependent on probability sampling for their generality. Conversation analysis, or CA, studies a corpus of data to reveal the formal (that is, sequential or syntactical) structures of talk. In this regard, the enterprise has been successful over the past 20 years (Heritage 1984a). One of the most insistent and recurring findings reported by conversation analysts is the "local character" of the organization of interaction (Sacks, Schegloff and Jefferson 1974; Schegloff, chapter 3 above). Conversation is organized so that only one speaker speaks at a time and with regular transitions between speakers. The transitions between speakers are achieved in an orderly fashion without overlap between speakers and without gap between adjacent turns. Furthermore, participants in conversation orient to these features of talk in the interaction (where "orientation" is defined in sequential terms). Importantly for our consideration of the macro–micro issue, the features of conversation are said to operate independently of such contextual variations as the identities of the speakers, the topic of the conversation, where it takes place, the number of participants in the conversation, the size or length of turns (Heritage 1984a; Schegloff 1987a).

Perhaps because CA has focused on the syntactic structures of talk that are presumably indifferent to participants and invariant across topics and settings of interaction, CA has given little analytic attention to the semantic and pragmatics aspects of language. But when conversation analysts have considered the identities of participants or institutional settings, claims of invariance have been challenged (Zimmerman 1984; Wilson, chapter 2 above; West 1984; Maynard 1984). The power relations in conversations among men and women is one such example (Zimmerman and West 1975; West and Zimmerman 1977; West 1979, 1982). Men are found to interrupt women more frequently than the opposite. This finding links interruptions, an important feature of conversation (a micro-level activity), with gender, an ascribed characteristic of the participants (a macro-level phenomenon).

There is another set of studies which discusses the power relationships among professionals and their clients in institutional settings, for instance, doctors and patients (Strong 1979; Silverman 1981; Fisher 1983; Todd 1983; Cicourel 1981b; West 1984; Waitzkin 1983), teachers and students (Philips 1982; Gumperz and Herasimchuk 1975; Mehan 1979; Michaels 1981; Collins 1986; McDermott, Gospodinoff and Aron 1978; Moll and Diaz 1986; Au 1980; Cook-Gumperz 1986), lawyers, judges and suspects (O'Barr 1982; Maroules 1985), and counselors and students (Erickson and Shultz 1982). These studies show different treatment options made differentially available across social class, gender and ethnic lines. In both the men/women and the professional/client cases, differentials in conversation become cast as differentials in status and/or power. The differentials are made manifest in the interaction of conversation.

Sharrock (1979) and Dunstan (1980) are critical of researchers who say that interaction in medical and legal settings is a conflictual discourse between unequal partners. Reanalyzing transcripts used by other researchers to claim that doctor/patient interaction was coercive, they propose that the parties are involved in producing and sustaining the medical interview. Doctors and patients are getting the work of legal interrogation done, but are not participating in an unequal relationship. They propose "practical activities" as an alternative to "coercive interactions" to explain the course of face-to-face interaction in institutional settings.

Schegloff, too, takes a chary view of status and power claims (1987a and chapter 3 above), suggesting that the studies of asymmetry in women's conversations with men and in those of professionals with their clients need to do more than ground their claims in statistical correlations; they must show that status and/or power characterizations are grounded in the participants' own orientation in the interaction. He says that differentials in conversation may not be affected by the attributes of the participants *per se*, and questions whether gender or status is the relevant attribute to invoke in the analysis. Perhaps status or gender are but proxies for a more general phenomenon of subordination–superordination relationships (Grimshaw 1981). Or, Schegloff argues, once the analysis of conversation is completed, the phenomenon of asymmetry may appear anonymous rather than gender specific.

I agree with certain aspects of this critique. From my point of view, Schegloff is correct in saying we must discover what high and low status (or any other "macro" construct for that matter) amounts to interactionally. Certainly, it is inappropriate to leap from a frequency count of the number of initiations by doctors versus patients or teachers versus students to conclusions that institutional officials automatically discriminate against clients. Indeed, many of the professional/client studies cited above (such as McDermott, Gospodinoff and Aron 1978; Mehan 1979; Erickson and Schultz 1982) do not base their claims only on statistical evidence. They show the participants' orientation to the structure of the relationship in the interaction.

Schegloff's critique of sociological claims inferred from frequency counts and correlations is important. However, the severity of his criticism extends the argument entirely too far in the opposite direction, leading to "micro-analytic myopia" (Wilson 1986). In (correctly) pointing out that people working in institutions have practical projects, the critics of conversational dominance studies have focused our attention on some of the basic mechanisms of everyday conversations. I am left with the impression, however, that these researchers believe that taking turns and vying for the floor is all that occurs in professional/client interaction. If this point of view is extended to its logical conclusion, then we need only analyze the syntactic structure of conversation because the sequential organization of conversation is all that matters in interaction (Schegloff 1987a).

There are more things happening in social interaction than are captured by analyzing the syntactic structure of conversation. Institutional officials and their clients are certainly engaged in taking turns, vying for the floor, and completing conditionally relevant utterances. But they are engaged in other activities as well, many of which are not as readily exposed by a syntactic analysis of conversation. And, some of these have the potential for stratifying people. Thus, managing a conversation is compatible with dispensing the work of an institution. Both the practical activity of getting the work of a medical interview, educational test or police call done and any coercive activity of unequal treatment can occur simultaneously. It would be productive to study practical and political activities because they are intertwined in institutionalized discourse.

Structures, practices and situated relevance

The CA and constructionist perspectives on the macro–micro issue share much in common:

1 they are not content with correlational and technical solutions to the problem, but seek to show that the social structures of society are to be understood as contingent outcomes of people's practical activity;
2 therefore, the everyday work practices of people are examined for the ways in which they generate the social structures of the relevant domain;
3 structures are taken to be "external and constraining" upon the social situation and not subject to change by individual actors;
4 the practices can not be simply a researcher's analytic device; they must be shown to be "members' phenomena."

In short, before admitting the importance of structure for interaction, members' orientation to it must be demonstrated on particular occasions of interaction.

While agreeing on matters of structure and practices, the issue of "members' phenomena" distinguishes the two perspectives. Claiming that "institutional contexts are created as visible states of affairs on a turn-by-turn basis . . . [and] . . . it is ultimately through such means that 'institutions' exist as accountable organizations of social actions" (Heritage 1984a:290), conversation analysts have adopted a stringent criterion for representing a member's phenomenon. The orientation must be demonstrated in the syntactic organization of a conversation. Those occasions of interaction when a "conditionally relevant" pattern which is normatively expected does not occur provide the test cases. If, on those occasions participants mark, index or otherwise formulate the *absence* of the normatively expected pattern in a succeeding turn of talk, then conversation analysts have a warrant for claiming that participants are oriented toward it on that moment of interaction.

While these canons of research provide a rigorous solution to the macro—micro problem, there are phenomena which do not lend themselves to a syntactic analysis. For example, working within the conversation analysis framework, Maynard (1984:126) found that the immediate sequential environment did not always make the functions of person descriptions by courtroom officials very transparent. Therefore, he had to consult a wider context, particularly segments of previous conversations between public defenders and district attorneys, in order to make sense of sequences of plea bargaining discourse.

Also working within the conversation analysis framework, Zimmerman (1984) and Wilson (chapter 2 above) point out that the mechanisms of syntactic analysis can be blinded to the differential distribution of discourse identities such as "requester" and "request granter." From the point of view of a strict conversation analysis, it is an accident that complaint takers (people operating a central emergency desk) ask questions and complaint givers answer them. While it is possible to account for why any particular individual in any given interaction is the one who asks questions by a sequential analysis, Wilson argues that the *uniformity across* episodes is not a matter of sequential organization, it is a matter of the social organization of police work. There are other phenomena in social interaction that do not yield to sequential analysis, for instance, the detailed configuring of social knowledge to organizational context – as when "street level bureaucrats" interpret the impact of laws or policies at the local level (Maroules 1985; Mehan, Hertweck and Meihls 1986) or when doctors or other "experts" consult a large stock of knowledge and decide its relevance on a particular occasion (Cicourel 1981b, 1981c). Because syntactic analysis (as defined in turn-by-turn terms) is not always adequate to the task of demonstrating the situated relevance of a so-called macro structure in the interaction, we must find other ways to solve the problem while at the same time remaining faithful to the criteria of members' orientation to structures and practices outlined above.

The Generation of Macro Structure in Social Interaction

In the analysis which follows, I explore a way of demonstrating the situated relevance of "macro structures" in social interaction. This procedure involves describing the ways in which circumstances which originate outside an organization (which I call distal circumstances) interact with circumstances which originate within it (which I call proximal circumstances) to influence the course of interaction and the work of an organization. I seek to locate the impact of both distal and proximal circumstances in the language of educators in the routine school activity of sorting students into various educational programs.

My procedure for locating the impact of these circumstances is contrastive. I first search for basic normative patterns in the corpus of materials (which include field notes of observations and transcripts of videotapes from classrooms, testing sessions, meetings and informal discussions). When I have a candidate normative pattern, I then look for occasions when it is expected to occur but does not. The absence of an expected normative pattern then becomes a warrant to search for reasons for the non-occurrence in the social organization surrounding the local circumstances to see if the participants themselves are oriented to its absence. Those familiar with conversation analysis will recognize this strategy. In fact, the *techniques* of my approach and the techniques used by conversation analysts have similar origins, as I explained elsewhere (Mehan 1979). The *scope* of my work, however, is much different than conversation analysis. I entertain a more far ranging set of materials than do conversation analysts because the phenomena I address require me to consider wider contexts than adjacent conversational pairs.

School sorting practices

I examine specific settings of concrete work activities in order to reveal the conventional practices through which social objects are created as outcomes or products which become detached from those practices. In the following, the constructed object is a child, or rather a step in a child's career in school as either a "handicapped" student or a "normal" student. The conventional practices are those institutionalized devices which sort children and thereby define them.

When educators have been observed, they have been found to be engaged in varieties of this construction work at their various worksites.

They "do assessment," they "do testing," they "do classification." In the classroom, this "bench work" takes the form of moment-to-moment decisions about the correctness of answers to teachers' questions during lessons or more enduring decisions to place students into various ability groups for the purposes of instruction. In the testing room, it takes the form of a tester examining students' behavior to determine their IQ or achievement levels. In committee meeting rooms, the work becomes the final decision to place a student into one or another educational program. These sorting practices contribute to the construction of students' educational careers.

This study, then, is in the social constructionist tradition of research (reviewed above) which is directed at analyzing the practices which compose the moment-to-moment, day-by-day work of daily life, including those portions of daily life which are carried out in bureaucratic organizations. Educational sorting practices are a particular form of "social practice" (Garfinkel 1967; Garfinkel and Sacks 1970; Cicourel 1967, 1978). To "practice" social life is, literally, to work at its production, maintenance and transformation. Practice constitutes social life; it is not an incomplete rendition of some ideal form. Practice encompasses people's application of ideals and norms as well as practical action in concrete situations of choice.

A social fact of the school system: handicapped students

Some aggregate data from our study is presented in the table. In the analysis which follows, I will be proposing that in order to understand the meaning of the aggregate, we must come to understand the organization of talk in a series of social events which occur routinely in a school context. Then I will present some fragments of talk and propose that in order to understand the organization of that interaction, we must come to understand the organization of the school and the way it does its work.

The table shows the number of students processed by "evaluation and placement" committees during the 1978–9 school year in the "Coast School District." All but two of the students considered by the "E and P" committee were placed into some sort of a special education program; the majority (68 per cent) were placed into an educational program in which the students worked in their regular classroom for a part of the school day and in a special education program (the "learning disabilities group" – LDG) for the remainder of the school day. A considerably smaller number (7 of 53 cases) were placed into an educational program in which

The disposition of 53 cases considered by placement committees

Placement	Number
Educationally handicapped (EH)	7
Learning disabled (LDG)	36
Severe language handicapped (SLH)	3
Multiple handicap	2
Speech therapy	3
Off campus placement ("private schooling")	0
Counseling	0
Reading	0
Adaptive physical education	0
Bilingual education	0
No placement (returned to classroom)	1
Placement process interrupted	1
Total	53

the students spent the entire school day under the supervision of a special educator (the "educationally handicapped" program). Especially important for my purposes, *no* students were placed in programs outside the district ("off campus placement") during the year of this investigation.

These figures, which represent the aggregate number of students placed into educational programs, would conventionally be accepted as an example of a "macro structure." Furthermore, each number in the table represents a point in a student's educational career, that is, his or her identity as a "special education" or a "regular education" student. Hence, we have two senses of macro social structures here: aggregate data and social identities.

Now, what practices produce this array, these careers, these identities? To answer this question, I propose that these "social facts" of the school system are constructed in the practical work of educators in their person-to-person and person-to-text interaction. In so doing, I hope to convey a sense of school organization as constituted by the ongoing situated practices of its members, not as an objectified reification.

Deciding whether students are "regular" or "special" is a practical project that occurs routinely in US schools. While this activity is as old as schools themselves, in response to recently enacted state and federal legislation (notably PL 94-142, The Education for All Handicapped Students Act) the classification and sorting activity has become more formalized in school districts. There are now legally mandated procedures concerning the referral of students, the temporal parameters in the assessment of students, and the participants involved in decision making.

In order to uncover the discursive and organizational arrangements which provide for an array such as the one in the table, we made field observations, read federal laws and policies, reviewed school records, conducted interviews, taped and analyzed the interaction in key events within the Coast School District during 1978–9 (Mehan, Hertweck and Meihls 1986). We discovered, upon the analysis of the materials gathered by these diverse research techniques, that the student classification process in the Coast District had a number of components.

The schools' work of sorting students most frequently starts in the classroom, with a referral from the teacher, continues through psychological assessment and culminates in evaluation by the E and P committee, which is composed of educators and the parents of the referred student. Thus, a "macro structure" – the aggregate number of students in various educational programs or their identity as "special" or "regular" students is generated in a sequence of organizationally predictable "micro events" (classroom, testing session, meetings) (cf. Collins 1981). An important feature of this process is that texts generated from the previous occasion become the basis of the interaction in the next step in the sequence.

The committee had 11 placement options available for consideration (ten special education placements plus the option of returning the student to the regular classroom). The *possible* number of outcomes should be compared to the *actual* number of outcomes used in the Coast District during 1978–9. For the remainder of this analysis, I will be focusing attention on the final evaluation committee meeting. Although that will be my focal point, as I will indicate throughout, it is necessary to incorporate information which has its origins far away from the meeting room in order to understand the schools' work of sorting students.

Distal and proximal influences on the work of sorting students

The E and P committee meetings had a regular and recurring order. The first order of business was the presentation of information about the student's history, the second was devoted to making a decision about the placement of the student. These were regularly followed by a discussion of parents' rights. Meetings were regularly concluded by a discussion of the goals the committee expected the student to reach during the time of his or her placement.

Proximal influences

Circumstances which influence the course of interaction and originate inside the institution are "proximal" circumstances. These are circumstances which are close to the immediate situation, which include the practical project of getting the work at hand done, getting through a particular interactional encounter and on to the next one. These are often the kinds of features that are thought of when we say features or structures emerge in interaction.

The internal order of each phase of the meeting was regular and recurrent, showing the influence of proximal influences. During the "information presentation" phase of the meeting, for example, each of the participants reported what they knew about the child. This presentation of information went in round-robin style, with the school psychologist, classroom teacher, school nurse, and special education teacher reporting about the student. Information gathered from standardized tests dominated the proceedings. When it came time for the committee to reach a decision, a choice was presented to the committee by the school psychologist. Importantly for our consideration, only one or two of the 11 possible placement options were presented to the committee; in no committee meeting was the "private schooling" placement option presented or discussed in this phase of the meeting:

4.1
((Key: Psy = Psychologist; SET = Special Education Teacher;
Prin = Principal; DR = District Representative; Mo = Mother))

EDM #33
92	**Psy:**	Does the uh, committee agree that the, uh learning disability placement is one that might benefit him?
93	**Prin:**	I think we agree.
94	**Psy:**	We're not considering then a special day class at all for him?
95	**SET:**	I wouldn't at this point//
96	**Many:**	//No.

EDM #47
28	**Psy:**	Okay, in light of all the data that we have, I think that the program we want to recommend is the learning disability group pullout program.
29	**Mo:**	Pullout-I don't understand that//
30	**Psy:**	//For Tracy. You know, that's the program we sort of talked about that day, where he would be pulled out of the classroom for specific work on the areas that he needs, that, you know, are identified today.

EDM #57
35   **Psy:**   Okay. Now, okay, now then, let's, why don't we take a vote. Um, for the Learning Disabilities Group pullout program. Um, is there anyone, anyone who does not agree? (3.0) Okay. I think that was unanimous. ((soft laughter))

After the placement decision was reached but not before, parents were told of their rights to place their children out of the district at district expense:

4.2

EDM #57
35   **Psy:**   All right. Then what we have to do is sign. But, um, before we sign I'd like to have uh, Suzanna um, talk about the rights to private schooling and talk about your rights as parents.
36   **DR:**   I think you probably have these two forms but they talk about your rights as parents. I'm going to give you a copy anyway so, um, you are aware.
37   **Psy:**   I think you received it in the mail before.
38   **DR:**   Yeah. You probably did. I'd also like to inform you of your rights as parents to private schooling for Ricardo *if* the District should not have an appropriate program for the child. Uh, this is the law. However, under the same law, we feel that we *do* have a program for your child that would meet his needs. Okay? So I'm going to ask you to sign this form and you'll keep a copy and I'll sign the form too. And this is *just* only to inform you of your rights. Okay?
39   **Mo:**   ((inaudible utterances while forms are signed)) (8–9 secs)

EDM #33
97   **DR:**   Mrs. Ladd, if we, um after evaluating Shane find that, um, we don't have the proper placement, the classroom available, appropriate placement for Shane, that you can request- or you have rights to private school and you can request that. We've made the decision that we do have a class available for Shane to go into.

This interaction, defined as the order of speakers within each phase of the meeting, was a locally produced order. It was influenced by proximal circumstances, those which are close to the immediate circumstances. It occurred turn by turn, sequence by sequence – just as conversation analysts would predict.

Distal influences

Circumstances which influence the course of interaction that originate outside the institution are "distal circumstances." "Distal circumstances" are generated from afar, outside the immediate circumstances, but nevertheless influence the course of local interaction. Some of the distal sources include governmental agencies, public policies, administrative or fiscal constraints and the course of institutional practice – all of which reside in the history of an organization.

While the sequence of turns within each phase of the meeting was proximal and locally produced, the order among the phases and the meaning and consequence of what was said in a given turn was influenced by distal circumstances. Most certainly, the fact that there were no decisions to place students outside the district showed the influence of practical circumstances within the district and fiscal and legal considerations originating at state and federal levels.

The Education for All Handicapped Students Act (PL 94–142) directs school districts to find an appropriate education in the least restrictive environment for all students, including those with physical and educational handicaps. If students can not be educated within the "mainstream" of regular education, then special programs are to be provided. These include special classrooms set aside for handicapped students, "pullout" activities (in which students are removed from their classrooms for special assistance for a part of the day), and in-class remedial assistance (in which an aide or tutor works with the student within regular classroom hours, or assistance is provided to the regular classroom teacher). In the event that a school district does not have adequate facilities to educate students within the district, the district is directed to send the students to facilities outside the district.

Furthermore, PL 94-142 indicates that 12 per cent of the school-aged population will be served by special education programs. This quota provides a legal incentive to identify a certain percentage of special students. This legal incentive is reinforced by financial incentives. At the time of this study, school districts were provided with funds from state and federal sources for each student in regular classrooms, and a greater amount of money for students in special education programs. They received more money for students in pullout special education programs (LDG in the table), and still more money for students in "whole day" programs (EH in the table). School districts were not allocated funds for the education of students sent outside the district, however; they had to provide for these students with their own resources.

Just as there are incentives to locate and place students in special education in order to receive the maximum state and federal support, so, too, there are disincentives to find too many students. Funds for special education are not unlimited. A funding ceiling is reached when a certain number of students are placed in one EH classroom, with one LD teacher, etc. No additional money is provided if more students than the quota are assigned to particular classrooms. So, too, no additional money is provided for students referred to programs outside the district; these students must be educated at district expense – another fiscal disincentive implied by the law.

The reason that there were *no* out-of-district placements during the year we studied the Coast District is visible within the interaction of the E and P meetings. The influence of policies which were drawn up far away from the meeting room are reflected in the organization of talk within the meeting and the order of the meetings. In no case was the possibility of an out-of-district placement discussed when the placement options were presented to the committee for consideration. Invariably, one or two closely related programs (such as EH versus LDG) were discussed at the meeting (see EDM transcript #33: 92–7, #47: 28–30 and #57: 35–9 in 4.1 and 4.2 above). The topic of parents' rights to private schooling at district expense was always introduced after the decision was made to place the student within the district. These discursive arrangements effectively foreclosed the possibility of implementing the "out-of-district placement" – a legally prescribed and organizationally permitted option.

The juxtaposition of proximal and distal information enables us to assess the peculiar status of the out-of-district placement option. While the participants are oriented to the out-of-district placement option, their orientation is not found in the next available turn of talk, but in the more global organization of the discourse. By organizing the discourse in the decision phase of the meeting such that one or two options were discussed, neither of which was the private schooling option, and by ordering the phases of the meeting such that the decision to place students appears *before* the notification of parents as to their rights, the educators accomplished the placement of students in programs within the district, *and* displayed their orientation to this placement option.

Conclusions

The integration of macro structures and micro interactions is a routine bureaucratic practice within institutions such as hospitals, courts and schools. Bureaucrats routinely integrate what researchers have segregated as the micro and macro aspects of everyday life as part of their daily work. It has been a central concern of our research project to document how this integration is achieved in the everyday work of schooling.

By examining the language of groups of educators as they engage in the work of sorting students, I have tried to demonstrate the situated relevance of social structures in the practical work activities of people in social interaction. Political, economic and legal considerations constrain social interaction, while, simultaneously, interactional mechanisms generate aspects of social structure (in this case a student's career – as either a handicapped student or a normal student). Casting the relationship between features of social structure and interactional process in reflexive terms seems to be faithful to the goal of linking social structure and social interaction without either separating them or reducing one to the other.

I have employed a spatial metaphor to map the reflexive relationships between features of social structure and interactional processes (cf. Latour and Woolgar 1986). By talking about influences on the immediate interaction as proximal or distal, I am trying to counter the idea so prevalent in sociology that macro phenomena are separated from their generative micro basis. Features of the social organization of the school are linked to interactions which take place in various organizational subunits of the school, influenced by its surrounding bureaucratic organization and the society of which the school is a part. Administrative policy concerning student classification (like those influencing curriculum content, textbook choices, teaching methods, and testing practices) are established by school boards and state departments of education in organizational units far removed from the school site. Decisions in bureaucracies distant from the school impinge on educational practice in the school and its classrooms. Likewise, the interest of business for a technically trained and literate labor force make the school responsive to external forces. Furthermore, parents, having been to school themselves, voice opinions about what and how their children should be educated.

Educators carry out the routine work of conducting lessons, administering tests and attending meetings. The notion of work stresses the constructive aspect of institutional practice. Educators' work is repetitive and routine, to be sure. But its mundane character should not overshadow the drama of its importance, for steps on students' career ladders are assembled from such practice. The enactment of routine bureaucratic practices structure students' educational careers by opening or closing their access to particular educational opportunities, including, as I have discussed here, regular or special education.

The sequential order of turns at talk within the placement meeting was locally produced. The local character of the sequential organization of the interaction was not dictated by legal, fiscal, or other distal constraints.

While the syntax of the placement meetings were locally produced, semantic and pragmatic considerations (what was said or not said in meetings, what was meant) displayed the influence of distal constraints: the discussion of parents' rights to out-of-district placement at district expense after the decision to place students in some special education program, and the absence of discussion about the out-of-district placement reflect the influence of economic, practical and legal constraints. This influence is displayed within the language of educators as they engaged in the work of sorting students into available educational programs.

Finding strategies for determining the relevance of social structure for participants in interaction is a key issue in the enterprise. Searching for conditional relevance in adjacent turns at talk has been useful for locating some sequential structures in the fine-grain details of conversation. This approach is not sufficient for other aspects of social structure, however. In order to make sense of what the participants were doing in their committee meetings, we had to consult the institutional dimensions of context, those which incorporated discursive arrangements among the participants, the social organization of the school, practical, legal and fiscal constraints on local work routines.

No matter how carefully or exhaustively we conducted an analysis of the syntactic organization of the committee meetings, we would have located the relationship between the absence of the "off campus" placements and the organization of the "decision to place" and "parents' rights" phases of the committee meeting. Knowledge gleaned from ethnographic observations informed by reading of federal laws and school records enabled us to hear the *meaning* of what was going on when the educators informed parents of their rights after they decided to place students in certain programs. By juxtaposing our knowledge of the social organization of the school with our study of interaction in meetings we were able to understand the connection between the statistical array depicted in the table and the discursive arrangements in committee meetings and demonstrate that our description is relevant to the participants in the interaction.

Conversation analysis informs us about the sequential organization, the syntax of conversation and other speech events. It takes ethnographic analysis of institutions to say something about the meaning, function and use of language in social events. Sequential organization of interaction may be independent of context, since turn-taking seems to operate across speakers and situations. The *projects and practices* to which these mechanisms are applied, however – such as the work of sorting students, judging delinquents, assessing mental patients, making scientific discoveries – are constructed by participants who are oriented to social, semantic and pragmatic considerations.

PART II

Talk and Institutions

5

On the Institutional Character of Institutional Talk: The Case of News Interviews

John Heritage and David Greatbatch

1 Introduction

In this paper we examine some of the basic characteristics of turn-taking in broadcast news interviews using data derived from UK news sources.[1] Our objective is to show the ways in which these characteristics are involved in the constitution of the talk they organize as "news interview talk." In so doing, we aim to demonstrate some ways in which basic, but superficially unremarkable, features of the organization of talk in news interviews are deeply implicated in the recognizable production of news interview conduct as an institutionalized form of interaction. We further seek to show that turn-taking procedures for the news interview represent institutionalized resources for dealing with some of the fundamental tasks and constraints that bear on its management. We begin with a brief overview of conversation analytic approaches to forms of institutional interaction.

2 Institutional Context: The CA Approach

During the past decade, conversation analytic studies of talk-in-interaction[2] have branched out from the "home base" of ordinary conversation to "institutional" settings in which more or less official or formal task-based or role-based activities are undertaken: doctor–patient interaction, courtroom trials, job interviews, classroom lessons, news interviews and emergency calls to the police are clear examples of interactions of this type.

One major approach to the analysis of these settings has embodied a strongly comparative dimension. The rationale for this approach is relatively straightforward. Following the initiative of Sacks, Schegloff and Jefferson (1974:729–31), the practices underlying the management of ordinary conversation are treated as primary and as collectively constituting a fundamental matrix through which social interaction is organized. One way, then, in which the "institutional" nature of interaction in institutional settings may manifest itself is in a range of differences from ordinary conversation. Guided by this notion, a considerable body of research has focused on variations in the use of specific conversational practices and variations from such practices as, at least in part, constituting the "institutional" character of specific forms of institutional interaction. These variations, it has been suggested, should provide for the recognizability – both for participants and for professional analysts – of such distinctively nonconversational events as an "interview," a "cross-examination," or a "lesson."

Although this approach is easily described, it can be comparatively difficult to achieve. As Schegloff points out in chapter 3 above, if it is to be claimed that some interaction has a specifically "institutional" character, then the relevance of the institutional context in question must be shown to inhabit the details of the participants' conduct. Thus in addition to the normal CA tasks of analyzing the conduct of the participants and the underlying organization of their activities, that conduct and its organization must additionally be demonstrated to embody orientations which are specifically institutional, or which are, at the least, responsive to constraints which are institutional in character or origin.

These tasks are complicated by the fact that, as several authors have noted, CA works with an elaborate and complex approach to the analysis of social context. Rather than working with a conception of context in which some pre-established social framework is viewed as "containing" the participants' actions, the CA perspective treats each action within a sequence of actions as both context shaped and context renewing (Heritage 1984a). Within this perspective, CA researchers cannot take "context" for granted nor may they treat it as determined in advance and independent of the participants' own activities. Instead "context" is treated as both the project and product of the participants' own actions and therefore as inherently locally produced and transformable at any moment. Thus the methodological constraints raised above by Schegloff concerning the relevance of particular social identities and the procedural consequentiality of context are generic to CA approaches to the analysis of social interaction. The study of institutional interaction cannot by any means be exempted from this constraint (Heritage 1984a:280–90).[3]

Among published studies that have focused on institutional talk, several of the more significant and influential have dealt with data in which the institutional character of the interaction is embodied first and foremost in its *form* – most notably in turn-taking systems which depart substantially from the way in which turn-taking is managed in conversation and which are perceivedly "formal" in character. Following Sacks, Schegloff and Jefferson's (1974) initiative, interactions in courtrooms (Atkinson and Drew 1979), classrooms (McHoul 1978) and news interviews (Greatbatch 1985, 1988; Clayman 1987) have been shown to exhibit systematically distinctive forms of turn-taking which powerfully structure many aspects of conduct in these settings.

The studies which have reported these findings have been influential for two reasons. First, turn-taking organizations – whether for conversation or institutional contexts such as courtroom interaction – are a fundamental and generic aspect of the organization of interaction. They are organizations whose features are implemented recurrently over the course of interactional events. This characteristic gives them a special methodological interest for students of institutional talk. For if it can be shown that the participants in a vernacularly characterized institutional setting such as a courtroom pervasively organize their turn-taking in a way that is distinctive from ordinary conversation, it can be proposed that they are organizing their conduct so as to display and realize its "institutional" character over its course and that they are doing so *recurrently and pervasively*. The "problem of relevance" raised by Schegloff above is thus resolved – at least at the grossest level – at a single stroke.

The second source of interest in institutional turn-taking systems also derives from their generic and pervasive character. To the extent that the parties confine their conduct within the framework of some distinctive "formal" institutional turn-taking system, other systematic differences from ordinary conversation tend to emerge. These differences commonly involve specific *reductions of the range of options and opportunities for action* that are characteristic in conversation, and they *often involve specializations* and *respecifications of the interactional functions of the activities* that remain. The ensemble of these variations from conversational practice may contribute to a unique "fingerprint" for each institutional form of interaction – the "fingerprint" being comprised of a set of interactional practices differentiating each form both from other institutional forms and from the baseline of mundane conversational interaction itself. Both severally and collectively, the members of each ensemble of practices may contribute to what Garfinkel (Garfinkel, Lynch and Livingston 1981) has termed the "identifying details" of institutional activities.

These institutionalized reductions and specializations of the available set of conversational options are, it should be stressed, *conventional* in character. They are culturally variable; they are sometimes subject to legal constraints; they are always vulnerable to processes of social change; they are discursively justifiable and are often justified by reference to considerations of task, efficiency, fairness, and so on in ways that the practices making up the conversational "bedrock" manifestly are not. Associated with these various institutional conventions are differing participation frameworks (Goffman 1981), with their associated rights and obligations, different footings and different patternings of opportunities to initiate and sanction interactional activities. The special character of these conventions is also associated with subjective sentiments. Those elements of "formal" institutional interaction which are experienced as unusual, irksome or discomforting are experienced as such against a tacitly assumed background which is supplied by the workings of ordinary conversation (Atkinson 1982).

In several of these "formal" forms of institutional interaction – most notably "formal" classroom interaction, courtroom interaction and news interviews – turn-taking is strongly constrained within quite sharply defined procedures. Departures from these procedures systematically attract overt sanctions. The pattern of turn-taking in these settings is uniform and exhibits overwhelming compliance with these procedures. In the case of courtroom and news interview interaction, for example, it can be difficult to locate the "deviant cases" with which to exhibit the normativity of the procedures under investigation. It is notable that these settings all involve the production of "talk for an overhearing audience." In two of the settings (courtrooms and classrooms), the audience is co-present and the turn-taking system is designed, at least in part, to control or curtail the nature of audience participation in any ongoing exchange (Atkinson 1979b, 1982; McHoul 1978; Mehan 1979). In all three settings, the presence of an audience whose members may assess the moral character of the focal participants may also tend to limit the extent to which the latter depart from formal turn-taking procedures.

Objectives

This chapter represents an exercise in the analysis of a setting – the news interview – that is, we argue, constituted in substantial part in and through the participants' compliance with a formally distinctive turn-taking procedure. In the following discussion, we show

1   that news interview interaction is organized through turn-taking procedures that are normatively oriented to but distinctive from ordinary conversation;
2   that adherence to these procedures establishes and maintains the relevance of the local "news interview identities" of the participants; and
3   that these distinctive procedures embody systematic and institutionalized solutions to the management of core tasks and constraints that are central to the practice of broadcast journalism.

We further propose

4   that where the participants depart from the formal provisions of news interview turn-taking, they continue to manage the tasks and constraints that the turn-taking system would otherwise automatically handle through the use of identifiable ancillary procedures.

We begin our analysis with an initial characterization of turn-taking procedures in news interviews.

3   Turn-taking in the News Interview

In the news interview, turn-taking is organized through a distinctive normative procedure in which – unlike conversation – the types of turns that may be produced by each speaker are provided for in advance. These constraints on the production of types of turns operate with respect to the institutional identities of interviewer (IR) and interviewee (IE). They specify that news interview talk should proceed as sequences of IR questions and IE responses to those questions. Correspondingly, speakers who act as IRs may not properly engage in actions other than questions,[4] while those who take part as IEs should refrain from initiating actions (such as unsolicited comments on prior talk) or sequences (for example, asking questions to which the IR or other IEs would be obliged to respond). A further consequence of this turn-taking procedure – which, following foundational work by Atkinson and Drew (1979:61 ff.), we term a turn-type preallocation procedure – is that, subject to certain minor qualifications,[5] the order in which the speakers may talk is largely confined to the following pattern regardless of the numbers of IRs or IEs involved.[6]

IR:	Question
IE:	Answer
IR:	Question
IE:	Answer

Compliance with these procedures is, in part, what distinguishes a radio or TV "interview" from a "discussion." Similarly, in the ways that the participants adhere to these procedures, they constitute themselves – for one another and for the news audience – as IR and IE respectively. We stress that the terms "question" and "answer" only minimally characterize the data. IRs may, for example, challenge or cast doubt on IE statements and positions while IEs may resist or evade such challenges. Nonetheless, these challenges and responses overwhelmingly remain packaged within turns that remain minimally recognizable as questions and answers respectively.

Moreover, as we shall show, the management of this event as an "interview" is the collaborative achievement of the parties. Across their various questions and answers – whether hostile or not – IR and IE collaboratively sustain a definition of their joint circumstances as "an interview" (rather than a "discussion") by restricting themselves to the production of questions and answers.

The fact that news interview participants generally respect these constraining provisions in the design of their turns has a number of elementary consequences for the formal structure of news interviews which we summarily note without supportive discussion: (1) The provision that IEs are confined to responsive activities has the corollary that they cannot properly open or close interviews and this task is exclusively allocated to IRs.[7] Moreover (2), the turn-taking system makes no provision for IEs to allocate next turns among the speakers or, with the exception of a particular contingency,[8] to select themselves to speak next, in contexts where there are more than two parties (that is, two or more IEs and/or two or more IRs). Finally (3), IR questions have "agenda setting" characteristics which may require IEs to engage in complex courses of action if they are to challenge or evade IR questions within a turn-taking framework that essentially confines them to responses to IRs' questions.[9]

While these gross features of news interview interaction are plainly the products of an orientation to the provisions and constraints of the news interview turn-taking system, this same orientation is also manifested in more detailed aspects of news interview interaction. We will briefly look at some of these details in the management of questions and answers.

The interactional management of turn type: questions

In news interviews, substantial numbers of IRs' turns are built from more than a single "questioning" turn constructional unit (Greatbatch 1988; Clayman 1988). Instead these turns commonly take a compound form which, adapting a suggestion from Graham Button, we term a "question delivery structure." A simple example of this compound form is displayed as 5.1 below – in which an initial "prefatory" statement (arrow a) establishes a context for a subsequent question (arrow b).

5.1 (WAO:25.1.79)

> IR: a → .hhh *The* (.) *p*rice being asked for these
> letters is (.) three thousand *pou*::nds.
> IR: b → Are you going to be able to *r*aise it,
> (0.5)
> IE: At the moment it . . . ((continues))

In a conversational context, in which turn size is systematically minimized by a current speaker's initial entitlement to a single turn constructional unit (Sacks, Schegloff and Jefferson 1974),[10] the IR's initial turn component could be treated as a completed turn and responded to as such – for example, by a confirmation such as "that's right." In news interviews, where the expectation is that IE statements will be produced as responses to *questions*, such statements are only rarely responded to as complete IR turns.

By withholding responses until a recognizable question has been produced, IEs orient to and help to produce the "interview" character of the interaction in which they are engaged. They "do interview" (Schegloff 1989). Such withholding embodies the IE's acknowledgment that, in the context of an interview, s/he has no rights to a turn until a question is produced and the corollary expectation that the IR's turn should properly consist of a question (Greatbatch 1988).

By withholding responses at such points and thereby permitting IRs to proceed to a subsequent questioning turn component, IEs not only exhibit an analysis that such statements are "prefatory" to a question, they also collaborate with the IR in realizing that expectation as an accomplished fact (Clayman 1988). In turn, IRs rely on that collaboration so as to produce "long" multi-unit questions free of "early" or "interjective" responses by IEs. Very commonly, the "prefatory" status of IR pre-question statements is analyzable to IEs either from the substance of the initial statement or from an action projection which may precede it (Schegloff 1980; Greatbatch 1985; Clayman 1988). However there are many cases where such prefaces could readily be treated as turns in their own right and the general absence of response to these stands as unambiguous evidence for the general IE expectation that an IR's turn will properly be completed as a question. For example, in 5.2 below, the initial statement of the IR's second turn (arrow a) strongly challenges the previous statement of the IE (AS) that he does not describe himself as a Marxist.

5.2   (WAO:13.3.79)

IR:		.hhh er *W*hat's the difference between *y*our Marxism and Mister McGahey's Communism.
AS:		er The difference is that it's the *press* that constantly call me a *M*a:rxist when I do *not*, (.) and never *h*ave (.) er er given that description of myself.[.hh I-
IR:		⌊ But I⌋'ve *heard* you-
	a →	I've heard you'd be very *h*appy to: to: er .hhhh er de*scribe* yourself as a Marxist. Could it be that with an election in the
	b →	offing you're anxious to play down that you're a Marx⌈ist. ⌉
AS:	c →	⌊ er ⌋Not at all Mister Da:y.=And I:'m (.) *s*orry to say I must disagree with you,=you have *n*ever *h*eard me describe my*self* .hhh er as a *M*a:rxist.=I have o:nly ((continues))

Here, where the IE clearly might move immediately to reject the IR's initial statement as an object in its own right, he nonetheless waits for the IR to come to a question (arrow b) before initiating a response (arrow c).[11] Moreover, his response initially deals with the question as the sequentially implicative component of the IR's prior turn (Sacks 1987), and only then does he turn to reject the IRs initial assertion. Here, as in other less problematic multi-unit IR questions, the IE orients to the production of an IR turn over its course and withholds any response until a recognizable question has been produced. In all such cases, IEs collaborate (and IRs rely on their collaboration) in the production of multi-unit questioning turns. That collaboration is consistent with and conducted within the provisions and constraints of the basic turn-taking system for news interviews.[12]

The interactional management of turn type: answers

We have seen that IEs systematically orient to IR turns in a way that departs from normal conversational turn-taking practices which exert a systematic pressure towards the minimization of turn size (Sacks, Schegloff and Jefferson 1974). The character of IE turns also exhibits departures from these ordinary conversational practices. In general, IEs' responses normally take the form of extended multi-unit turns. In ordinary conversation the production of long multi-unit turns normally involves the active collaboration of recipients through the production of "continuers" and related objects (Schegloff 1982; Jefferson 1981b, 1984a). In news interviews, by contrast, long IE turns are not managed by such means. For example in 5.3 below, the IE's answer passes through a series of possible completion points (arrowed) without response from the IR.

5.3   (ATV T:15.11.79) (Interview with a man who claims he was jailed for a crime he did not commit)

```
IR:        Have you any sort of criminal connections or
           anything,=u:⌈h      ⌉
IE:   →               ⌊No⌋t at all.=
           =I- I was working for the Gas Board at the time
      →    as a salesman,=
           =I had no: (0.2) emphatically no er: associates
      →    that (wo(h)uld) had criminal records,=
           =or I did not associate with people with criminal
      →    records.
           .hhhh I- I- I was living a life o- o- of
      →    a family man in Stockton-on-Tees,
           .hhh where I was a representative for the Gas
      →    Board,
           .hhh and it was out the blue to me.
IR:        .hh Were you surprise:d when you: w- went to
           court, an- and indeed went down,
```

Extended multi-unit IE turns of this type are prototypical in the news interview. The creation of these extended turns is the product of shared expectations about news interview talk which are realized as a collaborative achievement in which, on the one hand, the IE talks extendedly and, on the other, the IR withholds any form of intervention that would influence the IE's extended talk. These turns clearly represent a departure from the ways in which turn-taking is managed in ordinary conversation and, in themselves, exhibit an orientation to the institutional character of the talk they embody.[13] The expectation that IRs will permit – and even require – IEs to occupy extended turns by withholding turn initiation until some nth possible completion point in an IE's turn is especially apparent in cases where IEs finish their turns at points where their answers are hearably unextended. Such occurences regularly engender gaps as in 5.4 and 5.5 below:

5.4   (WAO:21.2.79)

> **IR:**   And d'you ex*pect* these reforms to be pa:ssed?
> **IE:**   Yes I do:.
> →   (1.2)
> **IE:**   The *ma*jor ones certainly.

5.5   (AP:7.3.79)

> **IR:**   *Is* it *you*:r *view* that *vic*tims get a raw deal
>   in British justice?
>   (0.5)
> **IE:**   *Very.* uhhh
> →   (0.7)
> **IR:**   And- and *wh*at would you like to see *do*ne
>   about that.

Moreover, as Greatbatch (1985:154–8) and Clayman (1989) have noted, the generalized expectation that IEs will talk extendedly is further evidenced when IRs urge IEs to "be brief" in their responses in contexts where the interview is about to be terminated and time is short.[14]

In sum, the management of IE responses in news interviews indicates a strong contrast with ordinary conversation where turn-taking procedures tend to minimize turn size. In news interviews, IE turns are routinely extended as a collaborative achievement of IR and IE. The shared expectations informing this achievement further point to a shared orientation to the "nonconversational" character of the interview encounter.

The normative character of the turn-taking system for news interviews

The fact that news interviews overwhelmingly proceed as sequences of IR questions and IE answers, taken together with the features of turn management described above, constitutes massive evidence for the existence of a Q–A preallocated turn-taking system for news interviews that is distinctive from conversation. Moreover, this turn-taking system naturally manifests itself on an iterative turn-by-turn basis and thus constitutes extremely powerful evidence for the conclusion that their engagement in "news interview talk" – as IR and IE respectively – has an endemic and ubiquitous relevance for the participants.

That this turn-taking system and its associated relevances have a normative character can most readily be seen through "deviant case analysis" when interview participants depart, however briefly, from the provisions of news interview turn-taking. Such departures most commonly involve the IE in moving away from the provided-for *responsive* position within an interview by *initiating* an action or a sequence. A common context for such departures arises in multi-IE interviews where a currently unaddressed IE seeks to comment on some aspect of the talk in progress – in breach of the turn-taking provision that IE turns should properly be produced as responses to IR questions. In 5.6, a second IE (MW) requests permission for such a comment (line 6) and only proceeds after the permission has been granted by the IR (line 7).

5.6   (AP:7.3.79)

```
 1  LL:         . . . and therefore I'm not going to accept the
 2              criticism that I haven't tried to help victims=
 3              =I've (.) been trying to help them (0.2) off and
 4              on for twenty-five years.=
 5  ( ):        =.hhhh=
 6  MW:   →     =Can I- can I say something abou⌈t this.    ⌉
 7  IR:                                         ⌊Yes in⌋deed.
 8              (0.5)
 9  MW:         e:r (0.7) As (0.5) Frank (.) Longford knows so
10              well .hh er my views . . . ((continues))
```

Here the IE clearly orients to his restricted rights to volunteer a contribution to the topic on the floor of the interview. And this orientation is also visible in "token" requests for permission to speak, as in 5.7, where the IE proceeds to make his contribution immediately after

a turn component that solicits permission to do so and without waiting
for the IR to respond to his request.

5.7   (AP:7.3.79)

LL: . . . there was no evidence whatever that stiffer
              penalties di- diminish crime.=
MW: →   =Can I make a point about that.=.hhh Which is
              that (.) if only this country . . . ((continues))

In this case, although the IE's request is a "token" request, it nonetheless
acknowledges that his action represents a departure from the turn-taking
provisions of the news interview which, by this acknowledgment, he
treats as normative.

A similar orientation is manifested in the following case where, rather
than initiating a comment, the IE initiates a Q–A sequence addressed to a
co-IE.

5.8   (P:28.9.81) ((The "David" addressed by RH is the interviewer))

AS: . . . the sooner they join the Social Democrats
              the *better* f⌈o r   u s⌉ and better for them?=
RH: ⌊Well let me a-⌋
RH: →   =David may I ask Mister Scargill a question you
              asked him and he didn't answer a moment ago. I've
              been in the Labour Party for thirty two yea:rs.=I
              was cam*paign*ing for it in South *York*shire when you
              were campaigning for a *diff*erent pa:rty. .hhhh I
              think my socialist credentials stand up against
              yours in any an- analysis.
              .hh Do you think people like me ought to leave the
              Labour Party. (.) Do you want us in.=
AS: =That's a decision that *you* have to make . . .
              ((continues))

Finally an orientation to the normative character of the turn-taking
provisions of the news interview is manifested in a range of instances in
which IRs sanction IE departures from those provisions. In 5.9, the IE
(industrial magnate, Sir James Goldsmith) initiates a hostile Q–A
sequence directed at the IR. In this example, Goldsmith's complaint (lines
1–11) concerns the coverage given to his business affairs in a previous
edition of the program in which he is presently appearing.

5.9   (0:21.4.81)

```
 1  JG:    . . . despite the fact there were fou:r major
 2          factories that you knew about,=despite the fact
 3          there was a two hundred and thirty million capital
 4          investment programme that you knew about,=
 5          =.hhh that we dealt in companies you stated and
 6          restated toda::y, .hhh despite the fact that ninety
 7          one per cent of our companies are still there:,=
 8          =and only the marginal ones which you knew were
 9          sold, .hhh and you e:ven mislead people by
10          suggesting for instance that we owned the Parisian
11          publishing house Brooke. Why=
12  IR:    =s- s- s- Sir James=
13  IR:    =I⌈'m so sorry   (  )   I'm so s⌉
14  JG:     ⌊No,=I'm asking a question n⌋ow.=
15  IR:    =It's more conventional in these programmes ⌈fo:r ⌉
16  JG:                                                 ⌊Well⌋
17  JG:    I don't mind ab⌈out        convention.⌉=I'm asking
18  IR:                   ⌊me to ask questions,⌋
19  JG:    you why (.) you distorted those facts.
20          (0.2)
21  IR:    Well we didn't distort them. ⌈  I mean er  ⌉
22  JG:                                 ⌊Well w- then⌋
23          did you ((continues))
```

In this sequence, the IE's lengthy turn culminates in the claim (lines 9–11) that the previous edition of the program misled the audience about his business activities. He then proceeds (at line 11) with the beginning of a question that would demand an explanation for this coverage. This question is intersected by the IR (lines 12–13) who attempts to preempt its production. This action is, in turn, intersected by the IE (line 14) who sustains his questioning stance, overtly acknowledging and asserting his reversal of normal interview conduct. The IR again resists the IE's attempt to adopt a questioning role, sanctioning his conduct with an appeal to the normal conventions of news interviews (lines 15 and 18) already implicated in the IE's prior turn (at line 14) and this, in its turn, is resisted by the IE who rejects the appeal and again presses for a response with a fully articulated demand for an explanation (lines 16, 17 and 19). Finally the IR responds to the question by rejecting the claim that the program had distorted the facts (line 21).

Here then the central turn-taking provision of the news interview is explicitly formulated by both parties in the context of a major and contested departure from its provisions and this provision itself becomes the object of dispute.

So far, we have been concerned to sketch an outline of the turn-taking system for news interviews and to argue for the normative character of its provisions. We stress that the overwhelming mass of news interview conduct is compatible – and compatible in fine detail – with this turn-taking system and that departures from its provisions are routinely treated as normatively accountable. This turn-taking system is, by comparison with the turn-taking system for ordinary conversation, both distinctive and restrictive. By managing their talk so as to respect the provisions of this system, the parties collaboratively instantiate both its "interview" character and, simultaneously, their roles as IR and IE within the context thus created. Respect for this system thus encodes an orientation to both context and role that is pervasive insofar as it is collaboratively sustained, turn by turn, across the course of the interaction.

4   The Institutional Distinctiveness of News Interview Turn-taking Procedures

Having established that turn-taking procedures in the news interview are distinctive from those operative in ordinary conversation, we now proceed to our second objective of showing how this distinctiveness is related to the particular orientations, tasks and constraints which are characteristic of the news interview. The achievement of this task will not only establish the specifically "institutional" character of news interview interaction, it will also move us towards the task of showing the ways in which quite small-scale elements of conduct which are characteristic of the news interview are systematically related to the macro institutional structures within which the news interview is embedded. Among a range of important news interview tasks and constraints we will here focus on two: (1) the task of producing talk for an "overhearing" news audience, and (2) the constraint that interviewers should maintain a stance of formal neutrality towards interviewee statements and positions.

The news interview is, of course, a form of professional journalism. Its fundamental function is the communication of information or opinion from public figures, experts or other persons in the news for the benefit of the news audience. As such it stands as an alternative to direct reportage of the views of public figures. Within this process, the IR essentially functions as a catalyst whose task is, first, to provide a context in which IEs can communicate information and opinion, and second, to challenge or press IEs, where appropriate, on the views they express.[15] The primary recipients of the expressed information or opinions are the news audience for whose benefit the talk is ultimately produced. Within the news interview, it is conventional to maintain the news audience as primary recipients of the talk rather than attempting to create the impression that they are eavesdroppers on a putatively "private" interchange. This must be managed in and through the design of the talk. So a first task we will be concerned with is the production of talk for an overhearing audience.

Second, IRs must manage this task while meeting a constraint that specifically bears on broadcast journalists at the present. This constraint is that they retain a stance of neutrality towards the statements and opinions of the IE. Because IRs' questions often (and in many cases unavoidably) embody assumptions that are supportive or hostile to IEs' stated positions and cannot, strictly speaking, be regarded as neutral, we will speak of this stance as embodying a position of "formal neutrality" or, more simply, as a "neutralistic" stance.[16] A central feature of this stance is that IRs should avoid making statements – whether hostile to or supportive of an IE's stated position – that could be construed as a personal opinion or as the position of their employers – the news organization that is ultimately responsible for the broadcast. This general stance is required of news organizations by law in some countries (including Britain) and by convention in others. This neutralistic stance is, once again, something that must be sustained over the course of IR conduct in the interview situation.

In what follows, we will propose that the turn-taking system for news interviews is one which is geared to the management of these two tasks:

1 the task of producing talk that maintains an "overhearing" news audience as its primary recipients;
2 the maintenance of a neutralistic stance towards IE statements and positions.

We begin by looking at the management of the parties' talk as "talk for an overhearing news audience."

5   The Management of News Interview Talk as "Talk for Overhearers"

In this section, we seek to demonstrate that compliance with the turn-taking procedures for news interviews embodies a "footing" (Goffman 1981; Levinson 1988) in which the parties treat their talk as geared to the "overhearing" news audience. In particular, we will focus on the fact that while IE talk is produced in response to, and thus addressed to, IR questions, it is hearably geared to a ratified audience of "overhearers" – the news audience. Our proposal is that this footing is a generic product of the news interview turn-taking provisions outlined above.

At first sight it may appear distinctly quixotic to develop this argument when so many other facets of the news interview context already point to the relevance of the parties' orientation to the news audience. In the first instance, the general role of the news interview as a vehicle for conveying information to the general public is almost universally understood and is unlikely to be overlooked by the participants. IRs are, after all, professional broadcasters who, in commenting on their role, frequently characterize it as essentially one of asking questions on behalf of an audience. Similarly, IEs have normally arrived at the interview situation as a result of a prior decision by the news organization that their activities or positions are of significance to the general public. Additionally, both parties are surrounded on all sides by the physical apparatus of broadcasting technology and IEs are confronted by an individual with whom they may well have predetermined the main topics of the interview and who will have received explicit training in the tasks of interviewing. Moreover these background features of the news interview are comple-mented by many of the participants' own actions. For example, IRs' questions may make explicit reference to the news audience; they may embody information that is already known to IR and IE and whose inclusion can only be understood as aimed at the news audience. Further IRs commonly summarize IE answers and positions in ways that, insofar as they are of primary relevance to the news audience rather than the IE, can be heard to be audience directed (Heritage 1985a). These and other features of IR and IE conduct overtly display their orientation to the presence of an overhearing audience.

Against these considerations, however, two major points should be stressed. First, notwithstanding the obvious weight of the physical context and background understandings of the news interview, the parties may not comport themselves in ways that reflect those understandings. In a context in which, despite the physical and social context of the interaction, the participants did not operate within the conventions of news interview conduct but instead oriented to one another "conversa-tionally" or – as in the case of the recent Bush–Rather encounter – "confrontationally," we should be justified in concluding that an "interview" was not taking place (Heritage 1984a:280–90; Button 1987; Schegloff, chapter 3 above and 1989; Clayman and Whalen 1989). Second, the facets of conduct outlined above as evidencing an orientation to an overhearing audience only emerge intermittently during the course of an interview. Yet it is not the case that a news interview is only intermittently hearable as a news interview. It is a rare event to switch on a radio and to be unclear for more than a few seconds as to whether a news interview or some other form of social interaction (a "discussion," for example) is taking place.

These points suggest that the footing of news interview talk as oriented towards the overhearing audience is managed at all points over the course of the talk and not merely at those points where an overt reference to the audience or some other specially audience-directed activity takes place. Since the turn-taking system for news interviews is a facet of their organization that, as noted above, manifests itself throughout the news interview on an iterative basis, it is here that we may look for a basis for the general maintenance of news interview footings. In what follows, we will trace the connections between the turn-taking provisions of the news interview and these special footings. In particular, we will specify how the provision that IRs are confined to questioning turns is associated with the management of the IE's talk as geared to the overhearing audience.

IR conduct and the management of IE talk

As we have noted, almost all IE contributions to news interviews are built as responses to IR questions. We have also noted that they are almost always "long" responses that take the form of extended multi-unit turns that pass through several possible completion points. Examining examples of these long responses, however, we find that, while they are long, they are not attended by any forms of response from the IR over their course. A number of such response forms would be possible or characteristic of conversational conduct by a recipient of such a multi-unit turn. These would include response tokens such as "continuers" or "acknowledgment tokens" (such as "yes" and "mm hm" – Schegloff 1982; Jefferson 1984a) and news receipt objects (such as "oh," "really," "did you," etc. – Heritage 1984b; Jefferson 1981a, 1981b) which treat the prior talk as "informative" or "news" for the producer. Example 5.3 (see pp. 101), for instance contains a number of instances in which an IE's multi-unit turn is not accompanied by such response tokens. The systematic absence of these tokens in this example is wholly prototypical of IR news interview conduct both in the UK (Greatbatch 1985, 1988; Heritage 1985a) and the US (Clayman 1987).

As Schegloff (1982) and Jefferson (1981b, 1984a) have shown, response tokens such as continuers are produced in ordinary conversation at the boundaries of turn constructional units in multi-unit turns. In these contexts, they overtly "pass" on a substantive response to the talk-so-far and thus permit continued turn occupancy by the producer of the multi-unit turn. Such response tokens, in overtly passing on the opportunity to speak, also identify their producers as the primary addressees of the prior talk and, in principle, as having rights to respond to the talk at those points in virtue of the turn-taking procedures for ordinary conversation. The systematic withholding of these objects, conversely, is a means by which the IR can decline the role of primary addressee of the IE's remarks in favour of the news audience.

Although, as Greatbatch (1988) has noted, response tokens are sometimes produced in chat show and celebrity interview contexts in the UK, contrast cases in which IRs use response tokens to receipt IE statements over their course have proved impossible to locate in our corpus of news interview materials. However, contrast cases have been found in special data that approximate the "heavyweight" political news interview. Because we will employ other aspects of these data in subsequent sections of this paper, we introduce the data here with a rather full ethnographic description.

The data (labelled Williams in Conversation) derive from a series of interviews in which British (Labour) ex-cabinet minister, Shirley Williams, interviewed a number of prominent politicians for a BBC series that, significantly, was broadcast under the general title *Shirley Williams in Conversation*. By this title, the BBC indicated not only a departure from the normal procedures adopted by professional interviewers, but also that – because Williams was not a professional interviewer employed by the BBC – it was not to be treated as accountable for her expressed opinions. At the time of these interviews (1980), Williams had recently lost her parliamentary seat in the 1979 general election, but had not yet left the Labour party (in 1981) to found the, now defunct, Social Democratic Party. In the interview from which we draw extensively, she is interviewing ex-Labour prime minister James Callaghan who had been a cabinet colleague six months previously. In these data, IR response tokens, while occurring very much less frequently than would be apparent in a conversational context, are more frequently occurring than in any other interview data from any source that we have examined.

The response tokens occur, for example, after an initial component of a response to a question:

5.10   (Williams in Conversation 1980:71) ((The question concerns the control of wage inflation in the UK economy))

Williams:		.hhh *N*ow do you think that there's (0.2) a *mo*re permanent machinery some different way that we can get at this problem.
Callaghan:		I *d*on't think there's a *d*ifferent ma*ch*inery, I think you've got to have a different climate of *o*pinion
Williams:	→	mhm
Callaghan:		In *o*ther words you have *go*t to win the trade union:s *a*nd their *m*embers.=It's not the leaders of the trade *u*nions so much .hh as the *m*embers on the shop floo:r. ((continues))

They occur as receipts (arrow b) to a repair by the IE that was initiated (arrow a) by the IR (Williams):[17]

5.11   (Williams in Conversation 1980:221)

Callaghan:		.hh But going to (0.7) the *n*ext que*s*tion what do we do,=we've neg*l*ected edu*c*ation.
		(0.5)
		We've al*l*owed it all to fall into the hands of the *m*ili*t*ant group.
		(0.6)
		(I mean) *t*hey do more education than anybody else ⌈(i n M e r s e yside.) ⌉
Williams:	a →	⌊You mean *p*olitical educ⌋ation.
Callaghan:		*Ye*:⌈s. Yes. Political edu⌉cation.=I- they- they=
Williams:	b →	⌊Yes. mhm. mhm.⌋
Callaghan:		=.hh they do *m*ore than anybody *e*lse.=I'm- they've come into the *pa*r:ty and they run their newspaper and heavens knows *wh*at. .hh *Th*ey're making the *pa*ce on education . . . ((continues))

Significantly, they also occur (arrow b) after Callaghan has specifically targeted Williams (arrow a) as the primary addressee of a remark, in 5.12 and 5.13 below:

5.12   (Williams in Conversation 1980:71)

Callaghan:	My own *v*iew is and I *gu*ess the trade union leaders would *b*ear this out is that *n*o figure

could have satisfied them or their member:s
last year:.

. . . .

. . . .

.hhh Although I never disbelieved their good will
I didn't believe that they could do *it*. (0.6) er-
And I'm a*f*raid the result has *b*orne that out. I am
an unrepentent believer in an incomes policy. .h

a →   And *l*et me say Shirley this is not a post war
phenomenon.=

Williams: b →   =mhm

Callaghan: .hh You know *I* g- I was a trade union *of*ficial
literally in the early *t*hirties. .hh And I
remember Douglas Houghton who's still al*i:*ve
saying to me in about nineteen thirty
((continues))

5.13   (Williams in Conversation 1980:240) ((On the Labour Party))

Callaghan: It *m*ust survive:. (0.2) It must survive.
.hhh After all there will be *n*o real al*t*ernative
to a Conservative *Gov*ernment un*less* the *L*abour
Party sur*v*ives.

. . . .

. . . . ((7 lines of text omitted))

. . . .

there must be an al*t*ernative. We- we- and *w*e are
the natural al*t*ernative to the Conservatives.=I
think the Conservative *policy* .hhh although (0.6)
for my *c*ountry's sake I would li(h)k(h)e it to

a →   succeed if you will under*st*and what I'm saying=
⎡=i t's b⎤und- I *fear* it's going to *f*ail.

Williams: b →   ⎣m h m⎦

Callaghan: I- I- I .hh feel it in my *bones* it's going to fail.

Although, as noted above, the response tokens are by no means densely
present in these data by comparison with conversational materials, they
are strikingly prominent when they are viewed from the perspective of
regular IR conduct in news interviews. In the Williams in Conversation
data, the presence of the response tokens imparts a quasi-conversational
character to the talk in which the audience, rather than being the primary
addressees of Callaghan's remarks, are, at least momentarily, formulated
as nonratified "eavesdroppers" on – as the BBC title characterizes it – a
"conversation."

In sum, we propose that the consistent absence of IR response tokens in the news interview is systematically associated with the tasks and constraints of news interview conduct. As we have seen, the turn-taking system for news interviews provides only for IRs to engage in "questioning" activities. It does not provide for IRs to engage in other forms of activity that are responsive to IE statements. The nonproduction of response tokens in the news interview is thus consistent with the provisions of turn-taking for this context. These provisions and the conduct associated with them thus enable IRs to decline the role of recipient to IE talk while maintaining (through questioning) the role of its elicitor (Heritage 1985a). Thus the maintenance of the audience as the primary addressees of IE talk is managed as a product of IR conduct *during the course of IE responses* – conduct which is specifically consistent with the turn-taking provisions for news interviews that we have outlined.[18]

Departures from the news interview footing and their management

In the previous section, we have been concerned to show that the management of IE talk as directed to the news audience is, in substantial and systematic measure, accomplished through the conduct of IRs. IE responses to IR questions are "deflected" toward the news audience by virtue of the fact that IRs systematically withhold response tokens across the component segments of IE turns. However, the success of this procedure is ultimately dependent on the maintenance of news interview turn-taking procedures which provide that IE statements should be produced as responses to IR questions. This consideration suggests that departures from these turn-taking procedures may tend to undermine the overall audience directedness of the talk. In what follows, we briefly address this possibility.

As we have already seen, most IE statements are produced as responses to IR questions. However, some are not. Many of these cases, as we have seen, involve IEs in direct comments on a co-IE's previous remarks and, notwithstanding the fact that they formally depart from the provisions of the news interview turn-taking system, they are routinely allowed to pass without intervention or comment from the IR. It is noticeable, however, that in the course of these departures IEs are normally careful to maintain the IR, rather than the co-IE, as the direct addressee of their statements. If, in such a context, the IR continues to "withhold" response, the outcome is that the news audience is sustained as the primary, if indirect, addressee of the IE's remarks and the character of the news interview as "talk for overhearers" is maintained.

For example, in the following case, an IE (PJ) initiates a disagreement with the assertion of a previous IE in overlap with the initiation of the IR's turn. Notwithstanding this departure, the IE continues to address the IR – and through the IR, the overhearing audience – by referring to his co-IE in the third person (references arrowed).

5.14   (WAO:15.2.79)

```
SB:        The most important thing .hhh is that Mister
           Healey .h should stick to his gu:ns.=
PJ:        =⎡You s ⎤ ee
IR:         ⎣Well I-⎦
           (.)
PJ:    →   I disagree with- with Sam Brittan on a- in a
           most (.) fundamental way about this, (.) because
       →   (0.2) it may well be so.=I mean he would arg-
       →   Sam Brittan would argue from a monetarist point
           of vie:w.=But what Mister Healey does about the
           money supply over the next few months. .hhh will
           ((continues))
```

In this disagreement sequence, an ancillary procedure – third-person reference to a co-present IE – is used to sustain the overall footing of the talk. Here, where the turn-taking procedures for news interviews are departed from, the footing which adherence to those procedures embodies is nonetheless sustained by this ancillary means. The procedure of third-person reference to a co-present IE is a central means by which an IE can depart from ordinary interview turn-taking procedures while sustaining the footing of an IE.

As Greatbatch (forthcoming) has shown, however, when disagreements are escalated in extent and seriousness, IEs sometimes abandon this footing by entering into direct, unmediated disagreement with one another. Such cases are normally of limited duration, with IRs intervening to restore the Q–A format and the footing of the participants – sometimes sanctioning the IEs' conduct in the process.

The following case, which is a seriously escalated disagreement, involves an abandoning both of news interview turn-taking procedures and of the footings which they embody. Here an IE's (JK) initial "out of turn" disagreement (arrow a) with a previous IE is intersected by the previous IE (OM) with a post-response initiation continuation (cf. Jefferson 1981a:39–49) of her earlier remarks (arrow b). This continuation is then heckled with a series of interjective disagreements by JK (arrows c, d and e). It can be seen that with her remark, "unless they come under pressure from the kind of counselling organization that you have in mind such as Life" (lines 5, 6, and 8), OM does not employ the procedure of third-person reference and instead directly addresses her co-IE. Thereafter both IEs address one another, rather than the IR, in sustained disagreement and overlap competition (Jefferson and Schegloff 1975).

5.15   (AP:22.1.80)

((OM and JK are being interviewed about proposed revisions to the legislation on abortion. OM's initial turn (lines 1–3) completes a defense of abortion referral agencies. Her post-response continuation of this defense incorporates an attack (lines 5–6, 8, 11–12 and 14) on an anti-abortion organization ("Life") which JK supports.))

```
 1   OM:            The point i:s .hhh that by and la:rge when people
 2                  seek out an agency like that they have made up
 3                  their mi:nds.=
 4   JK:    a →     =Not necessarily because .hhh ⌈certainly the ones⌉
 5   OM:    b →                                  ⌊Unless they come ⌋
 6                  under pressure from ⌈the kin⌉d of counselling=
 7   JK:    c →                         ⌊ N o ⌋
 8   OM:            =organization that you ha⌈ve in mind, such as Life,⌉
 9   JK:    d →                              ⌊No I- I- I've u- this  ⌋
10   JK:    d →     is no- ⌈there's no pressure at all,=no. e:r ( )    ⌉
11   OM:            ⌊which tries to make a woman feel guilty and⌋
12   OM:            takes no respons⌈ibility ⌉for the
13   JK:    e →                     ⌊ N o :⌋
14   OM:            ⌈consequences (            )        ⌉
15   IR:            ⌊Now can I put one point to you,⌋that I- I- I- as
16                  I hear you arguing yet again,=
```

In this case, where both IEs have abandoned the turn-taking procedures for news interviews and abandoned the footing which those procedures sustain, the IR terminates the sequence (at lines 15–16) with a question whose preface sanctions the parties as "arguing yet again."

In sum, by managing their talk within the constraints of the turn-taking system for news interviews, the parties not only establish and sustain the accountable identities of IR and IE but also maintain the stance that their talk is directed to an overhearing audience. Departures from this turn-taking system occur, but are commonly associated with the use of ancillary procedures for the maintenance of this stance. These procedures are ancillary in that they emerge most commonly in the context of departures from the news interview turn-taking system and they clearly serve to maintain the "talk-for-overhearers" footing of the interview notwithstanding such departures. In the cases to hand, departures from turn-taking procedures that are not associated with the use of these ancillary procedures are the ones which encounter sanctions from IRs who simultaneously seek to restore both the turn-taking procedures and the footings of the news interview by asking a new question.

6   News Interview Turn-taking and the Maintenance of IR Neutrality

We now turn to consider the role of the news interview turn-taking system in relation to the second dimension of the IR's task which was mentioned earlier: the maintenance of a "neutralistic" stance over the course of news interview interaction. The IR's maintenance of such a stance is a facet of the broader range of external constraints that bear on news organizations in the UK and the US.

In the UK, which is the source of the data in the present paper, broadcast news organizations are controlled through a series of charters and licences which oblige them to maintain impartiality and balance in their coverage of news and current affairs and to refrain from editorial comment on matters of public debate or policy. Until recently the US Federal Communications Commission's "Fairness Doctrine" similarly required communications licensees to achieve "balance" and to present "contrasting viewpoints on controversial issues of public importance." Notwithstanding the new climate of deregulation in US broadcasting, there is little sign that this new context has resulted in major changes in news practice. In the context of the news interview – in which professional journalists are treated as representatives of their employing news organizations, these obligations effectively translate into the primary requirement, noted above, that IRs should (1) avoid the assertion of opinions on their own behalf, and (2) refrain from direct or overt affiliation with (or disaffiliation from) the expressed statements of IEs. Again as noted above, we refer to this as the requirement that IRs maintain a neutralistic stance towards the assertions of IEs.

There are a number of ways in which the news interview turn-taking system contributes to this neutralistic stance. First, the constraint that IRs are restricted to asking questions is one which limits the assertion of opinions. In the news interview data that we have studied, IR questions are not treated as expressing IR opinions. Rather questions are uniformly treated as designed to solicit the IE's viewpoint on the matters which the question raises. This stance is massively preserved regardless of the extent to which the questions may be understood as "hostile" or as presuppositionally weighted against the position of the IE. Let us return, for example, to the following exchange between Sir Robin Day and Arthur Scargill, reproduced from 5.2 above. Arthur Scargill was, at the time of the interview, a rival with the Scottish mineworkers' leader Michael McGahey for the presidency of the National Union of Mineworkers:

> (WAO:13.3.79)
>
> IR: .hhh er What's the difference between *your*
>   Marxism and Mister McGahey's Communism.
> AS: er The difference is that it's the *press* that
>   constantly call me a *Ma:rxist* when I do *not*,
>   (.) and never *have* (.) er er given that
>   description of myself.⌈ .hh I-⌉
> IR: ⌊But I ⌋'ve *heard* you-

The question rests on two claims about the individuals involved: first, that Mr McGahey is a communist, and second, that Mr Scargill is a Marxist. Within the format of the IR's turn, neither of these claims is overtly asserted as either a fact or as an opinion. Rather the claims are embedded within the question as factual presuppositions about the individuals involved (cf. Harris 1986). In his response to the question, the IE (Scargill) rejects one of its presuppositions – that he is a Marxist. But it is noticeable that this rejection (which is framed as an "answer" to the question – note the answer preface "the difference is") is managed as the rejection of an error of fact (ascribed to "the press") and not as the rejection of an opinion expressed by the IR. In this, and innumerable other cases, IEs treat IR questions – no matter how hostile or in other ways prejudicial to their viewpoints – as activities which are not accountable as the "expression of opinion." Further complex issues arise in relation to "question delivery structures" that contain preliminary assertions and these will be dealt with later in this section.

Second, the restriction of IRs to the production of questions also excludes other forms of affiliative conduct which are otherwise commonplace in conversational contexts. Such IR activities as news receipts and newsmarks (which accept, or project acceptance, of the factual status of the statements to which they respond – Heritage 1984b, 1985a; Jefferson 1981a) and assessments which overtly affiliate or disaffiliate with stated positions (Pomerantz 1984a) are not provided for within the turn-taking system for news interviews and are generally absent from the data corpus we have worked with.[19] Moreover, as we have seen, the turn-taking system for news interviews does not even provide for the production of "continuers," which, if they were produced, would not only undermine the footing of the interview (as discussed above) but in addition could potentially be treated as exerting an inappropriate influence on the shape and trajectory of IR responses.

In general then, the provisions of the news interview turn-taking system are strongly associated with the maintenance of the IR's neutralistic stance. In what follows, we explore this issue by discussing a range of departures from this stance that have emerged from our database.

IR-initiated departures from the neutralistic stance

Professional IRs very rarely depart from their questioning stance to produce turns that are fully occupied with assertions or assessments that involve overt agreement or disagreement with IEs. Such departures, however, can occasionally be found in nonprofessional interviews. For example, in the Williams in Conversation data described above, Williams briefly affiliates with an assertion from her ex-cabinet colleague:

5.16   (Williams in Conversation 1980:240)

Callaghan:		*There* is at the moment a *gap* (0.2) in our thinking. I think that's *got* to be *filled*. .hh er- Because a *nu*mber of the things for example that uhm .h *Tony* Benn *says* have got a *lot* to be be- er- er- er- have got a lot in them.= =I mean some of his an*a*lysis has got a .hh great de⌈al *in* it. ⌉
Williams:	→	⌊Oh yes.=*He*-⌋ he's got a *great* deal
	→	of er of ( ) think⌈ing. There's ⌉*no*=
Callaghan:		⌊O h *y* e s⌋
Williams:	→	=*d*oubt about ⌈it his are new ideas.⌉
Callaghan:		⌊ he's a- he's-⌋ he's a very fertile- well uh he- he- he e*xpounds* these new and fertile i- i*d*eas. .hh uhm And I think that we shouldn't neg*l*ect them wherever they come f⌈rom. ⌉
Williams:		⌊.hhh⌋
		But Jim what of the- you see the *cru*cial question in a way is- I ac*cept* that and you yourself said in Wales after the election ((continues))

Here Williams departs briefly from the standard neutralistic stance of an IR with a turn that agrees with Callaghan's assessment of a fellow member of the Labour party.

And in the following case, which is from a consumer affairs program and not from a bona fide news interview,[20] a famous professional interviewer (David Frost) directly attacks the position of his interviewee. This notorious interview was conducted with a businessman, Emil Savundra, who had sold his auto insurance company – effectively liquidating it – leaving many claims outstanding. Savundra was subsequently tried and convicted for fraud.

The interview took place before his trial and was conducted in front of a studio audience composed of individuals who had claims outstanding against the company. Savundra sat facing the audience which was highly animated, while Frost addressed him from a standing position – frequently standing over him. It is noticeable that, under the pressure of audience reaction and the abrasive questioning techniques employed, Savundra intermittently comes to abandon the interview footing. For example, the video recording shows that his remark at line 11 is directed to the audience rather than David Frost, and he acknowledges Frost's question prefaces on several occasions (lines 14 and 31) in ways that align Frost as a co-interactant rather than an elicitor of talk for overhearers.

In this extract, we particularly note Frost's direct accusatory disagreement with Savundra (arrows a) and his subsequent direct alignment with the interests of the studio audience (arrow b).

5.17   (O:21.4.81)

1	**Savundra:**		*By* selling out (0.7) I have no legal
2			responsibility, (0.2) and no moral
3			responsibility.
4	**Audience:**		Rubbish
5	**Audience:**		No moral responsi*bility*?
6	**Frost:**	a →	You have- (0.5) you have *total* moral
7		a →	respons⌈ibility for *ALL th*⌉*ese* people.
8	**Savundra:**		⌊I beg your pardo:n⌋
9	**Savundra:**		*I* beg your *PARDON* Mister Frost.
10	**Audience:**		You have.
11	**Savundra:**		I have *not*.
12	**Frost:**		How can you s- You *say* you're a Roman
13			Catholic and ⌈ its ⌉ the will of God.
14	**Savundra:**		⌊Yes⌋
15	**Frost:**		.hh *How* can you be responsible and head of
16			company when *all* these things happen. .hh

17		And you think by some *fake* deal with
18		Quincey Walker (.) four thousand
19		pou⌈nds (.) on June twenty third ⌉
20	Savundra:	⌊ You have already assume::d⌋
21	Savundra:	You have already assumed ⌈ a　　fake　　dea:l ⌉
22	Frost:	⌊ How d'you get rid⌋
23		of *mor*al responsibility.
24	Audience:	Yeah
25	Audience:	You can't
26	Audience:	You can't
27	Savundra:	How- you have already assumed (0.6) you've-
28		one thing: the fake dea:l
29	Frost:	Well *for*get the fake deal.
30	Frost:	⌈*How*⌉ do you sign a bit of paper ⌈.hh⌉ that
31	Savundra:	⌊Right⌋ ⌊Yes⌋
32	Frost:	gets rid of *past* moral responsibility.=
33	Frost:	=Tell me that.
34	Savundra:	By i- =
35	Frost:　b →	='Cause we'd *all* love to know.

This interview was widely regarded as a form of "trial by television" and indeed was cited by Savundra, in his appeal against his subsequent conviction for fraud, as having prejudiced a fair trial. In a summing up which strongly influenced the subsequent outlooks of UK news and current affairs producers (Tracey 1977), the appeal judge – commenting on this interview – concluded that "trial by television is not to be tolerated in a civilised society."

Parallel cases to these rarely, if ever, occur in news interviews. Moreover, when news interviewers do depart from their role as questioners to produce turns that are wholly occupied with assertions or assessments, they are normally careful to employ alternative ancillary procedures to maintain a neutralistic stance. The most common of these involves a shift in footing such that the assertion or assessment is managed as an object that is issued on behalf of others. The following sequence illustrates this procedure:

5.18　　(DP:27.9.81)

IR:	.h How can it be otherwise if the result *is* .hhhh=
IE:	=Because of the: ⌈because of- ⌉
IR:	⌊ almost　a ⌋ dead *heat*.
IE:	Because of the seriousness of the *pos*ition. .hhh The fate of the people of this country,=and the fact that we're the only alternative government.

```
                =And they've gotta let that transcend .hh any
                contest that they have among themselves.=
    IR:   →     =There will be quite a lot of Social Democrats
          →     watching who will say that the: .hh you are not
          →     the only alternative government.
    IE:         Well I heh huh you don't expect me to say
                anything good about the Social Democrats.=There's
                nothing good to say about them. (.) I mean they're
                not an alternative government ((continues))
```

Here, although the IR produces an assertion which runs counter to an aspect of the IE's prior claim, it is not asserted on his own behalf. Rather it is issued as a formulation of the standpoint of a segment of the news audience. In this way, the IR avoids making factual claims on his own behalf about the counter-assertion and hence avoids direct disagreement with the IE (cf. Clayman 1988, forthcoming; Greatbatch 1986b; Pomerantz 1984b).

IE-engendered departures from the neutralistic stance

Inducing the IR to take a position
As noted above, IR-initiated departures from the neutralistic stance are rare. More common, however, are departures that are engendered by IEs. There are several ways in which this may be done. First, and comparatively rarely, IEs may demand that IRs do something other than questioning by initiating questions directed at IRs. Such questions, once produced, may oblige IRs to abandon the "safety" of the questioning stance. Their production is normally strenuously resisted – as we have already seen in 5.9, set out again below, where the IR is finally brought to a response to the IE's question (arrow) only after a lengthy struggle:

(O:21.4.81)

```
    JG:         . . . despite the fact there were fou:r major
                factories that you knew about,=despite the fact
                there was a two hundred and thirty million capital
                investment programme that you knew about,=
                =.hhh that we dealt in companies you stated and
                restated toda::y, .hhh despite the fact that ninety
                one per cent of our companies are still there:,=
                =and only the marginal ones which you knew were
                sold, .hhh and you e:ven mislead people by
```

```
                    suggesting for instance that we owned the Parisian
                    publishing house Brooke. Why=
IR:       =s- s- s- Sir James=
IR:       =I⌈'m so sorry   (    ) I'm so s-⌉
JG:        ⌊No,=I'm asking a question n⌋ow.=
IR:       =It's more conventional in these programmes ⌈fo:r ⌉
JG:                                                   ⌊Well⌋
JG:       I don't mind ab⌈out        convention.⌉=I'm asking
IR:                      ⌊me to ask questions,⌋
JG:       you why (.) you distorted those facts.
          (0.2)
IR   →    Well we didn't distort them. ⌈I mean    er ⌉
JG:                                    ⌊Well w- then⌋
          did you ((continues))
```

Here, it may be noted that once the IE's question has been produced, the
IR is obliged to abandon his neutralistic stance in order to defend the
substantive objectivity of the television program team of which he is a
member.

A related context in which IEs may induce IRs to take an overt position
emerges from direct IE attacks on questions – as in the following case:

5.19   (AP:28.9.81)

```
IR:              . . . Isn't the overall impa:ct of this whole
                 procedure we've seen .hhh to: remind the country
                 that the Labour Party is very largely in the grip
                 of trade unions whose procedures are both .h
                 ramshackle and undemocratic, .hh and to call
                 what's just happened .hh an election of a deputy
                 leader .h is actually a farce:.⌈And has just ⌉
IE:                                             ⌊But-    But-⌋
IR:              demonstrated .hh to the country at large how
                 the ⌈Labour Party's affairs are conducted⌉
IE:     a →          ⌊Yeah. tha- tha- tha-     that'⌋s
        a →      good trade union bashing stuff but it's absolutely
        a →      irr⌈elevant (        )⌋=
IR:     b →         ⌊It's not trade union⌋
IR:     b →      =⌈bashing at all,=it's just des⌉cribing the way
IE:              ⌊(        ) (I'll tell you,)⌋
IR:     b →      things ⌈are.⌉
IE:     c →             ⌊I- I⌋ know. But let me- let me tell you
                 why . . . ((continues))
```

Here the IR responds to the claim (arrowed a) that his prior question is
biased against unions ("that's good trade union bashing stuff") by flatly

disagreeing and asserting that his question described "the way things are" (arrowed b). This counter-assertion, on this occasion, is allowed to pass uncontested (arrow c).

In each of these cases, the IR is induced to take an overt position in order to defend the substantive objectivity of a prior broadcast (see the recap of 5.9 on pp. 121–2) and of a prior question (in 5.19). In each case, the defence requires the IR to temporarily abandon his neutralistic stance as a questioner.[21]

Attacks on IR question prefaces

A second form of IE-engineered threat to IR neutralism is more common. We have already seen that IEs usually collaborate in the IR's production of a question delivery structure by withholding response to the prefatory components of IR questions. For example, in the section from 5.2 shown again below, the IE, as we have seen, withholds response to a challenging statement that prefaces a hostile question and only responds to that preface *after* he has dealt with the question itself.

> (WAO:13.3.79)
>
> IR: .hhh er W̱hat's the difference between your
>   Marxism and Mister McGahey's Communism.
> AS: er The difference is that it's the *press* that
>   constantly call me a *Ma:rxist* when I do *not*,
>   (.) and never *have* (.) er er given that
>   description of myself.⌈.hh I-⌉
> IR: ⌊ But I⌋'ve *heard* you-
> a → I've heard you'd be very *happy* to: to:
>   er .hhhh er de*scribe* yourself as a Marxist.
>   Could it be that with an election in the
> b → offing you're anxious to play down that you're a
>   Marx⌈ist.   ⌉
> AS: ⌊ er ⌋Not at all Mister Da:y.=And I:'m (.)
>   *sorry* to say I must disagree with you,=you have
>   *never heard* me describe my*self* .hhh er as a
>   Ma:rxist.=I have o:nly ((continues))

In withholding response at the first possible completion of the IR's turn, the IE collaborates in the maintenance of the IR's neutralistic stance of one who is merely asking questions (cf. Clayman 1988).

This collaboration is not inevitable, however. The following cases involve IEs initiating disagreements with IR prefaces at or near their first possible completion points and thereby formulating those prefaces as contentious statements of opinion rather than merely "background information." In the first of these cases, the initial intersecting IE disagreement (arrow a) amounts to little more than an "underscoring" of an element in the IR's previous statement. However, this "underscoring" is marked as disagreement-implicative by its prefatory "well" (Pomerantz 1984a).[22] The IE's second intervention (arrow b) is also begun with "well", but the projected disagreement component is immediately abandoned as the IR proceeds directly to the question component of his utterance.

5.20   (WAO:9.3.79) ((GR is one of 90 Tory MPs who have put their names to a motion of no confidence in a newly appointed national body for settling pay disputes.))

> **GR:** .hhh er It's *also* very noticeable *l*ooking at the *l*ist of appointments and we've spoken about the appointments as a *wh*ole: .hhh that there's been a *b*ias toward people who've been as*soc*iated with the trade union movement itself, .hh or with er rather aca*dem*ic aspects of industrial relations, .hh and there's an apparent *ab*sence of er em*ploy*ers who might be called upon to (.) *pay* .hh monies .h er that are recommended.
>
> **IR:** Well there's er mis- sir- sir- Sir William *Ry*lan:d u- formerly chairman of the Post Of⌈ fice, there's Mister ⌉ Gibson of of BP,
> **GR:** a →   ⌊well- formerly chairman⌋
> **IR:** Are ⌈ the ⌉se people *un*fitted to sit in=
> **GR:** b →   ⌊Well-⌋
> **IR:** =judgem⌈ent on these matters. ⌉
> **GR:**   ⌊ Well I- I- I- ⌋ I- the word *un*fitted i- is is- is perhaps a *s*trong word to use, but after all Sir William Ryland is a *form*er .hh chairman o- of- of the Post Office, ((continues))

This case exhibits what appears to be the standard IR procedure for dealing with preemptive IE responses to IR prefaces: namely, to proceed to the question component of the turn as directly as possible, in overlap with IE remarks if necessary, and in disregard of the content of those remarks. This procedure, which avoids overt acknowledgment of intersecting IE statements, thereby avoids acknowledging that the IR has been placed in a position of direct disagreement with the IE.[23]

In the case below, the IR's question is abandoned in the face of a determined attack on the question preface. Here it can be noticed that the

IR attempts to proceed with the question preface across the first two "interjective" disagreements of the IE (LL) (lines 4–5 and 7), only subsequently acknowledging them at the end of line 9:

5.21   (AP:7.3.79)

```
 1  IR:        .hhhh Lord Longford erm (0.5) we- we- we do
 2             take a lot of trouble (0.8) rehabilitating
 3             (0.5) criminals. .hhh er: ⌈and long⌉
 4  LL:   →                            ⌊Well I don't-⌋
 5             I ⌈don't ( )-⌉
 6  IR:        ⌊long term⌋scheme for the criminals.
 7  LL:   →   No I don't agree wi⌈th that at all (sir).  ⌉
 8  IR:                          ⌊But we don't seem ⌋
 9             to ⌈Sorry.⌉
10  LL:         ⌊( )-⌋er⌈ Sorry ( ) I⌉ don't agree
11  IR:                ⌊I- I see. Well-⌋
12  LL:        with that statement not a- no way.=
13             =⌈We d⌉o very little to rehabilitate criminal⌈ s ⌉
14  IR:        ⌊Well-⌋                                     ⌊W⌋ell
15  IR:        we seem to spend a lot of money on it even if we
16             do little.=
17  LL:        =Very little.=
18  IR:        =erm ((coughs)) What are your recommendations to
19             giving the victim a better deal.
```

Here the IR's preface (lines 1–3, 6 and 8) is moving toward a contrast between the (allegedly substantial) efforts that are made to rehabilitate criminals and an assertion (initiated at line 8 but left incomplete) about efforts made to help the victims of crime. This contrast is interdicted by Lord Longford at lines 4–5 and 7, and his disagreement is reasserted at lines 10 and 12–13. In his revised question preface (lines 14–16), the IR abandons the projected contrast. His new contrast (between the resources devoted to the rehabilitation of criminals and the actual achievements of the program) both accommodates Longford's disagreement (by modifying his prior assertion) and supplies information which can be heard to warrant the earlier, disagreed-with assertion from which he has retreated. It is only after this revised question preface, and after Longford has upgraded the IR's backdown by his uncontested intensification of the IR's contrast (line 17), that the IR is able to proceed to his question without further contest (lines 18–19).

In each of these cases, the IRs compete in overlap with the IE's early response with the objective of getting to the subsequent question. In 5.20

the IR is successful in this objective, in 5.21 the IR is unsuccessful. Regardless of the success or otherwise of this procedure, the IRs' efforts are geared to avoid being drawn into a direct response to the IE, while simultaneously establishing – by the production of a question – a neutralistic object to which the IE should properly respond.

Finally, in the following case, the IE interjectively challenges (arrow b) a lengthy question preface in overlap with the initiation of the questioning component of the IR's turn (arrow a). In this case, the IR responds by abandoning the projected question in favour of one that counter-challenges the IE (arrow c).

5.22   (NN:14.10.81)

IR:		. . . I couldn't help *notici*:ng when uh .hhh Sir Geoffrey Howe was *speak*ing this afternoon how while *all y*our other *m*inisterial colleagues were *clap*ping uh .hh *dur*ing his speech in between many of the things he was *say*ing .hh you hardly *clap*ped at *a*ll.=You hardly applauded at all. =*S*itting as you were beside Mister Heath.
	a →	.hhh ⌈Do you:⌉
IE:	b →	⌊Come o⌋ff it.
IR:	c →	d- (.) Well is it *n*ot true.=
IE:		=cu- Come off it.=( ) I *clap*ped . . . ((continues))

Here the IR maintains a neutralistic stance by a "retreat" to a revised question that addresses the contested facts. He thus overtly offers the IE a chance to rebut an assertion which he had presented as "background information" in his previous turn.

The differential vulnerability of question prefaces to IE interdiction

In concluding this discussion, it is instructive to compare two types of statement that may preface IR questions: third-party-referred statements such as that in 5.2 (see pp. 100 and 117), henceforth Type A prefaces; and statements – for example, in 5.20–2 – which are not so referred (henceforth Type B prefaces). While type A prefaces are routinely treated as neutralistic in character (Clayman 1988, forthcoming), type B prefaces are distinctive in that, considered in isolation, they are often vulnerable to a hearing that treats them as expressing a position attributable to the IR. They must, therefore, be supplemented by a question if the neutralistic character of the IR's turn is to be sustained overall. While an IE's response that is interjected between a type A preface and a subsequent question will not threaten the IR's neutralism, a similar interjective response to a type B preface may readily do so – especially in cases such as 5.20–2 in which the interjective response is one that constitutes the IR as *in disagreement* with the IE. IRs may thus be strongly motivated to compete with interjective responses to type B prefaces not only to proceed to a neutralizing question and to offer something to which the IE should properly respond, but also to avoid being drawn into dealing with an overtly formulated disagreement with the IE. This motivation is absent in the case of type A prefaces and indeed it has become relatively common for IRs to package challenges to IEs' stated positions using type A prefaces without proceeding to a subsequent question – as in 5.18 above (see pp. 120–1).[24]

Excursus: a note on the hostile use of continuers by IEs

In this section, we comment on the incidence of IE continuers as an incipient "first step" that is adumbrative of attacks on IR question prefaces or other hostile conduct in response to IR questions.

Within the turn-taking system for conversation in which each current speaker is treated as initially entitled only to a single turn constructional unit (Sacks, Schegloff and Jefferson 1974), the role of "continuers" (such as "mm hm," "uh huh" and, to a lesser extent, agreement tokens such as "yes") is relatively straightforward. Essentially it is one of "passing" on an opportunity to speak and returning the floor to the prior speaker who is thereby entitled to a further turn constructional unit (Schegloff 1982; Jefferson 1984a). By this means, a recipient can exhibit attentiveness to, and ongoing analysis and understanding of, what a speaker is saying. This conversational role of continuers is predicated on the restricted access to multiple turn constructional units that obtains in ordinary conversation.

As we have seen, in the news interview, by contrast, each participant has rights to an indefinite number of turn constructional units. Because IEs are conventionally restricted to answering questions, IRs have opportunities to construct substantial question prefaces free of the risk of "early" response. Similarly IEs, as we have seen, are expected to produce lengthy responses to IR questions. In the news interview turn-taking environment, therefore, the primary contingency that is addressed through continuers in ordinary conversation – access to more than one turn constructional unit – is dealt with by other means and the production of continuers is, in this sense, redundant.

Yet the production of continuers in the news interview context is by no means a redundant or insignificant activity. Their role, however, is quite distinctive in the news interview turn-taking environment. For whereas the conversational use of continuers is to entitle others to extend a turn at talk, their use in news interviews implicates that the user is actively "entitling" a co-participant to an extended turn at talk and hence that the user is asserting the right to interdict (or not) the progress of the co-participant's turn. Such an assertion is, of course, sharply at odds with the turn-taking procedures of the news interview and their associated rights and obligations.

This use of continuers by IRs would constitute a significant departure from professional standards and is exceptionally rare. Thus the main environment in which this use manifests itself is, predictably, incipient IE hostility to an IR's line of questioning. Thus, in the following case from the controversial Bush–Rather interview on CBS, Bush responds to the opening of Rather's question preface with "continuative" acknowledgment tokens (arrows a and b) roughly positioned at the clausal boundaries of Rather's first turn constructional unit.

5.23   (Bush/Rather:3.00)

```
Rather:              You have said that y- if you had know:n:
                     you sed th't'f hed known: this was an
                     a:rms for hosta⌈ges swap, ·hh that you
Bush:       a →                   ⌊Yes
Rather:              would have opposed it.=·hhh You've a:lso=
                     =⌈said that- that you ⌉did not ⌉=
Bush:       b →       ⌊Exactly. (M a n y-)⌋       May I-⌋
Rather:              =⌈know:: that you:   ⌉
Bush:       c →       ⌊May I May I  ⌋answer that.
Rather:     d →      Tha⌈t wasn't a ques⌉tion.
Bush:       e →         ⌊(Th-   right  ⌋
Rather:     d →      It was ⌈a statement.  ⌉
Bush:       e →             ⌊Yes it was ⌋a statement,=
                     =⌈an' I'll a:nswer it.= T h e President=⌉
Rather:               ⌊Let me ask the question if I may first.⌋
Bush:                =created this progra:m, ·hh has testifie-
                     er: stated publicly, ·hh he di:d no:t think
                     it was arms fer hostages.
```

Here Bush's acknowlegments take the form of agreement tokens (the second being an upgrade on the first). Such tokens, by comparison with passive continuers (such as "mm hm"), are adumbrative of incipient speakership in conversation (Jefferson 1981b). For the reasons discussed above, they are markedly adumbrative of incipient speakership in the news interview context. Bush follows them with an overt request to "answer" the question preface (arrow c) which he then proceeds to do (at arrow e) after his request has been rejected by Rather (arrow d).

IEs' use of continuers in news interviews is thus associated with

1   the abandonment of news interview turn-taking procedures;
2   the abandonment of the "footing" of the news interview that is associated with those procedures; and
3   incipient escalation into either disagreement with a co-participant or attempted interdiction of the continuation of a co-participant's turn at talk.

This tendency for the abandonment of the turn-taking procedures for the news interview (and their associated footings) to be associated with conflict is also found in disagreements between IEs (see 5.15 on p. 115 above and, more generally, Greatbatch, forthcoming).

Summary

In this section, we have argued that IE compliance with the turn-taking provisions of news interview interaction involves IE collaboration in the maintenance of the IR's neutralistic stance that is managed through the production of questions. Our proposal is that an IE who (1) responds to a question without challenging its presuppositions or character, and also (2) permits the IR question delivery structure to go to completion, ratifies thereby – at least temporarily – its status as an appropriate and valid question. Conversely, (1) IE challenges to IR questions – whether in the form of questions or of assertions about the character or presuppositions of IR questions – threaten that neutralistic stance. Additionally, (2) interjective interdictions of type B question prefaces similarly result in such threats by constituting these kinds of prefaces as statements of IR viewpoints. In a majority of such cases, IRs seek to sustain their neutralistic stance by renewing a questioning stance as soon as it is possible to do so and by avoiding, as far as possible, defences that involve the assertion of positions on their own recognizance.

The News Interview as a Social Institution: Turn-taking and its Tasks

In this paper, we have considered the news interview as a social institution, *sui generis*, that is constituted as such by a configuration of normative conventions that is distinctive both from ordinary conversation and from other institutional forms of interaction. We have attempted to outline its turn-taking system and to show the distinctive character of that system in relation to ordinary conversation. We have also sought to draw out some of the institutional significance of turn-taking procedures in the news interview by pointing to certain of the specific tasks and constraints of broadcast journalism that adherence to these procedures automatically handles.

Although complex in its ramifications, this turn-taking system can be simply stated as the rule that one party (the IR) will ask questions, while the other (the IE) will answer them. This turn-taking system is normative in character and, on occasion, may be overtly thematized within the interview as an object in its own right. A tacit orientation to it runs – like a spine – throughout the situated management of ordinary news interview interaction. Through their detailed respect for its provisions, the parties display their pervasive orientation to the institutional character of their talk and the relevancies of their local social and discourse identities as IR and IE. They thereby locally instantiate the character of their talk as "news interview talk" on a recursive, turn-by-turn basis and, more broadly, reproduce "news interview talk" as an institutionalized form of social interaction.

We have further argued that this turn-taking system is pervasively associated with a central task and a core exogenous constraint of the news interview – the elicitation of talk that is expressly produced for an overhearing audience by an interviewer who should properly maintain a formally neutral or "neutralistic" posture. Observance of the provisions of this turn-taking system is associated with the appropriate management of this task and constraint while departures from these provisions often render their management observably problematic. Thus compliance with news interview turn-taking provisions is not the fetishistic maintenance of an empty form. Rather it is the most economical means by which the parties manage the quintessential business of the interview.

As we have seen, departures from these provisions are systematically associated with the employment of specific ancillary procedures through which, first, appropriate IR/IE footings in relation to the overhearing audience and, second, an appropriate measure of IR neutralism may be sustained. But although observance of the turn-taking provisions is therefore not the only means by which the business of the news interview may be properly conducted, it is nonetheless the "default" means. News interview turn-taking procedures form the centerpiece of an array of associated practices through which this outcome is achieved. In this context, it is instructive of the relationship between the turn-taking provisions and the "interview contract" that they instantiate that it is those departures which are unaccompanied by the use of alternative, ancillary procedures that threaten the underlying proprieties of the news interview. And it is these, in particular, that attract overt references to its turn-taking provisions and engender strenuous efforts to restore a *status quo ante* that is managed in and through those provisions.

We conclude by stressing that the news interview conventions we have described and the proprieties they sustain bear all the hallmarks of a social institution as traditionally conceived within the discipline of sociology. They are culturally variable; they are somewhat subject to legal constraints; they are subject to processes of social change; they are the object of debate and discursive justification. The comparative and historical study of these practices has yet to be developed. The impact of technological change, of political processes and pressures, of economic competition between broadcasting organizations, and of institutional dynamics within them, has yet to receive an assessment.[25] Similarly, the impact of these changing practices on the shifting political cultures of contemporary societies awaits investigation. It is here that the study of news interview talk as a social institution will intersect with the study of social structure.

Prior to all of this, however, is the investigation of the practices themselves. Without an understanding of their dynamics and of the ways in which their historically variable configurations interlock to define the "parameters of the permissible," social-structural analysis will fail to reach the core framework through which the participants contingently, yet collaboratively, "make the news" on a daily basis.

Notes

We would like to thank Steve Clayman and Manny Schegloff for their valuable comments on an earlier draft of this paper. Conversations with Doug Maynard stimulated a number of our introductory remarks. This paper is abridged from a longer version of the same title, in P-A. Forstorp (ed.), *Discourse in Professional and Everyday Culture*, Linkoping Studies in Communication, University of Linkoping, 1989, pp. 47–98.

1   Although this paper is based on UK news interview data, earlier work on news interview turn-taking in the US (Clayman 1987) and in the UK (Greatbatch 1985, 1988) has found overwhelming similarities between the ways in which turn-taking is managed in the two countries. No information is currently available about non-anglophone news interview interaction.

2   We here follow Schegloff (1987a) in referring to the object of conversation analytic work as "talk-in-interaction" rather than "conversation" because the interaction now studied using conversation analytic techniques embraces a much broader range of material than ordinary conversation *per se*.

3   Several recent papers deal with dramatic breakdowns in the normal or routine ways that "institutional" interaction generally proceeds. In relation to the news interview, Schegloff (1989) and Clayman and Whalen (1989) discuss aspects of the breakdown of an encounter between CBS anchor Dan Rather and George Bush, then US Vice-President, from a "news interview" to a "confrontation." Similarly, Whalen, Zimmerman and Whalen (1988) discuss a disastrous telephone call to an emergency hotline in Dallas, Texas in which, as a result of an interactional breakdown, an ambulance was not sent to a dying patient. These studies illustrate the generic methodological point that a "context" of interaction – whether conversational or institutional – is something that is co-constructed by the participants to an encounter, and that "routine" exchanges – whether conversational (Schegloff 1986c) or institutional (Whalen and Zimmerman 1987) – must always be treated as the contingent outcomes of a collaborative achievement between the participants.

4   IRs may, additionally, engage in nonquestioning actions that open and close news interviews (Greatbatch 1985, 1988; Clayman 1987, 1989, forthcoming).

5   Exceptions to this ordering may occur (1) in a multi-IR interview context when an IR may use a turn to allocate the next turn to another IR and (2) in a multi-IE interview context when an undirected question may be answered by the IEs in succession without the intervention of the IR (Greatbatch 1988).

6   See Greatbatch (1988) for further details on this point and the other assertions of this paragraph.

7   Though see note 4 above.

8   Detailed in note 5 above.

9   See, *inter alia*, Greatbatch 1985, 1986a, 1986b; Clayman 1987; Harris 1986 and, for a general overview, Heritage, Clayman and Zimmerman 1988.

10 For further considerations of turn-taking in relation to the issue of the minimization of turn size, see Goodwin 1981; Sacks 1974; Schegloff 1979b.

11 In addition to the examples of IE withholdings of response in the context of "hostile" IR question prefaces that are discussed in the present paper and in Clayman (1988) and Greatbatch (1988), see also Schegloff's (1989) discussion of the opening question–answer sequence in the Bush–Rather encounter.

12 The database used for the present paper was collected using audio tape. However videotaped data can show that participants exhibit still more fine-grained orientation to the turn-taking procedures for news interview interaction. For example, in the following case, the IE visibly restrains

himself from responding to segments of the IR's question preface (at arrows a and b):

(Nightline 7/22/85:4–5) ((The IE is the South African Ambassador to the United States))

IR:		As Peter Sharp said in that piece it is a lot

> IR: As Peter Sharp said in that piece it is a lot
> easier to im*p*ose a state of emergency than it
> is to *lift* it. .hhh You *still* have the root
> ca*u*se when you *lift* it. And bl*a*ck leaders in
> that country have made it very *clear* .hhhh that
> this kind of situation there's no way of *stopp*ing
> this kind of situation unless there is an end to
> ap*a*rtheid.
> It seems to me .hh that by *do*ing this by eh
> imposing I guess this kind of repression you-
> .hh you *really* set up uh *sy*stem where
> you can do *n*othing it seems to me
>
> a →   #.hh when you *lift* it# except to ch*a*nge the
> system that exists there (.) the *ba*sic system.
> b →   #.hhh# Is that unf*air*? er
>
> IE: Uh *I- I* would think it's unfair what is being
> said . . . ((continues))

At each of the arrowed moments, the IR has come to what, in a conversational context, could be a possible turn transition point (Sacks, Schegloff and Jefferson 1974). At each of these points, the IE visibly gets geared up and ready to speak. Within the # marks at arrow a, the IE licks his lip, opens his mouth (with a possible inbreath) and then closes his mouth again. Within the # marks at arrow b, he opens his mouth (with a possible inbreath) but withholds speech until the IR produces the subsequent question. The initiation of these IE actions is organized by the turn-taking system for conversation while their subsequent inhibition is organized by the more restricted turn-taking system for news interviews. The IE visibly inhibits "conversational" responses in light of the fact that he is in a news interview context and should act appropriately. Cases of this type thus exhibit both the priority of conversational turn-taking procedures in the organization of respondents' conduct and the normativity of their inhibition in the news interview context. We are grateful to Steve Clayman for permission to use this example from his database in order to illustrate this point.

13   The fact that IE turns are conventionally "long," together with the fact that the IR is deprived of response token resources (Jefferson 1981b, 1984a) with which turn completion may be the object of negotiation, creates additional difficulties for the management of IE turn completion. The latter may be notably more difficult for IRs to project, creating turn-taking dysfluencies,

for instance, gaps and overlaps. For some discussion of how IEs project the overall shape and size of their turns, see Greatbatch (1985:154–8).

14 Thus in the following example, the IR indicates that this question is his last and should be answered briefly.

(WAO:15.2.79)

IR: Finally gentlemen and in a *w*ord,=do you regard this
new deal between the *gov*ernment and the TUC as .hhh
*b*etter than nothing=A constructive achievement, (0.2)
or a non-*e*vent. .hhh
(0.5)
IE   *I*t (0.2) *c*ould be . . . ((continues))

See Clayman (1989) for an extensive discussion of the management of news interview closings.

15 The extent to which IRs may challenge, probe or cross-question the expressed views of IEs is historically and culturally variable. In the UK context, for example, such challenges were generally absent until the mid-1950s. See Greatbatch (1985:26–47) and Greatbatch and Heritage (in preparation) for some discussion of this issue.

16 We here follow a usage developed by Robinson and Sheehan (1983:34) when they distinguished between "objective" and "objectivistic" news reporting. As they distinguished the terms, "objectivistic" describes a manner or style of reporting, while the term "objective" is treated in the conventional sense of a judgment about balance, truthfulness and the absence of bias in the news. We use the term "neutralistic" to refer to a pattern of IR conduct which can escape formal charges of "bias" – whether in the interview context itself or beyond – while refraining from any conclusions about the substantive neutrality or bias which may be held to inhere in particular questions or lines of questioning. For a subtle general discussion of a range of other aspects of what we are terming IR "neutralistic" conduct, see Clayman 1988, forthcoming.

It has been suggested (Harris 1986:54–5) that previous publications by both the present authors (Heritage 1985a; Greatbatch 1988) have embodied claims that the restriction of IRs to questioning activities of itself guarantees their "neutrality." If this claim were about the "substantive" neutrality of IR conduct and had, in fact, been made, it would be false. As Harris's paper shows, questions routinely embody presuppositional elements which may be more or less supportive of IE positions. Moreover other writers (see Hall 1973; Schlesinger, Murdock and Elliott 1983; Jucker 1986) have reported that different types of IE tend to receive supportive or hostile questioning on a systematic basis. However our earlier papers have specifically referred to the maintenance of "formal neutrality" and have specifically not made claims about the avoidance of substantive bias, hostile questioning or, more generally, the neutrality or balance of news interviewer conduct. It appears, therefore, that our use of the term "formal neutrality" may have been misunderstood. We hope that our use of the distinctive term "neutralistic" may serve to avoid any future misunderstanding on this point.

17　Clayman (personal communication) notes of his US data that, by contrast with our data from the UK, IR continuation receipts do routinely occur as third components of IR-initiated repair sequences:

　　IR:　Repair initiation
　　IE:　Repair
　　IR:　Repair receipt/continuer (such as "mm hm")

The greater incidence of these receipts in US data relative to comparable data from the UK may be an indicator that the trend toward an informal "conversational" style of interviewing is more advanced in the US than in the UK.

18　The following letter from the *Los Angeles Times* (October 15, 1988, V/2) complains of "on air" conduct among members of the broadcasting community that is conspicuously absent from the news interview form: "Why do TV reporters in the field talk directly to the anchor people when they give their reports? And why do sports announcers talk only to each other, as if they're alone at a game? And why are reports of 'news only' radio stations directed at one of the staff members? The airwaves are supposed to be public. We, the audience, have been reduced to eavesdroppers and voyeurs." The complaint of this letter is a minor index of an increasing tendency for news personnel to engage in informal interaction among themselves. It is a further facet of the general trend toward informality in broadcasting, briefly discussed in Heritage, Clayman and Zimmerman 1988. We are grateful to Manny Schegloff for drawing this letter to our attention.

19　The main exceptions to this generalization arise when the IE contests an IR statement in such a way as to undermine his neutralistic stance. See the discussion of 5.9 above (p. 105) and 5.19 below (p. 122).

20　The television program from which this extract is taken was an early example of an interview-discussion program focused on consumer issues. Current UK examples of this genre include *Watchdog*, *Checkpoint* and *The Cook Report*. In this genre, live or filmed interviews with aggrieved consumers precede an interview with the alleged wrongdoer. In this case, the interview subject had already been portrayed as "beyond the pale" before being subjected to aggressive cross-questioning.

21　Counter-assertion is, of course, not the only course of action open to an IR who is retroactively formulated as in disagreement with an IE. Other alternatives can involve (a) IR topicalization of the contested matter via a question (a simple instance is 5.22 below), (b) IR retraction of the contested assertion, or (c) conflict elision. For some preliminary consideration of this issue, see Greatbatch (1985:231–8).

22　Note that the "well" that prefaces this "underscoring" makes it clearly disagreement implicative (Pomerantz 1984a).

23 The following case shows the IR in a similar effort to proceed to the
    questioning component of a turn in the face of an IE's preemptive response
    to the question preface. In this case, the IE's early response anticipates a
    question that would (and did) imply a challenge to the impartiality of his
    sympathy for the dead and injured in Northern Ireland, and the IR's effort to
    proceed with the question is designed to forestall that preemption.

    (WAO:21.8.84)

>   IE: The *death* of Sean (Giles) was tra:*gic*, I've
>   ex*pre*ssed my sympathy to his *fa*:mily,=but it
>   is the *Brit*ish who decided to use *vio*lence (.)
>   to use *mur*der (.) to use *te*rrorism. .h *I* could
>   not have *fo*rseen that,=it was the *Brit*ish who
>   decided to use murder that *day*:. .hh And it is
>   *they*: (.) Margaret *That*cher who are en*tire*ly
>   re*spon*sible (0.4) for that murder, .hh *they* are
>   entirely responsible .h for the conflict in
>   *I*reland, .hh *a*nd I think the British *peo*ple .h
>   having *seen*: what is being done with *th*eir *t*ax
>   monies in their name: to *I*rish men women and
>   children .hh must *say* to themselves that *th*is
>   is *wro*:ng:, .h that we must consider this issue
>   .hh that we *must* with*dra*:w from *I*reland.
>   .h And allow the basis for peace in Ireland.
>   IR: →   You say you have *sym*pathy for the widow: and
>   the chi::ld of Sean Downes
>   .h⌈h h   *W*hat   do   you:⌉
>   IE: →   ⌊*I* have *sym*pathy for *every*⌋body
>   ⌈who has died in the ⌉⌈*past* fifteen years. ⌉
>   IR: →   ⌊ *W*hat (did you)⌋⌊*h*ave: for   the⌋
>   widows and the children of RUC
>   me⌈n and British Army soldiers.⌉
>   IE: ⌊   .h h   *I*   have   *sym*pat⌋hy for *every*body
>   who has died in the past fifteen years.
>   ((continues))

24 We stress that this use of "freestanding" third-party-referred statements as a
    legitimate IE activity is a practice of recent origin in the news interview and
    one that appears to be restricted to the packaging of IR *challenges* to IE
    positions (see also the data in Clayman, forthcoming). Together with second-
    party-referred statements – or "formulations" (Heritage 1985a) – it appears
    to be the only type of statement formatted turn that is currently permissible
    in UK and US news interviews. It should be noted that both types of
    statement involve a footing in which the IR avoids speaking on his own
    behalf – as the "principal" of the utterance (Goffman 1981). The more general

topic of the vulnerability of question prefaces to preemptive IE responses is a large and complex one. It is currently the object of investigation by both Clayman and Greatbatch.

25 For a start on these topics, see Scannell (1988; in preparation) and Greatbatch and Heritage (in preparation).

6

Talk and Institution: A Reconsideration of the "Asymmetry" of Doctor–Patient Interaction

Paul ten Have

The idea that interaction between physicians and their patients is "asymmetrical" is widely shared among both participants and observers of medical encounters. It is assumed as a "social fact" that the roles of doctors and patients differ, and that this difference corresponds to that of leaders and followers. This "fact" has been explained in various ways by contributors to medical sociology, whether causally or functionally, but it is only during the past ten years or so that research has been directed to the details of the interaction that are masked by a gloss such as "asymmetry." The accumulated findings of this research, and further work along these lines, can contribute to a radical reassessment of conventional reasoning regarding institutional behavior. While traditionally the asymmetry of doctor–patient interaction was considered as an effect of institutional structures, rules or resources, it now becomes possible to think the other way around, in the manner developed over the years by ethnomethodology, and see how asymmetries are produced *in and through the details* of physicians' and patients' situated interactions. In this chapter, I will show some of the ways in which participants in medical encounters "talk an institution into being" (Heritage 1984a:290) and thereby accomplish "asymmetry" (see also Heritage and Greatbatch, chapter 5 above).

Medical encounters are tightly organized events. At one level, they display a rather conventional organization in terms of phases devoted to specific consecutive tasks in the encounter, i.e. complaint presentation, verbal and physical examination, diagnosis, and treatment, prescription and/or advice (see also Heath 1986). But, on a more detailed level, this overall organization has to be realized through series of concerted activities that are sequentially organized. This chapter is focused at this more detailed level. It is there that "asymmetry" seems to be produced. But it will prove useful to reconsider the connections between these two levels of organization at various points in the argument that follows. I shall want to argue that locally organized sequential events contribute to the phased organization of the encounter as a whole, but that they are also framed by it.

In the discussion that follows I will explore and elaborate on general aspects of the constitution of asymmetry in doctor–patient interaction, drawing on two resources: (1) research findings of authors like Fisher, Frankel, Heath, Mishler, Todd and West, who have studied medical interactions in detail, and (2) my own work on general practice consultations in the Netherlands (ten Have 1987). To say that doctor–patient interaction is asymmetrical implies that two kinds of comparison are made. First, there is a comparison of what is done, and what may be done, by physicians and patients respectively during the encounter. Secondly, those asymmetries are compared with a model of symmetrical interaction assumed for informal conversation among peers. In other words, characterizations of medical interactions typically tend to contrast the action repertoire of doctors and patients and then contrast this pattern with ordinary conversation. While these comparisons may be analytically helpful, one should resist the temptation to accept these contrasts, especially when stated in absolute terms, as adequate empirical descriptions. In fact, both the differences in behavior between physicians and patients, and the differences between consultations and conversations are relative, changing from one occasion to another and from one moment to the next. It is only in their actual dealings with each other that participants in medical encounters "produce" asymmetry in various ways and to a variable extent. Institutional structures are not only external constraints on participants' actions; they are also actively used as a resource for those actions (cf. Maynard, chapter 7 below).

The contrasts mentioned are used primarily analytically and descriptively, but moral overtones are not always absent. It seems that a "morality of equality" is hard to avoid and more symmetrical or conversational forms of interaction are somehow preferred. On the other hand, it may be argued that making consultations more like conversations would either tend to be a hypocritical masking of unavoidable asymmetry or would actually destroy the consultation as such. While this is certainly an interesting debate,[1] for present purposes I will try to avoid it. Following a policy of "ethonomethodological indifference" (Garfinkel and Sacks 1970), no moral judgments are implied in my use of the contrasts, although some of the authors I discuss – especially Mishler – either implicitly or explicitly tend to introduce such judgments into their contrasts.

Aspects of Asymmetry

Basically, asymmetry in doctor–patient interaction is of two kinds. First, there is an asymmetry of topic: it is the patient's health condition that is under review, not the doctor's. Associated with this, there is a second kind of asymmetry: of tasks in the encounter.

Patients' tasks mainly involve reporting their symptoms, answering questions, and accepting physicians' decisions, while doctors are supposed to listen to complaints, to investigate the case, and to decide on a diagnosis and a treatment. Although the initiative for the encounter is primarily the patient's, this task distribution involves quite "natural" interactional dominance by the physician, enacted through questioning, investigating, and decision-making behavior, coupled with interactional submission by the patient, achieved through answering, accepting and generally complying with the doctor's orders and suggestions.

Recent research in the details of medical interaction, including my own work (ten Have 1987), would seem to support general conclusions such as the following:

1   Local initiatives that establish a conditional relevance for specific kinds of second actions, such as questions, orders and proposals, are mostly taken by physicians and seem to be "dispreferred" when taken by patients (Todd 1984; West 1984:71–96; Frankel 1990).
2   The interactional control that seems to follow from this is reinforced by restrictive ways in which these initiatives are often used, especially by questions that allow for only short factual answers (Frankel 1984, 1990; Mishler 1984:59–91).
3   Questions put by physicians come mostly in series, in such a way that answers by patients are enclosed in and framed by the doctor's contributions: that is to say, the preceding question and the acknowledgment that follows it, and/or a next question, that in many cases comes interruptively (Frankel 1984, 1990; Mishler 1984:59–91; Todd 1984; West 1984:53–64).

4   The questions themselves, together with their topical flow and topic changes, are generally not accounted for by physicians; in particular, motivation for physicians' questions is not provided, and topic changes – which may be initiated quite abruptly – are not marked as such (Mishler 1984:95–121). In this way the patient is not informed on the reasoning process that supposedly guides the doctor's actions.

5   A similar lack of information is engendered by physicians' use of the "third turn" in questioning sequences: items like "okay," "uhuh" and "yes," as well as summarizing formulations, do not display for the patient what the physician makes of the answer, but only mark whether or not further elaboration is needed (Atkinson 1982; Frankel 1984; see also Heritage and Greatbatch, chapter 5 above; Maynard, chapter 7 below).

6   These tendencies often seem to be instrumental in a noted biomedical selectivity in that physicians tend to ignore those aspects of patients' utterances that report on subjective experience, personal circumstances and social conditions (Frankel 1984; Mishler 1984; Todd 1984). Elliot Mishler (1984:164) has called this a "context stripping" *def'd* approach. An important exception to this tendency is found in those cases where the physician specifically focuses on context in an approach that stresses psychosomatic aspects of diagnosis and treatment (ten Have 1989).

7   Finally, the asymmetries mentioned will accumulatively, so to speak, result in a tendency for decisions that are mainly based on the doctor's perspective on the case, guided by his questioning and relative lack of knowledge of the relevancies stemming from the patient's orientation to the problem (Paget 1983; Fisher 1984; Todd 1984). That is, in all the above instances, it takes specific efforts on the part of patients to counter tendencies leading to such a result, unless physicians take steps to provide them with occasions to influence the proceedings.

In essence, then, the literature reviewed suggests two major trends in the interactional style taken by physicians in their dealing with patients, one of monopolizing initiatives, and another of withholding information. ① ② Studies of medical interaction have, as their major focus, the phases of the *major areas* consultation producing data, especially the physician's questioning of the *studied* patient. Questioning is analyzed as a series of two-part or three-part sequences: a question followed by an answer, with the optional addition of a "third turn component" by the questioner (cf. Frankel 1984). In the following sections, I discuss some aspects of the ways these sequential possibilities are used by the participants, that is how "asymmetry" is locally produced or circumvented. In so doing, I will not only consider cases that conform to the major trends, summarized above, but also instances that run counter to those trends.

Asymmetries of initiative

Generally, as noted, patients take the initiative for the encounter as such: it is their decision to consult at this specific moment. Within the encounter, however, they seem to "lose" this initiative when the doctor's questioning takes over. It is this "takeover" that is of special interest in studying the accomplishment of "asymmetry."

While patients may decide if and when they come to their physician's consulting hour, it is the doctor who decides when they may enter his room. When inviting a patient to enter, a doctor acts like a host, inviting the patient to sit down and – possibly after some small talk – to provide the reason for his or her visit. In the initial invitation, the physician may refer to what he remembers or reads in his record concerning previous visits (cf. Heath 1981, 1982b). But, in the data for my study, typical invitations are quite direct: "Vertel het es," which amounts to "What's up?" or, more literally, "Tell me what it is." The "it" here appears to refer to the reason for the visit. In new cases, the patient will typically explain his or her[2] reason for coming by describing major complaints in one or two sentences, as in the following instances.[3]

> *6.1*   ((D = Physician, P = Patient))
>
>   9 **D:** Vertel het es
> 10 **P:** Ja ik ben zo geweldig aan diarh*ee* en 't wil niet
>   *ov*er gaan
>
>   9 **D:** What's up
> 10 **P:** Yes I have so m*u*ch diarrhoea and it won't go
>   aw*ay*

As can be seen, such a statement does not formulate a request, it states a reason for coming to the doctor and provides him with material for his upcoming questioning. In this way it functions as a request for diagnosis and/or treatment (see Wilson, pp. 33–4 above). When specific request forms are used, they tend to implicate a specified check-up, as in the following instances.

6.2a

7	**P:**	E:h kunt u kijken of ik zwanger ben
8		(0.4)
9	**P:**	(Ghh)

7	**P:**	U:h can you check to see if I am pregnant
8		(0.4)
9	**P:**	(Ghh)

6.2b

27	**P:**	Ja daar zitten we weer heh
28	**D:**	Daar zitten we weer ja
29	**P:**	Ik heb t'r nog twee dingen bij dat e:h moet u dus even naar kijken
30	**D:**	En dat is
31	**P:**	(Eerst es) naar m'n keel (1.2) en naar deze knie

27	**P:**	Yes here we are again huh
28	**D:**	Here we are again yes
29	**P:**	I have two more things that uh you have to take a look at for a moment
30	**D:**	And that is
31	**P:**	(First uh) at my throat (1.2) and then at this knee

In responding to the doctor's invitation in this subdued way, patients defer to the professional to decide what should be done next, whether a diagnosis and/or treatment is necessary and/or possible. These first utterances of the complaint also specify the body region that deserves his attention. Thus, patients provide their doctors with material for questioning in their very first utterances and physicians get an opportunity to "take back" the initiative they gave their patient just one moment ago (see also Wilson, chapter 2).

Both patients and physicians thus contribute to the start of an interaction format, namely questioning, that is oriented to the establishment of medically relevant facts. Within this format, the physician has the initiative and the patient is restricted to a responding role. In some cases, however, one can observe the emergence of a different format oriented to the history and the larger context of the complaint(s), rather than to just the facts. This format implies a more active role for the patient, as a teller of his or her own story. Extract 6.3 may be considered as an instance where such an alternative format is seen to emerge.

6.3

17	D:	Dat is een hele:: hh 'h geschiedenis met jou
18		geweest in eh januari heh
19	P:	Ja ( )
20		(.)
21	D:	En dat is toen dat is (.) sindsdien goed gegaan?
22	P:	Ja
23		((interrumperend telefoongesprek))
24	P:	('t is namelijk zo) ik ben al een paar maanden
25		(.) verkouwen en dan is 't weer over en dan is
		't weer weg
26	D:	Ja
27	P:	En eh zondag kree'k in een keer eh (.) g hoofdpijn
28	D:	Ja
29	P:	('k moest helema-) aan aan deze kant helemaal
30	D:	Ja
31	P:	En zondagavond kree'k eh pijn in m'n borst hier
32	D:	Met hoesten of zo of nou-

17	D:	That has been quite a history with you in uh
18		January huh
19	P:	Yes ( )
20		(.)
21	D:	And that has then that has been (.) going
		alright in the meantime?
22	P:	Yes
23		((telephone call interruption))
24	P:	(it's just that) for a couple of months I
25		had (.) a cold and then it was over and
		then it was gone
26	D:	Yes
27	P:	And Sunday I suddenly got uh (.) a real headache
28	D:	Yes
29	P:	(I had it all-) all over this side
30	D:	Yes
31	P:	And Sunday night I got uh pain in my chest here
32	D:	With coughing or something or whatever-

We have entered the consultation at the moment the physician finishes reading the patient's record card. Presumably referring to the last entry, he displays an interest in the sequel to the "history" he finds recorded there (line 21). In other words, he provides for a story to be told. The patient, then, does tell a story of sorts (lines 24–31). It is a tightly organized "unit" (cf. Houtkoop and Mazeland 1985), especially in the sense that the earlier parts display their own incompleteness, that is, that the major point, what may be called the "pressing complaint," is yet to come. This is achieved in a number of related ways:

1 by starting earlier in time (line 24), thus suggesting that the very reason for the present visit has not yet been discussed;
2 by mentioning relatively permanent states (lines 24–5), this effect is strengthened,[4] suggesting its status as "background information";
3 by adding a second item (line 27) to a previous one (line 24), it is suggested that a "list" is being constructed, which again heightens the expectation of more to come, that is, a third item to the list (cf. Jefferson 1990 on lists in casual conversation, and Atkinson 1983, 1984, on lists in various other contexts).

While in this case interactive structuring by the physician and the patient seems to complement and facilitate the production of a fuller historical account, this need not always be the case. Physicians may suggest fuller accounts, while patients stick to "just the facts," as well as the other way around. In the latter instance, patients are observed to use devices, those mentioned above and others, to change their local interactional identity from that of a "respondent" into that of an "informant."[5]

What these observations indicate is that although patients generally play their submissive part in the established "asymmetrical" format, possibilities also exist for patients to extend their chances to bring in materials on their own, which are sometimes successfully used. We should note that the devices for doing so are quite ordinary ones, regularly deployed in casual conversations (cf. chapter 1), as well as in various other settings. What is noteworthy, however, is their "covert" character: they seem to hide their action potential, the initiative their user is taking. In other words, patients seem to disguise their interactional initiative by refraining from formulating requests, by giving the initiative back to the physician rather quickly, or by using quite subtle and covert devices to hold off the doctor's questioning interventions.[6]

Questioning

Most researchers who have studied doctor–patient interaction in detail have given their primary attention to questioning sequences and consider the doctor's handling of these sequences as their primary instrument of interactional control. The central idea, summarized above, is that physicians have a privileged access to the first position in such sequences, which gives them control of what can coherently be said in the second position as an answer, and provides them with a possibility to come back after a minimally complete answer with a third position item, or a next question. In this way access to the first position is seen as a major entry into interactional control (see also Wilson, chapter 2 above, and Heritage and Greatbatch, chapter 5).

In this section, I will consider the concept of asymmetrical questioning *per se*, while in the next I will focus on some uses of the third position within it. The thesis of a dispreference for patient-initiated questions was, to my knowledge, originally developed by Frankel (1990). This concept was also used in a study by West in her analysis of 21 family practice consultations (1984; see also West 1983). West examined all questions that figure in this collection; most, 91 per cent of the total number asked, were initiated by the physicians, and these were also more successful (98 per cent versus 87 per cent answered). But West does not restrict herself to such an overall quantitative analysis. As she writes:

> Stronger evidence for the dispreferred status of patient questions is furnished by closer inspection of the form they take. In the course of this analysis, I assembled a collection of all patient-initiated questions from these exchanges. What is most striking in this collection is the presence of marked speech perturbations in the speech objects used by patients to construct their queries. . . . In fact, of the total of 68 questions posed by patients, 46 per cent (31) displayed some form of speech disturbance in the course of their production. Put simply, patients displayed considerable difficulty "spitting out" their questions. (1984:88–9)

She continues, later: "By and large . . . physicians' formulations of questions exhibited little evidence of speech disturbances" (West 1984:168).

Although I do not want to dispute the general thesis of a party-bound preference or dispreference for questions in consultations, I do have some difficulties with this research. Firstly, in my view, the analytic category of "question" is a difficult one. Although West (1984:73–80) deals briefly with some problems, I also see others. For instance, in my observation patients very frequently formulate their "ignorance" or "doubts" in various medical matters. These utterances do not have a question form and do not create a "conditional relevance" for an answer in the next slot. But they do display what the patient would like to know, or on which issues he or she would like to have an expert's opinion. Such utterances are often ignored by the physician, but sometimes they are taken up, possibly much later in the encounter, as in the next example:

6.4   (from the same consultation as 6.3)

```
 51  P:                        'hh ma- 'k ben gister expres
 52       een beetje op bed gebleven ik denk 't zal wel
 53       iets van kou zijn ik heb die- (.) die- in laten
          smeren met Dimedalgam heet dat=
 54  D:  =Dimidalgam (.) ja dat is tegen spierpijn
          (en ⎡zo)
 55  P:       ⎣Ja maar dat
 56  D:  'h⎡h dat helpt n⎡iet
 57  P:    ⎣e:h          ⎣(helpt) weinig
                                :
 96  D:  Want ik hoor d'r niks aan (.) in je longen (.)
 97       aan de binnekant is d'r niks (.) en eh je hoest
          ook niet
                                :
126  D:  Ik denk dat het toch eh die dat 't iets is met
127       spieren ⎡wat je daar hebt heh die pijn 'hh dat 't
128  P:           ⎣(Merkwaardig)
129  D:  een soort e::h spierpijn is
```

```
 51  P:                        'hh but- yesterday I
 52       especially stayed in bed a bit I think it is
 53       something like a cold I have di-di- (.) di-
          smeared it with Dimedalgam it's called
 54  D:  Dimidalgam (.) yes that is for muscular pain
          ⎡(and such)
 55  P:  ⎣Yes but that
 56  D:  'h⎡h that doesn't he⎡lp
 57  P:    ⎣u:h              ⎣(help) much
                                :
 96  D:  Because I don't hear anything there (.) in your
 97       lungs (.) there's nothing inside (.) and
          uh you also aren't coughing
                                :
126  D:  I do think that after all uh that that it's uh pain
127       something in your muscles ⎡that what you have there
128  P:                             ⎣(Strange)
129  D:  'hh that it's a kind of uh muscular pain
```

The physician, in this case, can be seen to check the two lay diagnoses that the patient reports to have considered earlier (lines 52–3), concluding that the first cannot be confirmed while the second is plausible.

In other words, it is difficult to set clear limits on the category of "question." Patients have a variety of ways in which they can make known to their physician their informational needs. Moreover, some of these more covert "questioning" approaches would be unlikely candidates for inclusion in West's analysis, although they may, in fact, be quite practical ways of getting physicians to provide desired information.

Secondly, while many questions put by physicians have a constraining effect on what *may* be coherently said as an answer to them, this is not *necessarily* the case. Although many questions provide for only yes/no or other kinds of short and factual answers, others specifically leave it to the patient to structure his or her report in the manner he or she sees fit (see also Maynard, chapter 7 below):

6.5   (from different encounters)

   13 **D:**   Waar dacht je zelf aan?
                  :

   32 **D:**   Waar kan dat nou vandaan komen denkt u?
                  :

   38 **D:**   E:n hoe komt-tattan?
                  :

   43 **D:**   Wat is dat allemaal?
                  :

  118 **D:**   Hoe ging het verder met u de laatste tijd?
                  :

  179 **D:**   Hoe voelt u zich verder?

   13 **D:**   What are you thinking of yourself?
                  :

   32 **D:**   Where does that come from do you think?
                  :

   38 **D:**   A:nd how does that come about?
                  :

   43 **D:**   What is that on the whole?
                  :

  118 **D:**   How have you been beside that lately?
                  :

  179 **D:**   How do you feel beside that?

In other words, West's analysis, by not differentiating as to the amount of control exercised by questions, runs the risk of overstating the interactional restrictions actually imposed by physicians.

Thirdly, also lacking in this type of research is a consideration of the sequential environment in which the objects under review are used. Specifically, I want to suggest that a dispreference for patient-initiated questions is most strongly present in the data-gathering phase at the beginning of the encounter. In that phase, a period of rapid and restrictive questioning – labelled "differential diagnosis" in the professional jargon of physicians – is often found. At other times during the consultation, however, and especially after the physician has stated his conclusions regarding diagnosis, treatment or advice, patient-initiated questions seem much less dispreferred or not at all. In fact, in my data, most patient questions posed in the environment of what I call the acceptance are uttered without any disturbance or other displays of a dispreferred orientation.[7]

In summary, I am proposing that while a questioning format is dominant in the data-producing phases of most medical encounters, and patient-initiated questions are largely dispreferred then and there, this should not be generalized to suggest that patients are automatically, so to speak, restricted in their possibilities to give and request new information throughout the encounter. Physicians can moreover frame their questions in ways that are less restrictive, and patients can use their answering slots to provide new information or suggest that they would like to be informed on specific points, as noted. Furthermore, the dispreference for patient-initiated questions seems to be phase specific. Patients have options to bring up their own points both before and after questioning, as part of their complaint(s) or as questions attached to the physician's decisions. West (1984:95–6) quotes Frankel saying: "It would be inappropriate to view the issues of control and responsibility in the medical encounter as properties of individuals," and she adds: "Instead, we are compelled to view such matters as micropolitical achievements, produced in and through actual turns at talk" (1984:95–6). Although in full agreement with these statements, I am suggesting that they be taken even more seriously than they have been until now. This is not to deny that physicians largely control the proceedings during medical encounters, but it is important to stress that this is not the automatic effect of institutional forms: rather it must be enacted by both parties and both of them have possibilities for less asymmetrical interaction.

Physicians' Uses of the Third Position: Assessments

Earlier, I summarized the literature on medical interaction as indicating two major trends in the style taken by physicians in their dealing with patients, one of monopolizing initiatives and the other of withholding information, at least during questioning. Having discussed the first trend above, I now turn to a consideration of the second. Atkinson (1982), Frankel (1984) and Heritage (1984 a and b) variously suggest that physicians and other professionals use "third turns" in quite specific ways when dealing with clients (see also Mehan 1979). Specifically, they tend to refrain from commentary, utterances displaying alignment, or any indication of their own information processing (see also Heritage and Greatbatch, chapter 5 above). Thus physicians, as well as other professionals, use two kinds of strategies, one active and one passive, to achieve an ongoing asymmetric display of knowledge, feelings and functioning.

Atkinson (1982) has suggested that a variety of routine utterance types – such as second assessments, second stories and newsmarks – are generally absent in professionals' contributions to lay–professional interaction; Heritage (1984a, b) has also specifically noted the absence of "Oh" as a "change of state" marker in these settings (cf. chapter 5 at p. 109 above). Both authors maintain that the specific character of "formal" or "institutional" interaction is especially, but not exclusively, observable in such third turn usage. Heritage calls this – referring to Garfinkel – one of the "identifying details" of such interactions (see also Zimmerman 1984).

Researchers who have given attention to physicians' use of the third position report a variety of turns such as acknowledgments, assessments, corrections and summaries (Fisher 1984; Frankel 1984; Todd 1984; Houtkoop 1986). Frankel, for instance, has analyzed over a thousand questioning sequences in the data-gathering phase of ambulatory care encounters. In over 60 per cent of them a third turn option was used. Dividing the utterances into two classes, acknowledgments and assessments, according to the absence or presence of contrast terms like good/bad, right/wrong, etc., he finds that assessments were almost never used by physicians, accounting for less than 3 per cent of his cases. Acknowledgments, on the other hand, were very frequent and were mostly given in short forms like "uhuh," "okay" and "I see." And he adds:

> One explanation for the large number of acknowledgements found in these data is that acknowledgements are used primarily to accomplish sequential as opposed to interpretive operations in discourse. Neutral third turn responses such as, "Mmh hmh," "okay," "I see," etc., operate without any obvious intrusion on the style or content of that which follows. Instead, their major effect is to invite speaker continuation by signalling receipt of prior information and nothing more. Assessments differ from acknowledgements functionally by introducing the speaker's reaction to, or interpretation of, the information supplied in an answer. (1984:157–8)

Generally, these tendencies roughly correspond to what I observe in my data from the Netherlands. Although perhaps to a lesser extent, Dutch physicians also seem to avoid assessments and newsmarks, for example. The fact that they do not always do so, however, offers the possibility of analyzing the exceptions. By investigating what may be done when such objects are in fact used, we may gain insight into what is accomplished by avoiding such use.

As a first approximation of such an analysis, I would like to propose a typification of episodes within medical encounters, as follows:

1 Episodes which have a marked "conversational" quality and in which non-medical topics are discussed, such as "small-talk."
2 Episodes which have a less marked "conversational" quality, which have more or less to do with medical topics, but are relatively marginal to the consultation's main "agenda."
3 Episodes in which the main medical agenda is being developed explicitly.

conversational
↑ *a continuum*
↓ *medical*

Quite often, in medical encounters, parties' talk does not continuously address the main topic(s) of the occasion, that is, the major complaint(s). In particular, immediately before or after dealing with their main business (type 3), parties tend to indulge in some non-medical small talk (type 1). This can also happen when the major activity does not require talking as such, for example during the physical examination (cf. Frankel 1983). Such occasions, especially toward the closing of encounters, can also be used by patients to elicit some minor medical advice, or to submit some medical idea of their own, even if it is not related to the major agenda (type 2). Elsewhere (ten Have 1987, 1989) I have tried to demonstrate that this variation in topic corresponds to a variation in interactional style. The style in type 3 tends to be the most formal, with type 1 the least formal in regard to such issues as the use of address terms, conversational restraints, and general asymmetry of interaction. In the following discussion we will observe a similar variation as regards the use of the third turn.

When objects like assessments and "Oh"-receipts *in type 3* are used in environments otherwise marked as belonging to type 1 or type 2, they may be seen to contribute to a process which we may gloss with a term like "informalizing." The following instances may serve as examples: *meaning?*

6.6a   ((during an "inserted conversation"))

> P: (Nou ja) die verhuizerij da's natuurlijk een
>   verv[elende (zaak)
> D: [Da's een ramp=
> P: =O::h

P: (Well yes) that moving business that's of course
a ted⌈ious (affair)
D: ⌊It's a dis*a*ster
P: O::h

6.6*b*   ((during the writing out of the prescription the patient has suggested that his colds are caused by the airconditioning at his workplace: the physician reacts as follows))

223 **D:** E:hm (.) als-tie aldoor uit dezelfde h*oe*k waait
224   (.) 'hh als je st*aa*t (.) dus ik zal maar zeggen
          tegen die ze⌈re *zij* aan⌈ 'hh dat zou h*ee*l best
225 **P:**   ⌊Hmm   ⌊hm
226 **D:** =kunnen ja (.) ik vind het altijd w*aa*rdeloos die
227   *ai*r-conditioning=
228 **P:** =Ik v:- ik heb ter een bl*oe*dhekel aan

223 **D:** U:hm (.) if it always blows from the same c*o*rner
224   (.) 'hh when you are standing (.) as it were
          on the a⌈ching side ⌈ 'hh that v*e*ry well
225 **P:**   ⌊Hmm   ⌊hm
226 **D:** =could be it yes (.) I always think
227   it's useless that airconditioning=
228 **P:** =I th- I really h*a*te it

Many instances of physicians' assessments in environments of type 3 also seem to do a job of "informalizing." In the instance quoted next, a strong negative assessment (in line 8), related to a central complaint, seems to be "a tease," which signals that the physician does take the complaint rather lightly, as have others before him (cf. line 11).

6.7   ((O = Observer))

7 **P:** Ik heb me gebr*a*nd (.) zondag=
8 **D:** =St⌈om
9 **P:**   ⌊Ik dacht h*ee*l ev- *ja*⌈   inderd⌉*aa*d (.) ik heb
10 **O:**   ⌊(huhhuhhuh)⌋
11 **P:** het eenenander*aa*n (ge) moeten horen (uhHUHhuh)
          ('K wou) toch maar even *zie*:n=
12 **D:** =J*a*

7 **P:** I burned myself (.) S*u*nday=
8 **D:** =St⌈upid
9 **P:**   ⌊I thought for a mo- yes⌈   inde*e*⌉d (.) I've
10 **O:**   ⌊(huhhuhhuh)⌋

11 **P:** had to listen to something-or-*oth*er (uhHUHhuh)
  (I would) see for a moment yet
12 **D:** Y*es*

The next excerpt concerns a case of a patient who stumbles into the consulting room because of an ankle that should have healed by now but hasn't. Here the doctor's strong assessments of her condition seem to function to ward off her possible complaints about this lack of medical success.

6.8

 1 **D:** Ja
 2 **P:** Morgen ⌈(uhm)
 3 **D:**   ⌊*Is* het nog zo erg
 4 **P:** Jaha
 5 **D:** O:h nee
 6 **P:** Ja *eerlijk*
 7 **D:** Ja
   ((voorstellen observant))
 9 **D:** N*ee* u bent verdorie een invalide als je zo loopt zeg
10 **P:** Ja

 1 **D:** Yes
 2 **P:** Morning ⌈(uhm)
 3 **D:**   ⌊*Is* it still so b*a*d
 4 **P:** Y*e*hes
 5 **D:** O:h no
 6 **P:** Yes *hon*estly
 7 **D:** Yes
   ((introduction of observer))
 9 **D:** N*o* you are an invalid damn it when you do walk like that
10 **P:** Yes

The two cases to be considered next stem from an encounter where a "biomedical" questioning is followed up with an episode during which the biographical background of the medical complaints is discussed (cf. ten Have 1989). In both instances quoted, the physician assesses parts of the patient's report with "difficult" (lines 102, 216). This report concerns problems the patient experiences in her dealings with her 18-year-old son.

6.9

 99 **P:** Ja en hij heeft dus om de haverklap geen werk
100 **D:** (Nja)

101	P:	Dus nou ja dat vind ik dus wel eh: (3)
102	D:	Moeilijk heh
103	P:	Ja: vind ik wel

:

212	P:	Jaha maar ja nu weet-ie natuurlijk dat ik
213		geweest ben (.) krijgt-ie te horen
214	D:	Okee
215	P:	(Huh)
216	D:	Zeh- 't is erg moeilijk een dieetje (.) vie-
217		vier weekjes (.) deze poeders

99	P:	Yes and so he is often out of work
100	D:	(Nyeah)
101	P:	So well yes I think that so well uh (3)
102	D:	Difficult huh
103	P:	Ye:s that's what I *really* think

:

212	P:	Yehes but now he knows naturally that I've
213		been there (.) he will hear about that
214	D:	Okay
215	P:	(Huh)
216	D:	Say- it's very difficult a little diet (.) fo-
217		four little weeks (.) these powders

The first instance fits in a strategy in which the physician focuses on the mother's feelings in order to be able to discuss them later as "part of the problem" (ten Have 1989). In the second instance, the assessment is delayed, comes after "okay" and "say," and creates the impression of an inserted afterthought. The doctor has just suggested that she should keep in the background regarding details of her son's life, that she should avoid the impression that she is continually concerned about him. But now she mentions a complication to that, he will learn that she has been around at his place. By hastily inserting "it's very difficult" the physician accepts that it may be hard to follow his advice, while at the same time making it clear that he is not going to discuss these difficulties any further. His accepting assessment makes further detailing on her part superfluous. In fact, this assessment is part of a successful effort to initiate a closing of the encounter.

While the uses of assessments in the preceding cases seem to be tied to the specific occasions involved, some other instances are, in my view, examples of a more systematic application of assessments: in fact, they mostly come in series. In the following cases, and in others like them, such a string of assessments is used *vis-à-vis* children and seem to display a specific orientation to their identity *as* children. That is, uses of assessments here and elsewhere are part of a certain style of speaking to children that is not bound to a specific topic or occasion, but is chosen by some adults in any kind of talking to the children. Some aspects of this style are displayed in the transcripts quoted in 6.10. In the first example, for instance, the doctor uses "sir" as an address term to a six-year-old boy, while the "pseudo-curse" in line 7 has the same "jolly" unseriousness. In the second example we see that the assessments are given to both medical and social aspects of the little girl, while in line 16 the mother displays an understanding of the doctor's efforts as trying to engage the child in conversation.

6.10a

```
 5  D:  Zo (.) vertel het es meneer
 6  P:  Ik heb steeds hoofdpijn
 7  D:  Wel (.) potverdorie hoe komt d⌈at
 8  P:                                 ⌊En als ik gaat
 9      hoesten danna (.) ko- gaat het hier pijn doen en
        op m'n hoofd
10  D:  J⌈a?
11  P:   ⌊En als ik niest ook
12  D:  O:h (.) moet je veel hoesten Peter
13  P:  Ja
14  D:  Ja? (.) vervelend joh
```

```
 5  D:  So (.) what's up sir
 6  P:  I have a headache all the time
 7  D:  Well (.) by Jingo how c⌈ome
 8  P:                          ⌊And when I cough
 9      then-uh (.) co- it starts to hurt here and on my
        head
10  D:  Y⌈es?
11  P:   ⌊And when I sneeze too
12  D:  O:h (.) And do you have to cough a lot Peter
13  P:  Yes
14  D:  Yes? (.) that's annoying lad
```

6.10b   ((M = mother))

```
 8  M:  Maja heb zo'n last van maaien
 9      (0.7)
10  M:  H⌈eh?
11  D:   ⌊Da's lastig (.) kriebelen ze Maja?
12      (0.4)
13  D:  Rotdingen heh? heb je je diploma gehaald? ja heh?
```

```
14        (0.5)
15   D:   Schitterend zeg
16   M:   Nou kun je praten
17   P:   Jha
```

```
 8   M:   Maja is very much troubled by maggots
 9        (0.7)
10   M:   H⎡uh?
11   D:    ⎣That's annoying (.) do they itch Maja?
12        (0.4)
13   D:   Terrible things hm? Did you get your diploma?
     D:   Yes huh?
14        (0.5)
15   D:   Really splendid
16   M:   Well can you talk
17   P:   Yhes
```

So we may conclude that at least some physicians use a special "conversational" line of conduct when they deal with children, even when the main topic is being developed.

A similar "conversational" approach is sometimes discernable in the ways in which physicians deal with elderly patients. It may not be a mere coincidence that the patients who are "praised" for their "good behavior" in the next two examples are, to judge from their voices, elderly persons.

6.11a   ((after the patient has told his physician that he hasn't been taking any medicine recently))

```
135  D:   Helemaal niks (.) ⎡Da's knap
136  P:                     ⎣(    )
137  P:   Jah jah
138  D:   Heh?
```

```
135  D:   Nothing at all (.) ⎡Well done
136  P:                      ⎣(    )
137  P:   Yes yes
138  D:   Hey
```

6.11b

```
28   P:   En ik ben op de weegschaal gaan staan en ik weeg
     P:   nou a⎡chtennegentig
29   D:         ⎣O::::h
30   D:   dat zijn goeie
```

31	**P:**	Jah
32	**D:**	ber*i*chten

28	**P:**	And I went to stand on the sc*a*les and I now
		weigh *ni*⌈nety eight
29	**D:**	⌊O::::h
30	**D:**	th*a*t is g*o*od
31	**P:**	Yes
32	**D:**	news

So, generally speaking, use of assessments in physicians' reactions to patients' answers, or other kinds of telling, displays an orientation to that telling that treats it lightly, as part of small talk, of marginal topics, or it is part of a wider "conversational" approach taken especially with persons with a non-adult status.

"Oh" in physicians' third turn

As noted above, both Atkinson and Heritage maintain that "Oh" is one of the kinds of items that professionals rarely if ever use in their talk with clients, while it is quite commonly used in ordinary conversation. Heritage summarizes some of his findings in this latter area as follows:

> Through the use of the particle, informed, counterinformed, or questioning parties can assert that, whereas they were previously ignorant, misinformed or uninformed, they are now informed. Correspondingly, the informing, counterinforming, or answering party is reconfirmed as having been the informative, knowledgeable, or authoritative party in the exchange. By means of the particle, the alignment of the speakers in their sequence-specific roles is confirmed and validated. (1984b:315)

So through the use of "Oh," a preceding item is labelled as having been informative, and, at the same time, the respective roles of the parties *vis-à-vis* the informing process is displayed. While patients quite often mark what their physicians tell them as news by the use of "Oh," doctors rarely do the same with patients' informings.[8]

Thus, I have been looking for exceptions to this general tendency in my corpus, locating 30 instances in which a physician receives a patient utterance with "Oh." Using the same typology of episodes as I did earlier, I observe that ten cases were used in environments that can be characterized as non-medical (small talk, etc.: type 1). Another ten cases were found to occur in episodes that, although more or less medical as to the topic under discussion, could be seen as relatively marginal in relation to the main medical agenda (type 2). *This is also in type 3.*

An example of the first type may be seen in the following extract which occurs at the beginning of the physical examination, often a moment when the physician starts some kind of small talk (cf. Frankel 1983):

6.12 ((at the start of the physical examination))

72	**D:**	(Hmhm) (.) In welke bar werk je? in welke bar werk je?
73	**P:**	Paradiso op de Markt
74	**D:**	Ohh (.) 'h als je eventjes dit uitdoet

72	**D:**	(Hmhm) (.) Which bar do you work in? which bar do you work in?
73	**P:**	Paradiso on the Market
74	**D:**	Oh (.) 'h if you could take this off

An instance of the second type, below, is taken from an episode toward the end of a consultation in which the physician has asked the patient how her husband is doing. When she mentions a side-effect of tablets the physician prescribed, he receipts this with "Oh" (line 3).

So this is w/i clearly talk — medical when his medical treatment

6.13 ((near the end of the consultation, about patient's husband))

1	**P:**	Ja: en 't is niet zo erg maar nou die tabletten
2		die: e:h krijgt-ie 't van aan z'n maag
3	**D:**	Oh (.) da's vervelend (.) moet ie ze met een beetje melk innemen
4	**P:**	Beetje melk innemen
5	**D:**	Ja (Da's beter)
6	**P:**	Oh

1	**P:**	Ye:s and it's not so bad but now those tablets
2		tho:se uh his stomach hurts from them
3	**D:**	Oh (.) that's bad (.) he has to take them with a bit of milk
4	**P:**	Bit of milk
5	**D:**	Yes (That's better)
6	**P:**	Oh

In relation to the collections from type 1, small-talk environments, and type 2, those marginal to the consultation, we might say that apparently physicians feel free to relax their professional habitus, since they are not being informed as a professional at these moments, at least not concerning the topic that is the major reason for the consultation. So we might conclude that the major discrepancy concerning the use of "Oh" is to be found in the type 3 data on the main business of the consultation. For this reason I will give most attention to this last set.

Before I do so, however, I will present a summary description of my findings concerning the type 1 and type 2 collections, as well as some suggestions from Heritage's essay on the use of "Oh" in ordinary conversation, in relation to these findings. In most cases from these collections, the information receipted with "Oh" is of a kind to which the teller has a privileged access, for instance, biographical details. In many cases, also, the information involved contradicts apparently existing expectations, either as displayed by the recipient or as set up by previous information given by the teller. In some cases, "Oh" marks the moment at which the recipient understands a point the teller is trying to make, a moment of recognition.

These observations are mostly in line with the conclusions of Heritage, although the frequency with which Oh-receipted information has a biographical character may be specific for the types of situation considered in the present essay. An important point made in scattered remarks throughout Heritage's paper is that an important difference exists between "Oh"s followed by inquiries, assessments, or formulations, on the one hand, and what Heritage calls "freestanding" "Oh"s, on the other. The last type is often used in such a way that a further elaboration of the topic under discussion is not invited, or is even discouraged. As he writes: "Whereas 'oh' may propose a change of state in response to an informing, it is entirely opaque as to the quality or character of the change of state proposedly undergone by its producer" (1984b:325). For this reason, informers may wait for an "unpacking" of this opaque message, and when none is coming conclude that the recipient is unwilling to give one. At the same time, an oh-receipt makes it clear that the informing has had some effect, and that further informing may be superfluous. Because of these suggestions, "Oh" often has a sequence terminating effect. Heritage notes that freestanding "Oh"s are less common. In my data, I count one in the type 1 collection, four in the type 2, and three in the type 3. In the interest of space I will only discuss the latter examples.

In the ten cases that make up my type 3 collection, most of the general findings mentioned above are recognizably relevant. For example, biographical information is clearly involved in the next case,[9] which also illustrates a process of counterinforming.

6.14   ((woman about her menopause))

```
270  D:  En tot die tijd heeft u g⌈ewoon
271  P:                           ⌊(     )
272      ()
273  D:  regelmatig gemenstrueerd
274      ()
275  D:  Ne⌈e?
276  P:     ⌊Nou niet regelma⌈tig,=
277  D:                      ⌊(  )
278  D:  =Oh 't was nooit regelm⌈atig
279  P:                         ⌊Neu
280      (0.9)
281  P:  Nee want ik ben (hier) 'n paar jaar terug hier
282      ook wel 's voor geweest
```

```
270  D:  And up to that time you ⌈just
271  P:                          ⌊(        )
272      ()
273  D:  menstruated regularly
274      ()
275  D:  N⌈o?
276  P:   ⌊Well not regular⌈ly
277  D:                    ⌊(    )
278  D:  =Oh it was never regu⌈lar
279  P:                       ⌊No
280      (0.9)
281  P:  No because I was (here) a few years back
282      for this too
```

The specific aspect on which the physician is informed is clearly displayed
by him in his "oh it was never regular" (line 278). In this way the topic is
kept open for further elaboration.

A similar display of understanding is given in the next case,[10] where the
information concerns another kind of private information, the location of
pain in the body.

6.15

```
32  D:  En waar zit dat precies die kramp?=
33  P:  =Hier is 't=
34  D:  =Oh daar echt in die kuit ja
```

```
32  D:  And where is that cramp exactly?=
33  P:  =It's here=
34  D:  =Oh right there in that calf yes
```

In three other cases, "Oh" is also followed by a formulation of the produced understanding, although in these the formulations are not restricted to the "gist" of it, but also extend into an "upshot formulation" – to use the terminology developed by Heritage and Watson (1980). In all these cases an "oh" plus formulation displays confident recognition.

This leaves three remaining cases in which "Oh" is not followed by a formulation or something similar, and where the "Oh" is not part of some kind of "conversational" series, as in the cases quoted earlier. In the interests of space, I shall merely summarize my analyses of these three instances. These are "freestanding" occurrences of "Oh" where the "quality or character of the change of state" is left entirely "opaque" – as Heritage has formulated it – and where the physician initiates a topic shift or change soon afterwards. This condition has the effect of confronting the analyst, too, with an opaque action, allowing for only tentative interpretation at best. These oh-receipts occur in environments that can be seen as somehow awkward or delicate. In two of the three instances, the physicians seem to challenge the information provided, but when the patients confirm their previous stance, they subsequently acknowledge this with a freestanding "oh" and change topic soon thereafter. In this way they mark that they have noted the "opinions" expressed without offering any assessment of the information "noted" in this way.

These interpretations are far from definitive. The opaque and hinting quality of a freestanding "oh" and its tendency to contribute to a subsequent termination of the current sequence makes it difficult to provide any interpretation from further sequential development.

My analysis of the 30 instances of "Oh" produced by physicians during consultations has suggested two generally valuable interpretations. On the one hand, the use of "Oh" may be a part of, and contribute to, a "conversational" quality an episode in which it occurs may have. And, on the other, it may indicate that the information so receipted may be seen as one to which the informer has some kind of privileged access. The latter may concern biographical information as well as private opinions and feelings. In some special instances this last marking was tentatively interpreted as part of a challenging episode, occurring when a patient stuck to a contested report on her feelings. In this way the "Oh" seemed to give an extra mark of "this is your private opinion." While such a use is not uncommon in informal conversation, its rarity in professional reactions to clients' informings could add to its impact.

Asymmetry Reconsidered

I have suggested throughout this chapter that "asymmetry," often conceived of as a given and constant feature of medical interaction, should instead be seen as an interactionally achieved and varying aspect of the interactional stream produced by doctors and patients. It is not my intention to deny that phenomena that can be glossed as "asymmetries" are massively present in medical encounters. But I should like to stress that the choices participants have to act more or less in accord with institutional expectation, that is, in a more or less "asymmetrical" or "formal" way, can be exploited by them to create specific kinds of episodes and to achieve analyzable interactional effects. More research is needed to specify what has only been suggested in broad terms here. The strategy pursued, to give specific attention to practices that depart from the routine, seems to be a promising one. The covert ways in which patients can try to influence the course of the consultation, alternatives to restrictive questioning, and alternatives to the third turn "uhuh," are all topics deserving more detailed exploration in the near future.

Consultations are sometimes almost like conversations. At other times they resemble interrogation. But mostly they are somewhere in between, zigzagging between the two poles in a way that is negotiated on a turn-by-turn basis by the participants themselves, whether they are Anglo-Saxons or Dutchmen.

Notes

Earlier versions of this paper were read at the Talk and Social Structure conference, and subsequently at the 11th World Congress of Sociology, Research Committee for Sociolinguistics, in New Delhi in August, 1986, and at the International Conference on Discourse in Institutions at the University of Dortmund in October 1986.

1 This debate could start with Atkinson's (1979a) observations concerning efforts to "humanize" judicial proceedings by making them less "formal" and more like "conversations." He suggests that such efforts tend to ignore the inherent functionality of many institutional arrangements, such as the achievement of "shared attentiveness."

2 Except for fragment 6.15, all physicians quoted are male; patients, however, are both male and female. I have adapted my use of pronouns to this circumstance.

3 The data extracts are presented in a simplified form (see appendix); the Dutch

version will be followed by an English gloss, which is intended to capture the utterance as it was spoken, and not to provide fully colloquial English.

4 Harrie Mazeland pointed out to me that this can be done by using verbs like "to be" or "to have" for background items, as opposed to verbs like "to get" for the pressing complaints: compare, in 6.3, lines 24–5 with lines 27 and 31.

5 This contrast between "respondents" and "informants" as locally constituted identities is currently being developed by Harrie Mazeland in a conversation analytic study of sociological research interviews.

6 This discussion, being restricted to "talk" as its topic, does not consider non-vocal devices. Christian Heath (1986) makes it clear that movements of the body can be used very effectively as "covert initiatives."

7 These findings are partially similar to what Frankel (1990) reports. He also mentions that most of his patient-initiated questions were put forward towards the end of the consultation, specifically at "unit boundaries," but – contrary to my findings – his examples display many dispreference markings, such as pauses, token acknowledgments and announcements, preceding the questions, even at those locations.

8 Just how rare this is cannot at the moment be specified. As far as Heritage knows it is very rare indeed in English language material. In eight complete consultations from my corpus, however, where patients used "Oh" 31 times, I have found that physicians produced 14 cases of "Oh." My intuition is that this does not represent a "language" difference. "Oh" seems to function in a similar way in both languages. It may be an aspect of a more informal style practiced by Dutch physicians, especially by general practitioners who know their patients for years.

9 This excerpt is a simplified version of a transcription made by van Mierlo and Driessen.

10 This excerpt is taken from a transcript made by Kaag, Koffieberg and Vreeburg.

7

The Perspective-Display Series and the Delivery and Receipt of Diagnostic News

Douglas W. Maynard

At medical facilities, patients often go through a battery of examinations, after which clinicians meet with them or their representatives (guardians, parents, or other relatives) in an event called the *informing interview*, to present findings and diagnoses. Within the discourse of informing, as it is partly constituted through practices for the delivery and receipt of diagnostic news, participants' ordinary interactional concerns and their orientations to social structure coalesce. In presenting a diagnosis, for instance, clinicians may preliminarily ask recipients for their view of the matter.

7.1   8.013 (simplified version)

```
1   Dr. E:   What do you see as his difficulty.
2   Mrs C:   Mainly his uhm- the fact that he doesn't understand
3            everything and also the fact that his speech is very
4            hard to understand what he's saying lots of time.
5   Dr. E:   Right . . . I think we basically in some ways agree
6            with you, insofar as we think that David's main
7            problem you know does involve you know language.
```

Such a practice contrasts with the strategy of presenting clinical information in a more *straightforward* way. Thus, in another interview, a pediatrician characterized a six-year-old boy as being at the level of a two-and-a-half year old. Justifying this characterization on the basis that "you have to have a fairly good idea of what he can and can't do," the doctor then presented the diagnosis:

7.2   57.116 (simplified version)

```
1  Dr N:  But um uh K is a retarded child, and it's not mild,
2          it's moderate retardation as far as we can
3          estimate.
```

When compared with straightforward presentations like this, the practice of asking recipients for their view is *circuitous*. But this circuit, and the straightforward delivery with which it contrasts, involve a social organization of talk for handling both convergent and divergent perspectives regarding whether something is wrong with someone, and if so, what it is. That is, the use of different forms in the delivery and receipt of diagnostic news maximizes the possibility for presenting clinical findings as in agreement with recipients' view and minimizes the potential for disagreement. The interactional implication is that participants structure the informing, like much ordinary interaction, to preserve a visible social solidarity (Heritage 1984a:269–72). The structural effect is to exhibit various institutional characteristics of the encounter, including (a) participants' orientation to the existence of a clinically relevant problem, and (b) the parties' consequent involvement in the lay–professional relationship as a continuing course of action.

Background to the Study

Data were collected at clinics specializing in developmental disabilities (mental retardation, autism, attention deficit disorder, etc.).[1] At such clinics, children go through an extensive evaluation process, which may include speech, psychological, psychiatric, pediatric, educational, and other kinds of examinations. When these tests are completed, clinicians meet with parents to tell them about the clinic's findings and diagnoses, and to make recommendations as to how to handle identified problems. This meeting or informing interview may last from 20 minutes to two hours as participants discuss a wide variety of concerns. At its beginning, clinicians often formulate the report of findings and of recommendations as being the purpose of the interview:

7.3   3.004

```
1  Dr. H:  Well (0.5) what uhh (0.6) we have brought you here
2          for is to sort of (0.2) give you all the (0.2)
```

3   results of all the tests that we did on uh (0.1) M.
4   (0.9) A::::nd sort of recommendations of:- of what
5   we feel should be done for uhh (0.2) M.

Sometimes, a clinician may ask the parent(s) for this sort of formulation:

7.4   14.008

1   **Dr. E:**   Okay do you know the uh- the purpose Mrs D of this
2   uh::: meeting?
3   **Mrs D:**   Mmm hhh I think uh you're suppose to tell me uh just
4   what you find wa- what you found out about my son
5   and what you think is wrong with him, and .hhh what
6   you think can be *done* about it
7   **Dr E:**   Right. General idea.

Thus, the tellings and recommendings are discrete and focal events within the conference.

The Perspective-Display Series

When clinicians ask recipients for their view, they do so before delivering findings, diagnoses, and recommendations. Thus, these preliminary queries occasion "mentionables" (Schegloff and Sacks 1973) from the parents that clinicians can utilize in particular ways when presenting their own information. For example, they can find out what and how much parents know regarding the child (Davis 1982). Of more interest here is that, after parents display their view, clinicians regularly deliver diagnostic news by marking or formulating agreement or degrees of agreement with the parental perspective (see also example 7.1 above):

7.5   41.079 (Simplified)

1   **Dr. E:**   I tell you in many ways I think- you know after this
2   great big work up, you know I think we- more we-
3   you know more substantiate what you- what your
4   feelings are.

7.6   30.121 (Simplified)

1   **Dr. C:**   . . . you know, we agree with you, you know to a
2   certain degree.

7.7   52.103 (Simplified)

1 **Dr V:** . . . I found that in*deed* M uhh *did* have uhh a
2   language problem.

Following such formulations, clinicians present findings and may further
indicate their relation to parental views – as additions to, upgrades from,
specifications of, more technical than, or contrastive with what the
parents say.
    Given this serial relation between the clinician's query, the recipient's
view, and the diagnostic news delivery, it is possible that generic
procedures are here employed to bring off what the participants regard as
the focal event of the staffing or informing interview. Thus, in everyday
conversation, one participant may ask another to give an opinion
regarding some social object:

7.8   15.092

    A: So what do you *thi::nk* about the bicycles on campus?
    B: I think they're terrible
    A: Sure is about a *mil:lion* of 'em

Opinion queries of this kind not only invite recipient to display an
attitude or perspective regarding the social object, but ultimately occasion
asker's own such display (Maynard 1989a; 1991). I call the generic form a
perspective-display series (PDS),[2] which consists of three turns:

1 Clinician's opinion query or perspective-display invitation;
2 Recipient's reply or assessment;
3 Clinician's report and assessment.

The first two turns are similar to what Sacks has called a pre-sequence.[3]
Pre-sequences include the summons–answer type, by which participants
provide for coordinated entry into conversation (Schegloff 1968); pre-
invitations ("are you busy Friday night?"), by which a speaker can
determine whether to solicit someone's co-participation in a social
activity (Sacks 1964–72), and pre-announcements ("have you heard?")
through which a speaker can discover whether some news-to-be-told is
already known by a recipient (Terasaki 1976). Depending on what a
speaker finds out by initiating a pre-sequence, the conversation,
invitation, or announcement may or may not ensue.
    In ordinary conversation, the perspective-display invitation and its
reply operate like a pre-sequence and seem to have alternative trajectories.

1   Sometimes, the asker follows a reply with his own report, or with further questions or "probes" and then with his report. In this case, the third-turn report is akin to a "news announcement" (Button and Casey 1985), providing for at least some "receipt" of the report or possibly a "topicalizer" in the next turn; this topicalizer then occasions elaboration of the topic by the one who initiated the series. In the clinical environment, the "topic" is the diagnosis, although recipients of a diagnosis often remain silent when it is delivered, and the clinician moves to a discussion of prognosis and treatment or management of the problem (Heath, in press).

2   At other times, the reply to a perspective-display invitation will be followed by further questions or other topicalizers that permit the recipient to talk at length on some topic. The questioner, never announcing any independent information or perspective, appears to "interview" a recipient and provide for that person to do extended topical talk. However, in the clinical environment, the relationship between the first two turns and the third-turn report in the perspective-display series appears more fixed or *rigid* than in conversation; only one of the alternative trajectories occurs. After asking parents for their view, clinicians unfailingly provide their assessment of the child (for discussion, see Maynard, 1991).

Marked and unmarked perspective-display invitations

As a mechanism for the delivery of diagnostic news, the PDS involves three turns or components that must be understood in relation to one another. Of particular interest is how clinicians fit their diagnostic news delivery to the occasioned display of the parents' perspective, especially by formulating agreement in such a way as to "co-implicate" the parents' perspective in the diagnostic presentation. A complete discussion of this phenomenon is beyond the scope of this chapter (but see Maynard, in press). Instead, the analysis is concentrated on the first two turns of the sequence, the perspective-display invitation and its reply. Although I de-emphasize the third turn, or delivery of diagnosis, I will later discuss differences in this delivery between interviews in which the PDS appears and those in which a clinician employs a more straightforward strategy.

Invitations to parents to display their perspective or view of a child appear in a variety of forms. A major distinction is between those that are *marked* and those that are *unmarked*, depending on whether or not they

initiate reference to a problem as a possession of the queried-about child.[4]
If the invitation contains such a reference, it is marked:

7.9   8.013

1	**Dr E:**	What do you see? as- as his difficulty.
2		(1.2)
3	**Mrs C:**	Mainly his uhm: (1.2) the fact that he doesn't
4		understand everything. (0.6) and also the fact
5		that his speech. (0.7) is very hard to
6		understand what he's saying.

marked – difficulty
says

7.10   14.012 (Simplified)

1	**Dr. E:**	What do you think is his problem.
2		(3.0)
3	**Dr. E:**	I think you know him better than all of us really.
4		So that ya know this really has to be a (0.8) in
5		some ways a (0.6) team effort to (0.4) understand
6		what's (0.4) going o:::n. .hh
7	**Mrs D:**	Well I know he has a- (0.6) a learning problem.
8		(1.2) in general. .hhh and s::::peech problem an' a
9		language problem. (1.0) a behavior problem, I know
10		he has all o' that but still .hhh in the back of my-
11		my- my mind I feel that (0.4) he's t- ta some degree
12		retardet.

That is, the invitation in these examples each contains a problem
proposal. Unmarked invitations do not propose a problem:

7.11   10.002

1	**Dr S:**	Now- (.6) uhh *since* (0.4) you've (0.1) been here and
2		through this thing h:ow do you see R now (0.4) Mrs C.
3	**Mrs C:**	I guess I (0.2) see him better since he here

7.12   9.001

1	**Dr S:**	Now that you've- we've been through all this I just
2		wanted know from *you:::*. (0.4) .hh *how* you see J at
3		this time.
4		(2.2)
5	**Mrs C:**	The same.
6		(0.7)

```
7    Dr S:   Which is?
8                                    (0.5)
9    Mrs C:  Uhm she can't talk . . .
```

We will see that marked and unmarked invitations have different
sequential effects, but an overall pattern suggests that they are still cut of
the same cloth. Each type, in particular ways, helps to collaboratively
establish the warrant for any given child's presence at the clinic, and the
clinic's involvement with the child. That is, both kinds of invitation help
establish a legitimate relationship between child and clinic. Analytically,
this has two dimensions. Clinician and parent mutually reach an
alignment, first, on the idea of the child having a problem and, second, on
the expertise of the clinic for dealing with the problem. Marked and
unmarked invitations propose such alignments through separate routes,
with different interactional effects.

On Children Having Problems

Marked and unmarked perspective-display invitations and replies are
involved in the work of establishing the idea that a child has a problem.
The relevance of the third part of the sequence, the delivery of diagnostic
news, depends on this premise.

Marked queries and presumptiveness

References to children's problems in marked queries can be considered as
suggestions or proposals, which require acceptance. This matter is
masked by the regularity with which marked invitations obtain replies
that similarly reference a child's problem. Segments 7.9 and 7.10 above
are exemplary. In response to each of the clinician's queries, parents
produce complaints in which they specify some problem of the child. In
the bulk of cases, the perspective-display invitation and its reply both
reference difficulties of a child in these routine and certain ways. That is,
parents converge with clinicians on the position that the child has a
problem, and the issue becomes one of what it is and what can be done
about it. After the parents display their views, clinicians can easily deliver
official findings and diagnoses.

Nonetheless, initiating the delivery of diagnostic news with a marked
perspective-display invitation is a *presumptive* move, which becomes
visible when parents disagree with a clinician's query (cf. Maynard

1985:15). Instead of responding with a complaint, recipients may take issue with the notion that there is a complainable aspect of the child.

7.13   22.007

```
 1   Dr N:       Now uh (0.8) from- from just the way you wrote up
 2               the application.
 3   Mrs G:      Mm hmm
 4   Dr N:       It's obvious that uh- you- understand a fair amount
 5               (0.2) about what Charles' problem i⌈s⌉.
 6   Mrs G:                                         ⌊Y⌋es. (yeh).
 7   Dr N:       And uh (0.2) from what I understa- you've also had
 8               other people who *have* looked at him too.
 9               So a⌈t this-⌉
10   Mr G:         ⌊Only ⌋ here.
11   Dr N:       Oh-oh. (0.4)  only   here?
12   Mr G:       On ⌈ly here⌉
13   Mrs G:         ⌊(Yes) ⌋
14   Dr N:       Uh huh.
15   Mr G:       Only in this clinic.
16   Dr N:       S::o at this point there is a certain amount of
17               confusion.
18                               (0.2)
19   Mrs G:      Mm hmm
20                               (0.3)
21   Dr N:       in your mind probably as to what the problem really
22               is?
23   Mrs G:      Mm
24   Dr N:  →    .hhh and we haven't really had a chance to hear from
25               *you* at all as to (0.7) what you
26               f⌈eel the situation-        ⌉
27   Mr G:        ⌊Well I don't think ⌋ there's anything wrong
28               with him.
```

Both mother and father are present at this interview. Mrs G, in affirming the doctor's inference that they "understand a fair amount about what Charles's problem is," also aligns with the position that the boy has a problem. However, when the doctor invites Mr G to display his view (arrow, line 24), the latter disagrees with that position (lines 27–8). To do such disagreement necessitates breaking the "frame" of the PDS; rather than producing a canonical reply to an invitation, a recipient may address the position implicit in it.

This contrarity is not a one-way street. Often parents make the first claim that a child has a problem, only to have a clinician disagree,[5] as the narrative elicited in the following excerpt indicates:

7.14   43.3-OTR (Simplified)

```
 1    Dr A:   Did you think something was the matter?
 2    Mrs Q:  Yeah.
 3    Dr A:   Did you ask a pediatrician?
 4    Mrs Q:  Oh, yes.
 5    Dr A:   What did he say?
 6    Mrs Q:  She kept on saying, oh, there's nothing wrong.
 7            There's nothing wrong. So you know I got very
 8            upset with her. And I told her, well you gotta send me
 9            somewhere because there is something wrong
10            because she's not doing this and not
11            doing that. And she would just give her a physical
12            examination you know and she couldn't tell if there
13            was anything wrong, just physically. And so she
14            didn't see anything wrong, so everytime I went to
15            visit her, I would complain you know.
```

How defined?

In fact, when clinicians produce a closed perspective-display invitation, they may be furthering someone else's claim, one that derives from the parents, the school, or some other source, rather than themselves making an initial proposal:[6]

7.15   39.036 (Simplified)

```
 1    Dr I:   Um C was referred to us from the school because of
 2            his behavior.
 3    Mrs B:  Mm hmm.
 4    Dr I:   He had a problem with behavior but you didn't see
 5            very much at home, a lo⌈t    at   ho⌉me
 6    Mrs B:               ⌊Mm mmm⌋
 7    Dr I:   Okay. Um when we tested him we found that there *was*
 8            a problem with the way his brain was functioning.
```

That is, even though clinicians deliver a diagnosis on the basis of an independent assessment, they may simply be confirming something that others first noticed elsewhere.

To argue that marked perspective-display invitations suggest or propose a problem as the possession of some individual child, then, is not to say that clinicians have unilaterally discovered a problem and coercively seek to label the youngster.[7] More accurately, marked queries exert or further a claim or presumption regarding a child's problem. When recipients of the invitation display their view by producing a description of the problem, they are agreeing with this presumption; and that constitutes acceptance of the problem proposal and continues the claim. Disagreement rejects the proposal and claim, and may, then, *pre-reject* the diagnosis and other findings and recommendations the clinicians have to present. When a marked query meets with disagreement in its occasioned reply, that does not forestall completing the perspective-display series. It does not prevent the clinician from delivering a diagnosis, that is, but it does engender attempts at remedying the disagreement.

In brief, then, use of a closed perspective-display invitation presumes the idea of a child having a problem. That presumption works as an interactive claim. It is most often honored, but it can be dishonored, and this results in initiatives to achieve the presumption as a mutual one before progressing through the series.

Eliciting problem proposals via unmarked invitations

Marked queries are visibly presumptive with respect to the issue of a child possessing a difficulty or problem. Unmarked invitations, which ask in more generalized terms about the child, are not presumptive in this way. This means they could be asking whether any problem even exists and, if so, wherein it lies. It would appear that clinicians are investigating parents' views as part of the diagnostic process, and using them in the attempt to discover whether any pathology exists. Or clinicians might be inviting a "troubles telling," with parents as speakers and themselves as recipients (Jefferson and Lee 1981). In fact, unmarked invitations, at least in this data, do not work in these ways, but rather, like their marked cousins, seek and require complaints about the child. When parents produce such complaints, they are the ones proposing the existence of a problem; this helps set up a turn in which clinicians can confirm that there is a problem and deliver a diagnosis. Having displayed openness with respect to topic, and after getting a complaint, clinicians align with the parents' position. In short, unmarked invitations, while not themselves containing problem proposals, elicit them from recipients.

This can be established in various ways. First, parental recipients regularly produce complaints about children's problems in response to unmarked invitations (recall the interview in 7.12 on pp. 169–70 above). Second, after a clinician produces a query, recipients may formulate it as asking for a problem proposal:

7.16   16.006

```
1   Dr V:      What is your impression of what's going on with A?
2                         (2.7)
```

```
 3   Mrs G:        (Uh::m) (mm)
 4                            (2.6)
 5   Mr G:    →    You mean what seems to be his problem?
 6                            (0.2)
 7   Dr V:         Yeah, what- what- how do you see your son.
 8                            (0.5)
 9   Mr G:         Uhm (1.0) well the main thing is not listening.
```

Both of these points suggest that recipients hear unmarked perspective-display invitations as asking for complaints in which a difficulty of the child would be proposed.

Third, when these queries fail to occasion an immediate complaint and problem proposal from parents, the clinician may employ various devices to obtain them. One is to remind parents of why they came to the clinic. This occurs in a case where the pediatrician asks, "How has M been?" The parent, Mrs S, replies that she does not "think anything is wrong with my son." Dr V then suggests there was a previous screening that turned up a speech or language problem, to which Mrs S responds, "right." Another strategy involves the clinician listening for or encouraging talk from recipient to which a problem proposal can eventually and relevantly be attached. This can be seen in an ordered relationship that exists between marked and unmarked invitations when they both appear in a single interview. Marked invitations may occur subsequent to unmarked ones (but not the reverse):

7.17   47.001 (Simplified)

```
 1    Dr E:    →    How's B doing.
 2    Mrs M:        Well he's doing uh pretty good you know especially
 3                  in the school. I explained the teacher what you
 4                  told me that he might be sent into a special class
 5                  maybe, that I wasn't sure. And he says you know I
 6                  asks his opinion, an' he says that he was doing
 7                  pretty good in the school, that he was responding
 8                  you know in uhm everything that he tells them. Now
 9                  he thinks that he's not gonna need to be sent to
10                  another
11    Dr E:         He doesn't think that he's gonna need to be sent
12    Mrs M:        Yeah that he was catching on a little bit uh more
13                  you know like I said I- I- I know that he needs a-
14                  you know I was 'splaining to her that I'm you know
15                  that I know for sure that he needs some
16                  special class or something
17    Dr E:    →    Wu' whatta you think his problem is
```

18	**Mrs M:**	Speech
19	**Dr E:**	Yeah. yeah his main problem is a- you know a
20		*lan*guage problem
21	**Mrs M:**	Yeah language

The marked query (line 17) is not issued after the (line 1) unmarked invitation (and its reply) in some kind of mechanical fashion.[8] It is clearly sensitive to the way that Mrs M, in reporting her discussion with B's teacher, displays a position implying that she sees B as having a problem ("I know for sure that he needs some special class or something", lines 15–16). Dr E's marked invitation, while containing a problem proposal, takes up this implication and in that way furthers the mother's own claim.[9]

Unmarked queries, in effect, can originate a circuit within a circuit. That is, the PDS itself delays movement to accomplishing the focal activity of the encounter, which is the delivery of diagnostic news. But that sequence can be done in two ways. Marked queries exert a presumption which, when honored, allows immediate movement to discussing the child's "problem." Unmarked queries, while ultimately working to elicit complaints and problem proposals, also occasion other kinds of talk, such that arrival at a problem proposal and delivery of diagnostic news can be more roundabout.

On the Expertise of the Clinic

By displaying, in the first two turns of a PDS, an alignment with respect to the idea that the child has a problem, participants to an informing establish the relevance of the clinician's third-turn report. In this turn, then, the clinician warrantedly introduces an assessment of the child. Thus, by virtue of its positioning as the concluding part of a series, the report or assessment is "sequentially implicative or projective of the range of issues to be discussed in following talk" (Schegloff and Sacks, 1974:239). The clinician's report or assessment and subsequent discussion, furthermore, are not just any diagnosis and explication but ones that participants regard as relatively authoritative. The relationship between clinic and child involves an assumption that the clinician has the expertise and right for speaking the diagnostic news that the PDS occasions. Within the sequence, participants converge on an alignment regarding this expertise and this right, which suggests that the authority of the clinic is not something imposed on the interaction, nor simply imported from a social structure that exists outside of the talk in this specific setting. In their conversational practices, participants constitute an authoritative relationship between clinic and child as a visible feature of the interaction.

Unmarked perspective-display invitations: seeing problems and seeking help

One manner in which participants construct the relationship between clinic and child can be seen in unmarked perspective-display invitations and their replies. Although asking in a generalized manner for the parents' view of the child, unmarked invitations regularly have temporal formulations, which include terms such as "now" and "at this time," and may contain locational formulations, such as "here" and "through this," which refer to the clinic as a "course of action, place, or location that is identifiable by what goes on there" (Schegloff 1972:101). When these formulations appear in the invitation, they are mirrored explicitly or implicitly in the reply. In example 7.11 on p. 169 above, the mother ties her utterance to previous temporal and spatial references in Dr S's query by repeating "since" and "here." In 7.12, the mother's utterance "the same" (line 5), as an indexical expression and as a comparative term, ties to Dr S's immediately previous utterance and thereby invokes "as before" and "at entry" for understanding the utterance. That is, because of the prior talk, "the same" can be heard as proposing "at this time" a condition of the child that has a relationship of identity with one that existed when the family first entered the clinic.[10] In short, unmarked queries elicit not just any descriptions and assessments but rather those that link the child in time and space to the clinic. Recipients' reproduction of, or indexical reference to, such formulations respond affirmatively to the elicitation; accordingly, when parents display their view of a child, it is by way of descriptions and assessments that incorporate the family's clinical rather than any other experience. Clinicians, in fact, seek just that talk regarding such experience.

The clinical experience is not confined to those processes through which the family goes after arriving at the clinic's doors. It includes common-sense knowledge of social structure (see Mehan, chapter 4, and Wilson, chapter 2, above), as displayed in speaking practices such as those that are intrinsic to the PDS, and as exercised as a course of action in which the family's arrival at the clinic is only a moment. Notice how conversational sequencing in the next excerpt suggests a particular order to the events of everyday life (Sacks, lecture 8, 1964:2–5).

7.18   33.007

```
1    Dr B:      How's he doing now?
2    Mrs M:     Y'know sometimes he- he comes, I call him, he
3               act like he didn't (   ) Uhhm I don't know,
4               like I told you, sometimes he plays, sometimes
5               he don't. (2.0) But he's uh::: like the toilet,
6               I still can't (get him toilet ⌈trained.)⌉
7    Dr B:                                  ⌊right    ⌋
8                       (1.4)
9    Dr B:      Well you've been through a lot of tests with
10              him, seen a lot of different doctors. Do you
11              have any idea of what you think is the problem?
12                      (0.2)
13   Mrs M:     I don't know, I (1.2) I don't know even myself.
14              Once me and my sister (            ) (1.7) She
15              said (2.8) maybe (0.6) my (      ) was too close.
16              Or maybe they was too close. My one sister told
17              me maybe I didn't need, you know, maybe if I just
18              had him by himself, he'll act (1.8) you know
19              (0.7) better.
```

After the clinician's initial (unmarked) query in this segment (line 1), the mother produces a series of complaints about her child. Then the clinician, before producing another (marked) invitation (lines 10–11), recounts the tests and doctors they have seen. In this, sequential ordering of the talk (that is, the clinician's recounting of the tests taken and doctors seen follows the mother's complaints) is a resource for understanding the testing and doctoring as a way of handling the complainable aspects of the child's behavior.[11] Put differently, the above segment suggests a proper course of action that involves (a) seeing, in another person, problems that are complainable problems, and (b) seeking help for those problems, in this case by getting tests and consulting doctors.

Lay and professional knowledge

The connection between (a) and (b), between seeing and seeking, involves the use of membership categorization devices that prescribe a correct pattern of requesting assistance (cf. Sacks 1972a:40). Requesting assistance may also include making a transition between "troubles talk" and "problem talk." Troubles talk, according to Jefferson and Lee (1981), is conversation about events that may be stressful for, and even disruptive of, people's everyday lives. These events are relatively familiar and capable of local or self-management, however; a troubles teller does not necessarily seek remedy (Jefferson and Lee 1981:13). If, in conversations between lay persons, a troubles telling obtains an offer of advice, the teller regularly rejects that advice. But when a person's trouble is proposed to be "problem," the person or the person's agents (parents, guardians) are obligated to engage in a search for help in specific ways depending on their use of membership categorization devices. Often, the parties employ a "relational" device to categorize themselves and others, and therefore orient to rights and obligations that organize help-seeking activity according to various kinship and friendship pairings. For certain kinds of problems, or at a certain point during the search for help, parties may learn to utilize a membership categorization device that is organized in terms of a distribution of knowledge for dealing with such problems. The categories from this device include "professionals" and "lay" people, and in terms of this "K" device, as Sacks (1972a:39) calls it, the parties and their relatives and friends are lay people who lack expertise. According to this device, therefore, parties with a problem have the right and obligation to seek aid from professionals, who have that expertise. Thus the clinical experience as a course of action involves, as part of the seeing and seeking process, an orientation to a social distribution of knowledge.

This orientation to lay and expert knowledge is exhibited, in various ways, within the PDS itself. Parents' replies to solicits of their view often contain, as in 7.18 on p. 177, disclaimers ("I don't know"), qualifiers ("maybe"), and other devices that downgrade the status of their exhibited view. Furthermore, in that same example, subsequent to recounting the doctors seen and tests taken, the doctor asks, in the marked form of the perspective-display invitation. "Do you have any idea of what you think is the problem?" Insofar as "you" is a contrastive term to the "we" of the clinic, it captures the lay–professional partitioning of the K device. The reference to "problem" (which may be a selection from alternatives such as "trouble") helps set up "advice giving" as opposed to "troubles telling" or some other activity as the focal event of the encounter (cf. Jefferson and Lee 1981:411). And, in querying the mother for her "idea" and what she "thinks" the problem is, the utterance elicits a reply that is *subjective*, an opinion, following which the clinic's report can be contrastively displayed as *objective*, as a finding. This can be seen in the next segment. It follows shortly after the talk in 7.18, and starts with Mrs M's reply to a probe from Dr B regarding the nature of M's problems:

7.19   33.059

1	**Mrs M:**		Uhhm::: I *know* he can hear (0.1) That's why I
2			don't see why he don't talk. .hhh And when he
3			gets (0.3) when he gets upset, he let you know
4			he's ma:d. Now he's (0.3) make a lot of noise,
5			(0.2) scream. (1.4) ( ) , may be
6			he can't (1.1)
7	**Dr B:**	→	Well, (0.5) No we- we: would, (0.4) we feel that
8			(0.2) the problem is that he *ca:n't* (.) yet.
9			(0.9) and that he (0.2) our (0.3) *all* our exams
10			show that he is quite re*tard*ed.

After the reply, the clinical assessment is also initially formulated in subjective terms (lines 6–7). Dr V displays a position on which Mrs S portrays herself as ambivalent, and he uses a "state marker" preface ("we feel that . . .") depicting the position ("the problem is that he *can't*") as contingent upon processes internal to the viewer(s). The state marker appears to do other work as well. By delaying production of the position report (as do the "well," and other hesitations at the beginning of the turn), the preface mitigates its assertiveness, and therefore perhaps is a strategy that is affiliative rather than confrontive (cf. Pomerantz 1984a). When moving to deliver the diagnosis, however, Dr V prefaces it with a phrase ("*all* our exams show") proposing the diagnosis as a conclusion from external evidence. In various ways, then, participants *produce* the visibility of the distinction between lay and professional knowledge.

Marked perspective-display invitations: the reflexivity of problems to seeking help

Marked perspective-display invitations (see 7.9 and 7.10, p. 169, for instance) do not ordinarily contain temporal and locational formulations that relate to the clinic. Nevertheless, several pieces of evidence that we have already seen, plus several considerations to be added here, demonstrate that marked queries, like the unmarked kind, clearly invoke the propriety of the clinic having been asked to test and diagnose the child. Examples 7.17 and 7.18 show that marked queries often follow unmarked invitations or other discourse events, such as formulations of the purpose of the interview, in which the clinician does make reference to the clinic. Also, the seeing and seeking connection described above demonstrates a *reflexive* relationship between making problem proposals and seeking help. It is partly through the ways that parties seek help that it is possible to see the existence of a problem, and clinicians draw on the fact that a search for help was undertaken to further the claim that there is a problem. Thus, when recipients of perspective-display invitations are resistive to producing problem proposals, a clinician may then recall the reason why the parents came to the clinic, and elicit agreement that there was a problem for which help was originally sought:

7.20   52.001 (Simplified)

```
 1   Dr V:        How has M been.
 2                     (0.7)
 3   Mrs S:       I tell ya, to me::::. (0.5) he's doing all right
 4                . . . to me as I say I don't think there is anything
 5                wro(h)(h)ng with my son I don't know.
 6   Dr V:        Well, I think y'know one of the reasons if we can
 7                go back (0.7) ta understand why you got here in
 8                the first place
 9   Mrs S:       uh huh
10   Dr V:  →     . . . y'know he was screened and it *was* a speech
11                problem. There was: some difficulty
12                     ⌈with⌉ language.=
13   Mrs S:       uh⌊hmm⌋
14   Mrs S:       =right.
15   Dr V:        Uhhh and *that*'s why . . . the OFfer was made that
16                more things could be done to *help* under- better
17                understand what the problems were here at the ____
18                Center and you said okay I'm waiting to see what's
19                happened.
20   Mrs S:       Right.
```

With marked queries, therefore, the mere suggestion that a child has a problem may be linked with a presumption that seeking expert help is part of the legitimate history by which the family and child arrived at the clinic. Finally, marked queries invoke the clinic as a proper mechanism for help not only because they presume a standard way of searching for help, but because the very term "problem" invokes the conversational relevance of discussing remedies rather than elaborating on the seeker's experiences.

For all these reasons, queries such as "Tell me what you feel is the problem," or "Do you have any idea of what you think is the problem?," while lacking temporal and locational formulations that invoke the clinic, still implicate an obligatory mode of help-seeking organized in terms of a social distribution of knowledge. These invitations do so by their contextual relations to other aspects of clinical discourse, by the way that the term "you" evokes distinctions between parent and clinician, lay person and expert, by means of asking for "feelings" and "ideas" that categorically contrast with "findings" and testing results, and through the very reflexivity of problem proposals to a specific course of action and to the giving and receiving of advice as the socially appropriate conversational event.

Overall, then, the perspective-display invitation and its reply, as turns of talk that are preliminary to the delivery of diagnostic news, aid in occasioning the delivery of that news and setting it up as the "expert" version of the child, and do so because of the obligatory pattern of help-seeking these turns render visible and the kind of talk they occasion. The well-known orientation to lay and expert knowledge and to the "authority" of the latter, then, is not entirely a cognitive backdrop (Cicourel 1974, 1981c) to conversation in the clinic. As a feature of the setting and the clinical experience, this orientation is a public matter whose visibility is an accomplishment of practices that comprise the discourse and the course of action of which it is a part.

Convergent and Divergent Perspectives

To say that marked and unmarked perspective-display invitations and their respective replies are cut of the same cloth is to say that, through them, deliverers and recipients collaboratively establish an alignment with regard to a pair of interrelated matters on which the delivery of diagnostic news depends: the existence of a child's problem and the expertise of the clinic for dealing with it.

Why, then, these two invitational forms? One answer to this can be offered in purely sequential and social organizational terms rather than on psychological, stylistic, or other grounds. As noted, perspective-display series regularly work to occasion the delivery of diagnostic news in an unproblematic way. But with respect to diagnostic assessments, it is inherent in the very notion of perspective that a recipient's position may diverge from the deliverer's. Sometimes clinicians, because they have previous experiences with parents, with other clinicians, or officials from a child's school, know this in advance of an informing interview. Other times, they may learn this within the interview itself. In any case, the two invitational forms are differentially sensitive to the possibility of divergent perspectives between clinician and parent. Moreover, the answer as to why the two methods of initiating a PDS exist is related to why clinicians may employ the series in the first place. Why does it occur in some interviews and not others?

Marked queries

Consider, first, the marked query as a presumptive way of asking parents for their view of the child. When parents agree with the problem proposal, talk is immediately directed to the nature of the problem. Clinicians can present their findings and diagnoses or, at the very least, probe the parents and then discuss clinical information. However, sometimes parents disagree with the problem proposal embedded in a marked invitation. Clinicians will then initiate repair of the disagreement. In ways that further their claim to expertise, they do this not by modifying their own position, but by asking recipients to change theirs. Two ordered possibilities follow. First, recipients can back down from their original stance to accept the problem proposal, thereby helping to repair the disagreement, whereupon clinicians can move to present the diagnosis in a regular way. In backing down, recipients have to perform what may be, for them, a status degrading act (cf. Labov and Fanshel 1977:64). Second, if the repair attempt fails – that is, the parents hold to their original position – then, when delivering the diagnosis clinicians will do so in an environment of disagreement. By proceeding in a conflictual context, furthermore, the actors engage in activities that are socially disruptive. As Pomerantz (1984a:77) has suggested, participants regard disagreement as uncomfortable, unpleasant, and difficult.

The ensuing talk from the interview in which Mr G thought nothing was "wrong" with his son (7.13 above, p. 171) illustrates these possibilities. After Mr G displayed his view, Dr N produced another query:

7.21   22.049

```
1  Dr N:   Mister Smith are there any things about
2          Charlie that worry you?
3  Mr G:   Not a thing.
4  Dr N:   Nothing?
5  Mr G:   Nothing.
```

Further solicits were similarly unsuccessful in obtaining any negative assessment from the father. Thus, while the clinician gives Mr G several opportunities to back down, he does not do so.

Finally, Dr N noted the existence of disagreement and forged ahead with the clinic's diagnosis:

7.22   22.125

```
 1    Dr N:    Well (1.8) there's (0.3) a disagreement on
 2             exactly (0.2) whether there is a problem or
 3             not. (0.5) I think rather than belabor the
 4             point of whether we- (0.3) whether there is a
 5             problem or not? (0.1) I think we should give you
 6             what (0. 5) we found (0. 4) which is a ⌈fter     ⌉ all
 7    Mrs G:                                        ⌊Mm hmm⌋
 8    Dr N:    what you came here for.
 9                                 (0.3)
10    Mrs G:   Mm hmm
11                                 (1.9)
12    Dr N:    F::rom (0.5) straightforward pediatric ⌈point⌉ of=
13    Mrs G:                                          ⌊Yeah ⌋
14    Dr N:    =view,
15                                 (0.2)
16    Dr N:    His general health, a:fter he got over that hundred
17             and three ⌈poin⌉t eight temperature (.hhh) i:s-
18    Mrs G:             ⌊Yeah⌋
19    Dr N:    has not been the problem.
20                                 (0.2)
21    Mrs G:   Yes
22                                 (0.4)
23    Dr N:    Uhhh (0.3) But a general evaluation. (1.7) it
24             was very noticeable some of what you described.
25                                 (0.2)
26    Mrs G:   (mm hmm)
27    Dr N:    Charlie has a problem with language.
28                                 (0.4)
29    Mrs G:   (mm hmm)
```

Several points are worthy of note here. First, Dr N precedes and justifies her presentation of findings by submitting that those are what they "came here for" (lines 6–8). As previously seen, in the face of parental resistance to problem proposals, a device clinicians use is to invoke a reason for the family visiting the clinic. Second, the doctor delivers the clinical assessment in a two-part format that has a good news/bad news structure (Maynard 1989b). What has "not been the problem" (lines 12–19) occurs first, followed by a description of what problem Charlie "has" (line 27). Sandwiched between the good news and the bad news is an utterance (lines 23–24) that prospectively characterizes the negative assessment as in agreement with what an intake form or application apparently indicated.[12] The clinician purports to package the diagnosis as confirming an earlier statement. Insofar as the presentation of a diagnosis itself (line 27) occasions some form of receipt and, more specifically, solicits a display of agreement, the clinician thereby encourages yet again an alignment on Charlie having a problem. The mother seems to provide displays of agreement or acknowledgment (lines 26 and 29), but the father remains silent during the entire delivery. If this means holding to his position stated earlier, then the problem proposal in the presentation at line 27 exhibits disagreement with that position, and in fact occurs despite that disagreement.

Thus, subsequent to disagreement with a problem proposal, the first suggested possibility occurred. Dr N initiated repair of the disagreement by re-asking the father for any complaint or negative assessment he had. But Mr G stayed with his original position that nothing was wrong, thereby refusing to back down. When the clinician completed her delivery of diagnostic news, she therefore did so in an environment of disagreement.

Unmarked queries

The unmarked invitation, while also seeking alignment on the issue of the child's having a problem, can entail a different route for achieving it. Of course, when family and clinical perspectives converge, parents may propose that their child has a problem immediately in reply to a perspective-display invitation. Or, they may produce troubles-oriented or related talk that discusses the child in more general terms. This suggests that a feature of topical organization may be operative here. Unmarked invitations provide recipients with the opportunity to adumbrate a first topic on something other than the focal aspect of the informing interview, the presentation of clinical findings and diagnoses. Because placing "mentionables" such as findings and diagnoses in first topic position accords them a special status, diverting them from that position can therefore lessen that status (Schegloff and Sacks 1973). Initially producing troubles talk or describing a child in general terms does not change participants' orientation to the interview's focal purpose, but it can indicate that there are other things to be discussed, and that those who are recipients of diagnostic news themselves have something to talk about besides "problems" for which the clinic may have solutions. If parents do take the opportunity to speak troubles or to describe the child in general terms, they may nonetheless eventually introduce a complaint about the child, or provide talk to which clinicians can relevantly attach an utterance with a problem proposal. In either instance, such talk

exhibits the warrant for the clinician to discuss the child's problem and
deliver a diagnosis. Unmarked invitations thus allow news deliveries that
are more visibly confirmatory and less presumptive than the marked
variety.

Furthermore, when parental and clinical perspectives diverge, and an
unmarked invitation meets with parental resistance to topicalizing a
child's problem, disagreement is not salient in the sense of being publicly
displayed. Clinicians can move toward delivering a diagnosis without the
parent backing down from a stated view, and without implicating
disagreement and the social disruptiveness associated with it. These
matters are evident in the next example. After the clinician invites a child's
guardian – his aunt – to display her view of the boy, she describes him but
offers no complaint, even in response to a probe. Eventually, however,
the clinician assesses the boy as "having some difficulty . . ." and obtains
agreement with that description (lines 33–6). The device is again that of
introducing the reason for the clinic visit. (The aunt's daughter is also
attending the interview.)

7.23   21.001

```
 1   Dr F:   We're all together here today.
 2   Mrs P:  Mm hmm.
 3   Dr F:   To talk about (0.7) uh the kinds of things that
 4           we've found out about Marvin.
 5                       (0.4)
 6   Mrs P:  Fi::ne.
 7   Dr F:   But before I- we do that I was wondering uhm (0.4)
 8           if you had any questions or anything you wanted to
 9           tell me about how things have been since I first
10           saw you ⌈and Marvin.⌉
11   Mrs P:       ⌊Weh I think⌋ he's fine.
12                       (0. 5)
13   Dr F:   Uh huh.
14                       (0.7)
15   Mrs P:  At least I (feel) so
16   Dr F:   You hav ⌈en't⌉
17   Mrs P:         ⌊My da⌋ughter can tell you ⌈too.   ⌉
18   Dr F:                                     ⌊There⌋ hasn't
19           been any changes since w⌈e  ⌉
20   Mrs P:                          ⌊No⌋
21   Dr F:   we saw you (that you want to report
22           ⌈or speak about)⌉
23   Mrs P:  ⌊Things have   ⌋ been fine.
24                       (0.6)
```

```
25    Dr F:   Okay. (0.9) Uh:m (1.4) Well (0.7) First of all
26            (0.3) Marvin (0.2) is a very appealing boy (0.2)
27            he's very: (0.4) he's very friendly
28    Mrs P:  Yes.
29    Dr F:   A::nd he likes to::: um (0.2) do as well as he can
30            and he likes to have contact, he's very cooperative.
31    Mrs P:  Yes.
32    Dr F:   This was very apparent to- (0.3) to myself and to
33            everyone else who's- has seen Marvin. .hhhh uhm
34            (0.2) the reason he was- (0.2) you know you brought
35            him here (0.2) was because he was having some
36            difficulty (0.6) in school with learn⌈ing. ⌉
37    Mrs P:                                      ⌊Yes,⌋ with
38            learning. Right.
39    Dr F:   ⌈A::::nd- ⌉
40    Mrs P:  ⌊I said as⌋ far as reading and his math.
41    Dr F:   Yes.
```

When asked her view of M (lines 7–10) and when queried about changes since they had first been seen at the clinic (lines 18–19), the aunt uses the neutral term "fine" (lines 11 and 23). This is something less than a fully positive evaluation of her nephew or his situation, yet neither is it a complaint or negative assessment in which a problem proposal would be displayed.[13] Then, following a series of disjunction markers (pause, line 12; "okay," pause, "uhm," pause, "well," pause, line 25) – items that regularly signal a topic change – the doctor produces the phrase "first of all" (line 25). This projects following talk as prior to something else, which is the doctor's eventual delivery of the main diagnostic findings.

However, our main interest is the utterance in which the doctor proposes that M "was having some difficulty . . . with learning" (lines 35–6) within a suggestion that this is the reason he and his caretakers came to the clinic. When the aunt confirms this suggestion (line 37), she thereby agrees with the problem proposal as well, although by repeating a phrase the doctor used, she clearly emphasizes the difficulty as being "with learning" (lines 37–8) and specifically "reading and math" (line 40), thereby bidding to delimit the extent of the problem. After this, the aunt is given the opportunity to expand on her assessment of the reading and math problems. During this talk (not reproduced here), she describes M as "slow." Subsequently, the doctor delivers the clinic's findings:

7.24   21.109

```
1    Dr F:   We found- we felt also that his main problem is
2            (0.4) that he's slow (0.5) too (0.6) that he's:
```

3   slower uhhh slower than let's say another
4   child of his age

The findings, then, are formulated as in agreement with the aunt's assessment, which relates to the work mentioned earlier of clinicians in co-implicating recipients' perspective in the delivery of diagnostic news (Maynard, in press). In short, when a problem proposal does not appear in reply to either an unmarked perspective-display invitation, or to a subsequent probe, the clinician returns with a different type of action. She prepares to deliver the diagnosis, but before doing so offers a suggestion incorporating "what everyone knows" regarding why the family is at the clinic.

Reminding the recipient of how she came to the clinic is a strategy similar to that employed in the prior example (7.22 on p. 183). Dissimilar is how the clinician first issues an unmarked invitation to the parent, who resists producing a negative assessment of the child, and can do so without disagreement because no problem proposal is on the floor. This means, firstly, that the clinician can move into delivering a diagnosis without initiating repair of disagreement or proceeding in an environment of disagreement. Secondly, when the clinician reminds her of the reason for originally visiting the clinic, Mrs P, without backing down from any previously-stated position, and by way of assenting to Dr F's reminder of how the family arrived at the clinic, can also agree on the boy's having difficulty. To achieve the purpose of the interview, therefore, neither party has to perform a status degrading or socially disruptive action.

Marked and unmarked perspective-display invitations, in seeking material with which to agreeably fit the presentation of clinical findings and diagnoses, also work to occasion an alignment regarding the existence of a child's problem and the expertise of the clinic for treating it. At the same time, they have different sequential consequences. Marked queries presumptively ask recipients for their view, immediately occasion talk that is relevant to the purpose of the interview, and, when parents are resistive to producing negative assessments of their child, entail conversational difficulty in the form of disagreement. Unmarked queries are less presumptive regarding the existence of a child's problem, allow an opportunity to topicalize matters other than that problem, and, when parents defy solicitations of complaints, allow disagreement to be avoided as a warranted movement is made to the presentation of clinical findings. Thus, depending on clinicians' prior knowledge of, and relationships with, parents, children, schools, diagnoses, treatments, and other matters, they can choose a strategy that, in sequential terms, is more or less presumptive, more or less topically direct, and more or less implicative of disagreement. Or, having no such prior knowledge and relationships, they can employ devices that are more or less capable of easily handling convergent and divergent positions as these are exhibited within the informing interview itself. Marked invitations seem most easily fitted to convergent views, while the unmarked variety facilitates dealing with both convergent and divergent perspectives.

Conclusion

Informing interviews in clinical settings may be of two types: straightforward or circuitous deliveries. The latter involve a perspective-display series initiated either by marked or unmarked queries. When clinicians present information straightforwardly, without asking parents their view of the child, that still depends on an assumption of the child having a problem and the clinic being a relevant agency to diagnose and treat it. The PDS merely shows that and how this assumption, rather than being a static fixture of the clinical experience, is a collaborative achievement, an outcome of interactive work. When the series is not utilized, this points to a whole series of prior encounters and ceremonies in which the complainable aspects of a child were already proposed as problems in need of professional attention (Mehan, Hertweck and Meihls 1986: 164–5).[14] Thus, to a degree, the PDS itself reproduces, in the immediate informing interview and local setting, the visibility of features (the child-as-problem and clinic-as-authoritative-service) that are embedded in and as the course of action by which the family arrived at the clinic. Thus, a conversational series such as that identified here, which is thoroughly and independently organized as an interactional phenomenon, may also actuate and display accountable aspects of the institutional order (Maynard 1991).

A further dimension to this discussion pertains to why clinicians employ the PDS in some informing interviews and not others. The reason here is similar to why there are marked and unmarked queries. One outcome of eliciting the parents' perspective is to allow a clinician to formulate findings and diagnoses as in agreement with that perspective. In some cases, however, clinicians may know or find that parents think nothing is wrong with their child. If, before announcing clinical findings, they query these parents, then clinicians will have to deliver the diagnosis in an environment of disagreement that this delivery partially constitutes (see example 7.22). This is because clinicians apparently orient to the "service" nature of the encounter (Jefferson and Lee 1981:411) and take it as their task to forge ahead with the disagreeing diagnosis. Contrariwise, the clinician who straightforwardly delivers diagnostic news puts the parent who has a divergent perspective, and who is willing to exhibit that perspective, in the position of disagreeing with the clinical view.[15] Parents, however, can and do withhold displays of disagreement after a diagnosis is presented.[16] As recipients of straightforwardly given diagnoses, parents do not have to state their perspective at all. A characteristic way of dealing with diagnostic news, as Heath (in press) suggests, is to simply not say anything.

In summary, the clinician who asks parents their view of a child may do so to obtain material with which to agreeably fit clinical findings and diagnoses. When they do not so ask, they may be presuming that clinical findings converge with the parents' view. Or, if this presumption is not warranted and a discrepancy between clinical and parental perspectives possibly exists, the effect of straightforwardly delivering a diagnosis may be to avoid any public disagreement. A result of strategically employing these various procedures – straightforward or circuitous news delivery, and marked or unmarked perspective-display invitations – is to maximize the potential for presenting clinical assessments as agreeing with recipients' perspectives or in a publicly affirmative and nonconflicting manner. This demonstrates participants' sensitivity to the interactional context of news delivery and receipt. Additionally, in a situation where the informing interview may foreshadow further encounters between professionals and family, it is as if participants may deploy ordinary conversational devices not only for some here-and-now interactional concerns, but also for long-term institutional relationships that the delivery and receipt of diagnostic news itself instantiates and projects.

Notes

I would like to thank Aaron Cicourel, Deirdre Boden, Richard Frankel, Hugh Mehan, and Emanuel Schegloff, all of whom made extensive and extremely helpful written comments on earlier versions of this chapter. I also benefited from discussions with Pam Laikko, Courtney Marlaire, Albert J. Meehan, and Ann Rawls. Finally, special gratitude is due to Don Zimmerman, who kept pushing and pushing to make this better than it otherwise might have been.

1 The data were collected under Grant HD 01799 from the National Institutes of Health, Stephan A. Richardson, principal investigator, and Grant HD 17803–02, Douglas W. Maynard, principal investigator. Bonnie Svarstad, who worked on the former grant with Helen Levens Lipton, with permission generously made the Richardson data available to me.

2 The reason for referring to the series as a perspective display (as opposed to a "news delivery," for example) is that the news does not just report a change

of status for the social object, as is often the case with other deliveries (Terasaki 1976); the news evaluates this social object. Participants package their assessments as "my side tellings" (Pomerantz 1980), as being differentiated according to the subjective position of the observer. Clinicians ask parents how they "see" their child, what they "notice," what their "impression" is, what they "feel" the problem is, and what their "understanding" is. After obtaining the parents' opinion, clinicians may then suggest they try to "see it our way" (Interview #30) or try to "accept this view of the facts about our experience" (#32). However, as compared with recipients' views, the clinicial position is buttressed with commonsensically more "objective" evidence (i.e., by references to tests, examinations, findings, and so on). See the discussion below "on the expertise of the clinic."

3 In his lectures of 1966, see Sacks 1964–72. The early Sacks lectures have been published as a special issue of *Human Studies*, see Sacks 1964–5, and the remaining lectures are planned for publication by Basil Blackwell in two volumes, see Sacks, forthcoming.

4 There are also gradations between the marked and unmarked varieties of invitation; i.e., the invitation can be mixed. In the mixed invitation, the clinician may make reference to a problem but not attach it to the child:

(a)   20.001

> **Dr N:** Now (1.8) tell me (0.6) what you feel is the problem.
>   (0.4)
> **Mrs F:** Mm he's not learning.

(b)   1.OTR–1

> **Dr L:** I really don't know what's happening in Juan's life
>   at the moment, whether- how he's managing in school,
>   whether there is a problem? or there isn't a problem.
> **Mrs A:** He has a problem.

Moreover, the clinician is able to be more or less firm as to whether a problem even exists or not. In (a) the doctor is firm; in (b) he portrays himself as in a dilemma over the issue. In either case, in replying to the invitation, recipient takes a position as to whether a problem exists and apparently takes the clinician's reference to "a" problem to mean "the child's" problem.

5 This kind of experience is not infrequent among parents (see Booth 1978). Although they notice something is amiss with a child, it may be years before their sense is confirmed. In their attempts to construct meaning, the lack of definition puts parents in an anomic position that is analogous to that of chronic pain sufferers (Hilbert 1984).

6 As Davis (1982:137) suggests, the informing interview is not a "single point at which parents were notified things have changed for the worse," but a "last

referral" in a system that "created a context of doubt and ambiguity around the child's identity."

7   A critique of the "labelling" approach to educational handicaps, and also of "realist" assumptions (that problems exist as the "private and personal possessions" of children who await identification and treatment) can be found in Mehan, Hertweck and Meihls (1986:159–64), who favor an interactionist perspective: "Disability, we conclude, exists neither in the head of educators nor in the behavior of students. It is, instead, a function of the interaction between educators' categories, institutional machinery, and student conduct" (p. 164).

8   Compare 7.17 to 7.18 on p. 177 below (lines 1 and 10, 11), in which a marked invitation is also issued subsequent to an unmarked query.

9   The way in which the clinician encourages "complaint" talk can be very systematic. In an example which is too long to reproduce and analyze here, a mother, in answering an unmarked query, talks extendedly about her life and her activities with her son. During this talk, the clinician in a number of ways indicates disinterest – by producing silences, delayed minimal responses, and continuers ("mm hmm") – at points where stronger displays of understanding are relevant (cf. Jefferson 1978; Schegloff 1982; Zimmerman and West 1975). In contrast, when the mother complains about her son's ability to "express himself," Dr I produces agreement tokens and invites further specific talk regarding the topic of the boy's language behavior (cf. Scheff 1968). He is then able to characterize the "upshot" (Heritage and Watson 1979:141) of Mrs J's talk and ask for confirmation:

25.066 (simplified)

> **Dr I:** So he answers in short words rather than in
> sentences. That is- so you've noticed that that is
> one of his problems
> **Mrs J:** Yeah

10 Some unmarked invitations may lack temporal and locational formulations. Nevertheless, in this data, immediately preceding utterances link the question to the parent's clinical experience, which suggests a general principle. The conversational and interactional context is crucial to the activity performed by any given query. Thus, as a comparison to this study, see that by Silverman (1981), who found clinicians in a pediatric cardiology clinic using what I call unmarked invitations with the parents of Down's Syndrome children as a way of constituting these children as "social" and familial rather than "clinical" objects. That is, in questioning these parents, clinicians regularly omitted reference to a "problem" so as to focus away from potential medical difficulties. With parents of other, "normal" children, clinicians more often used marked queries and thereby displayed a willingness to deal with medical and particularly heart problems.

11 Sacks (1978:252) discusses temporal and sequential organization in narratives,

and shows that they are distinct kinds of ordering. The importance of
sequential organization is to allow an appreciation of some point in the
narrative to be appreciated in terms of its position as "subsequent to some
other point."

12 I am inferring that "what you described" (line 20) refers to "the way you
wrote up the application" (see 7.13 on p. 171, lines 1–2).

13 See Sacks (1975:69–70) on "personal" state descriptors, i.e., evaluations that
apply to the self of the speaker. Here, we are concerned with similar
evaluations of "third" parties.

14 For a general discussion of the "interpenetration" of one episode of
interaction with other arenas in an institutional setting, see Cicourel (1987).

15 See example 1 in Maynard (1989b). A way of being accountably "confrontive" is
for a clinician, who already knows of a parent's disagreeing perspective, to
deliver a diagnosis straightforwardly.

16 See example 2 in Maynard (1989b).

PART III

Structure-in-Action

8

The Structure of Direction-giving in Interaction

George Psathas

In everyday interactions, persons can be heard to ask others for directions to their homes, places of business and other locations. Others take up such requests willingly (though not always) and, through the course of a series of utterances, provide for the direction asker a "set of directions" which, if it were to be followed, presumably would enable the person to "find" the place.

In this chapter, then, I wish to propose that sets of directions can be analyzed, as have stories in interaction, for their features as a sequentially organized activity.[1] As a "coherent conversational unit" or "activity" (Jefferson 1978:219) the set involves organized ways of entering or beginning the activity and closing or exiting out of the activity. Further, as a set, the directions are also monitored for their coherence (Sacks 1964–72) in terms of such matters as the progression of a sequence of operations with orientational and directional references until "arrival" at an end point is proposed. Internally, as the direction set is produced, various matters may be addressed through sequences inserted into the main body of the operations by either party, thereby suspending the sequenced production of operations until a point is reached where both parties agree to resume. This paper will examine openings or entry into direction-giving, suspensions and resumptions introduced via insertion sequences in the body of the operations, and closings or exits out of direction-giving.

The significance of this analysis is that a *social action*, direction-giving, is found to be accomplished in and through the *talk* of the parties. The action (activity) is shown to be socially structured, that is, as one involving a coordinated and sequenced series of utterances by the parties. The analysis and explication of the structure of this complex social action reveals for us ways in which multi-turn extended sequences of talk may be examined to discover the organization of any such action. An activity as complex (or simple, depending on the readers' view) as direction-giving can be shown to have structures which are recurrent and patterned, and which hold across a number of direction sets and direction-giver/recipients.

The Direction Set

The type of direction set which will be examined in this paper is that in which the direction-giver produces a route ("how to get there"), or a series of operations, to bring the recipient from a starting point to the destination. Once the direction-giver begins the activity of giving directions, the recipient becomes actively involved in what becomes a collaboratively produced direction set. Consider the following example:

8.1   (Insight Workshop)

```
            ((ring))
  1   A:   Insight Workshop?
  2   C:   Yes uh (.) I'm uh (0.4) looking fer Peter Lorenzes
           class tanite is it meeting at the Academy?  (1.0)
  3   A:   U::h as far as I know it is (0.4) u:m (1.4) thats:
           the fine print? (0.4) ⌈-or:
  4   C:                        ⌊anh the zone system that th⌈ee
  5   A:                                                    ⌊The zone
           system °oh thats the other one. ° um- (1.4)
           yeah that should be meeting eight ta ten thirdy?
  6   C:   Ye:s, (0.2)
  7   A:   Over at (0.4) the Academy. (0.2)
  8   C:   .hh Okay do yu-can you tell me where the Academy
           is?
  9   A:   Yeah, where ya coming from? (0.2)
 10   C:   uh Newton. (0.4)
 11   A:   Oka:y why dontcha come up one twenty eight? (0.2)
 12   C:   Yes. (0.2)
 13   A:   An take two A, (1.0)
 14   C:   Yes, (.)
 15   A:   u:m (0.4) Two A will take ya right across Mass
           avenoo an ya just stay on two A, (0.6) uh until
           ya get to Lowell Street.
                          (1.4)
```

```
16  C:  Is it marked? (0.6)
17  A:  uh, Lowell Street? (0.4)
18  C:  Yeah (0.4)
19  A:  a::h Yeah I think there's a street sign there, (.)
        its a- (0.6) u::m (0.6) an intersection with lights.
20  C:  °Okay°
21  A:  an ya turn right on Lowell Street. (1.2) an its
        about (.) quarter to a half a mile (0.4) um, pt (.)
        take another right on Bartlett Avenoo. (1.0)
22  C:  °Okay°.
23  A:  an that takes ya right to the Academy. (1.0)
24  C:  °Okay° an its one building? (0.2)
25  A:  Yeah, um (0.4) Bartlett avenue sortsuv- sort of
        curves around and (0.2) its a great big school. (0.4)
26  C:  °uh°
27  A:  an they'll be somebody (0.2) near the door taking
        registrations
                      (0.2)
28  C:  °uh°
29  A:  saying=hello=tellin=people=where=to=go. (0.4)
30  C:  °Okay° (0.4) good. (.) tk ⌈ .hh  ⌉
31  A:                            ⌊okay?⌋
32  C:  Thank=you. (.)
33  A:  yur welcome.=
34  C:  =°bye°=
35  A:  =bye=
36  C:  =bye.
```

The route produced by the direction-giver is given over a series of utterances and turns. As the direction-giver speaks, opportunity is provided for the direction-asker to produce various indications of understanding or nonunderstanding, requests for clarification, etc. Whatever the recipient produces is implicative for the continuation of the set, particularly for the utterance by the direction-giver in next turn. An indication of mishearing or nonhearing may produce a repeat or a repeat with expansion, whereas a misunderstanding or request for elaboration may produce an insertion sequence of one or more turns until the elaboration is understood.[2] Since what is being produced is a route in which a series of operations are to be performed in a particular sequence, what the recipient does in those places provided as possible next turns is also closely attended to by the direction-giver for its relevance for the operation produced just before and for the next operation to be produced. That is, questions concerning orientational reference points may differ from inquiries concerning directional movement and differ from displays of misunderstanding in terms of their implication for the direction-giver's next utterance. We, therefore, will examine insertion sequences[3] in terms of their relevance for the direction-giving activity itself as a coherent unit.

The produced set does not appear to be a predesigned and preformulated set which will, once started, go off as planned. Rather, what recipients say in their turns shapes or affects the route being constructed. Direction-givers at places such as businesses and organizations, which presumably receive such requests frequently from varieties of callers with varying amounts of knowledge, do appear in some of our data to have predesigned routes marked by carefully specified landmarks, roads, turns, etc., seemingly designed to avoid travelers losing their way or not understanding the directions. However, even these direction-givers do not proceed without providing opportunities for recipients to speak in the course of the production of the direction set. Thus, there is ample opportunity provided for indications of trouble, misunderstanding, requests for elaboration, etc.[4]

A gross characterization of direction sets, without yet examining in detail the sequential structures which they contain, such as the one provided in the example, may be offered as follows:

1 they are sequentially organized;
2 they are undertaken in response to a request initiated by the recipient (direction-asker) or solicited by the direction-giver;
3 they are designed for a recipient (direction-asker);
4 they consist of a next turn(s) in which the set of directions is begun; and of
5 next turn(s) in which the recipient-asker co-participates as an active recipient with displays of understanding, acceptance, or requests for elaboration, repetition, clarification, etc., which are a coordinate part of the set of directions and not new topics; and of
6 a next turn in which the direction-giver proposes "arrival" at the destination; and of
7 a marked ending of the set with such possible moves to end as
    (a) an acknowledgment/acceptance/understanding display by the recipient and a move to a next topic or to a closing, or
    (b) a request for confirmation by the direction-giver and a confirmation/ acknowledgment/appreciation by the recipient and a move to next topic or to a closing.[5]

Elsewhere (Psathas 1986b) I have shown that for the set of directions, by virtue of the sequences of utterances within which the operations are produced, a sequence of operations is also produced, that is, the sequence of utterances provides for the sequence of operations as an embedded property. We can speak of this as *sequential operations embedded in utterance sequences.* Or, alternatively, say that *the sequence of operations is organized by their production in sequences of utterances.*

By "operations" I refer to the production of a series of steps or procedures which are presented as implying or describing movement and which connect places and points along the route being constructed. Operations include such matters as "take," "go," "turn," "stay on," "get off," "go down," "bear," "cross," "head," "get to," "come on," "make (a turn)," and so on. Operations are connected to particular points or places at which, or in relation to which, the operations are to be performed.

From a general description of these features, I would now like to move to more detailed discussion of direction-giving activities such as openings, suspensions and resumptions of operations, and closings.

Openings or Entry into Directions

Entry into direction-giving is marked in conversation by various entry devices, but primarily by a request initiated by the direction-seeker. The activity of direction-giving which is being considered here is that which I have described as "route construction," or "how to get there." This form may be distinguished from another form of requested spatial orientation to a destination which is characterizable as "where are you." This latter type can have location descriptors and orientational reference points provided without a series of operations or steps referring to movement through space. For example:

8.2
(Shanghai Restaurant)

    C: Where are you located?
    A: Twenny-one Hussan Street Chinatown Center.
    C: Twenny-one *Hudson?*
    A: Yes (righ-)
    C: °Hudson Street Chinatown° (0.4) okay thank *you:,*

(Lectra City)

    C: Oh-yeah, tell me where you're located
    A: We're at ninety-five First Street
    C: Yeah

A: Right across the street from Lechmere Sales
C: Oh, across from Lechmere?
A: Yep
C: Okay, terrific

The "where are you" request can produce a location descriptor which would include such matters as name of street, area names, and named places nearby as in these examples. Note that the answerer does not start the recipient from a starting point along pathways to the destination.

The prototypical entry into direction-giving activity of the route construction type is a request by the recipient for a route proposed in the form of a "how to get there" request. Instances are:

8.3
(Ski School)

   C: Yeah uh::: I'm tryin a find out how ta get *the*re

(FH)

   A: Ahm sorry ta bother you with this, but you don't know
          where Faneuil *Ha*ll is, do ya:
   B: Yeah, it's downtown.
   A: Do ya know the directions?

(Cherry Orchard)

   C: Yeah (0.2) okay, what's the best way to get out there
          from the Mass Pike?

(Apple Orchard)

   C: .hh Okay. uhm how- what's the best way to get out there?

(JP)

   Q: Can you tell us how to get to Jamaica Plain?

An alternative mode of entry into route construction is the conversion of a "where are you" form of question into a "how to get there" request by responding to the initial question with a request for a starting point location formulation, that is, where are *you*, the caller, located. I have elsewhere referred to these as "conversion sequences" (Psathas 1986b). The following displays two such sequences:

8.4

(TSE-1 Walnut in Burbank)

> C: Right an lets see now Walnut Avenue in Burbank where
> is that?
> A: Awright. Where- where you coming from Eaglerock?
> C: uh huh The store
> A: Get on the *free*:way

(Crestview Plaza)

> C: . . . .hhh Can you tell me where you are?
> A: uh, Where are *you*. hah That's easier if I can dir-
> give you directions.
> C: Oh *yes* uhm in ah Newton.

In direction-giving, there are two key locations, a starting point and the destination. The construction of a route involves the direction-giver describing a set of operations which would bring the recipient (direction-asker) *from* a starting point *to* the destination. The starting point named or assumed in the direction set need not be the current physical location of the recipient, since it is possible to make inquiries now for some future journey, and for the proposed journey to start from any place known or presumed known by the direction-giver and direction-asker. The time when the journey is to be taken, that is, when the directions are to be "followed" and the operations actually carried out, is not necessarily specified though it would appear that some understandings as to the parameters of time are involved. That is, an indefinite "now" seems to be assumed, rather than what was a possible route in the "past" or would be in an indeterminate "future." It seems to be assumed that the trip would be made under the present circumstances of the local topography. The matter of temporal references or assumptions is not analyzed in these data at this time.

Matters which are presupposed or made explicit in these first or initial interchanges are:

1 starting point
2 destination
3 mode of travel
4 time of travel
5 membership categorization by each of the parties of each other

The emergence and solution of any problems which the absence of these matters (or misunderstandings about them) may produce for the activity of direction-giving is not necessarily limited to these first or "prefatory" interchanges. The absence of the specific topicalization of these matters may indicate that the problems they pose are solved in passing, that is, in the normal course of the interaction, and this may be the preferred structure for the activity of direction-giving. The maxim which seems to operate is "presuppose these matters rather than topicalize them if you can." That is, hearer and speaker are "discovering" through what is said what is presupposed with regard to these matters.

The following example will be considered in detail in order to show how these matters are dealt with by interactants.

8.5   (Ski School)

         ((ring, ring))
1 **A:** Ski school (0.2)
2 **C:** Yeah uh::: I'm tryin a find out how ta get *there*
         (0.6)
3 **A:** Ya take exit sixty *four* N (0.5) off of (.) one
         twenny eight
4 **C:** °Off of one twenny eight.° (0. 2) yeah

The destination name is provided by answerer's way of answering the phone which caller accepts by referring to it as "there" (line 2, caller's first utterance), an indexical location formulation. The caller's starting point is not requested by answerer but a starting point is supplied (line 3) by naming a major highway. Answerer presumes caller knows 128 and thereby treats recipient as one who knows the local area and the names and locations of major highways. The membership category proposed by answerer for caller is that of a "local area person" in contrast to a "stranger to the area," "visitor" or otherwise nonknowledgeable person. Caller has already offered a basis for this categorization by calling the school, accepting the answerer's self-identification as an adequate formulation of the destination and thereby indicating that it is to this particular named place that he wishes to go. By not specifically naming his starting point (as a particular named place or area or road) he allows the answerer to select *any* possible starting point (or, alternatively, to inquire about it directly). By turning over the selection of a starting point to the answerer (direction-giver) the recipient implies possession of adequate knowledge until proven otherwise. When answerer mentions 128 as a starting point, this is accepted as understood by caller ("°Off of one twenny eight° (0.2) yeah") thereby, confirming answerer's categorization and the presumed level of knowledge of the caller.

Time of travel is assumed to be an indefinite now with present tense used by caller in line 2 ("I'm tryin a find out . . .") and time of travel implied as possibly immediate future.

Mode of travel is assumed by answerer to be by car as highways and their exits are named and no counter indication is given by caller.

In 8.6 and 8.7, some of these matters are specifically inquired about.

8.6   (FH)

    A: Do ya know the directions?
    B: uh (.) You driving or walking?
    A: Walking (0.2)
    B: Get on the subway . . .

8.7   (DirTape)

    S: You tell us to get to route nine (0.2) from here
    H: Route nine yup. You driving a car.
    S: Yeah

In these instances, the parties are co-present and on foot. The co-presence in the first instance on the sidewalk and in the second at a gas station is perhaps not sufficiently informative for the direction-giver to proceed with an unstated assumption of mode of travel. Nevertheless, the topicalization of mode of travel at this point indicates its relevance for the route construction which follows, namely, that a different route would be produced if the asker were walking rather than driving. In 8.6, answerer's immediate next "get on the subway" displays an acceptance of the requester's categorization of him as potential direction-giver, and a relevant operation which can be performed by a traveler on foot, without a car.

8.8   (SBL 1)

    6 **A:**   I don't know just where the-uh-this address/ /*is*.
    7 **B:**   Well where do- which part of town do *you* live.
    8 **A:**   I live at four ten east Lowden
                   (2.)
    9 **B:**   Well you don't live very far from me. If you go
                   on the State (1.0) High- no if you go out past
                   the courthouse/ / to Elmhurst.
    10 **A:**   / /yeah

In 8.8, the destination is known by both parties (line 6), but the direction-asker's starting point is requested by B with a part of town location formulation (line 7) and provided by a street name and number (line 8). Mode of travel is proposed by car ("go on the State (1.0) High- . . .") and accepted by caller (line 10). Answerer categorizes caller as a local person ("you don't live far from me . . ."), a categorization which is accepted by caller.

8.9   (Insight Workshop)

```
  8   C:   .hh Okay, do yu- can you tell me where the Academy
           is? (.)
  9   A:   Yeah, where ya coming from? (0.2)
 10   C:   uh Newton. (0.4)
 11   A:   Oka:y why dontcha come up one twenty eight? (0.2)
```

Here the caller's starting point is requested (line 9) with an indefinite "where" and only after a name of town is provided does answerer begin the route construction. We should note that location formulations of where the asker is located or coming from are examinable for what they might provide or enable the direction-giver to assume about the asker's state of knowledge of the area. For example, to say "I don't know exactly where I am" or "home," or "Fifth and Main" or "Weston" (a suburb of Boston) are each indicative of different circumstances of the asker. In the following example the direction-asker provides an unsolicited starting-point location formulation.

8.10   (Topsfield)

```
  1   A:     (Tha) bell capns desk (0.2)
  2   C:     Hi I have a reservation there nex week an I'm
             wondering how ta
       →     get there from Topsfield.
```

In this example, the direction-asker provides a name of town (city) as a starting point. The answerer can hear this as indicative of knowledge of the local area adequate for the location of major roads and highways and as therefore not requiring a further, more detailed specification of exactly where within the named town (city) the asker would start. The direction-giver can then begin with *any* nameable highway or road that any presumed knowledgeable local person would know. Such roads are then used by direction-givers as the starting point for the direction set and only if not accepted by the asker are alternative beginnings provided.

8.11   (Topsfield)

3 **A:**   From Topsfield?
4 **C:**   Yes
5 **A:**   Yeah jus come down route *one*. . . .

Here "route one" is proposed as a route that anyone coming from Topsfield would be expected to know. If caller accepts this, then it is not necessary to inquire where within Topsfield the caller is located in order to then provide a route from that location to route one.

8.12   (Colman)

6 **C:**   Could you direct me I'm coming from Boston
7 **A:**   ohh (0.4) Coming from Boston oh/ /kay
8 **C:**   / /on the Expressway?
9 **A:**   Yes the Expressway. (0.2) umm lets see (0.2) get off
         at the: (0.4) Washington Street in *B*raintree.

In 8.12, the direction-asker provides the first named road which direction-giver can use as the starting point. It is provided after some indications of uncertainty and a pause before the direction-giver indicates that she might be able to provide a route. It is recognized and accepted by the direction-giver who then produces the name of the exit to take from the named roadway. This example further indicates how direction-askers can collaborate in the production of a route by supplying items which are of assistance to the direction-giver. Also illustrated here is the potentially problematic matter which those who are asked to provide directions contend with, namely, whether they can or will respond to the request and offer themselves as adequately knowledgeable to undertake the activity of direction–giving.

Another formulation of a starting point as provided by direction-askers is that of named roads.

8.13   (Cherry Orchard)

   C: Yeah (0.2) okay, what's the best way to get out
         there from the Mass Pike?

In such an instance, the location formulation of a named town or area may or may not be provided. The named roadway serves as a starting point. However, since roadways are presumed to be directional, that is, as going "from" and "to" various directional points, the provision of a named town or area, in conjunction with the named roadway, serves to orient the direction-giver as to which direction the recipient will be coming *from*. In this instance, "out there" can be heard to mean that the asker is "in" the city. This conjunctive provision of area plus roadway serves to provide orientation for subsequent operations. Coming from one direction may mean a right rather than a left turn, or one particular named exit rather than another, or a first traffic light rather than the second, etc.

Thus, starting point as an orientational reference point is consequential for subsequent operations. This may be referred to as the *orientational referential adequacy of any starting point for subsequent orientational and direction operations.*

Insertions: Suspension and Resumption

Given that the coherence of the direction set is achieved by providing (and for the recipient attending to) a sequence of operations produced in the sequence of turns, any insertions within the sequence which are oriented to repair or to requests for clarification, elaboration, etc., provide for a suspension of the ongoing main activity. Such suspensions deserve close examination in order to discover how they are patterned and organized and what relevance they have for the ongoing – and resumable – character of the production of the direction set.

Evidence of how direction-giving is suspended is available in some of these data. By suspension, I simply mean that in a next turn, after the route construction has begun and before it is acknowledged to be completed by the parties, is inserted something other than a next operation and its acceptance. For example,

8.14   (Insight Workshop, lines 16–20):

13	**A:**		An take *two A*, (1.0)
14	**C:**		Yes, (.)
15	**A:**		u:m (0.4) Two A will take ya right a*cross* Mass avenoo an ya just stay on two A, (0.6) uh until ya get to *Low*ell Street.
			(1.4)
16	**C:**	→	Is it marked? (0.6)
17	**A:**	→	uh, *Lowell* Street? (0.4)
18	**C:**	→	Yeah (0.4)
19	**A:**	→	a::h Yeah I think there's a street sign there, (.) it's a- (0.6) u::m (0.6) an *in*tersection with *li*ghts.

20 **C:** → °Okay°
21 **A:**   An ya turn *right* on *Lowell Street* (1.2) an it's about
            (.) quarter to a half mile (0.4) um (.) take another
            right on *Bartlett avenoo*. (1.0)
22 **C:**   °okay°

In 8.14, the inquiry by the caller (line 16) concerns the recognizability of Lowell street since at that point in the sequence of operations some change of direction is about to occur. This change is marked by the phrase "just stay on two A, (0.6) uh until ya get to *Lowell* street." The "until" signals the significance of recognizing just that place along the route which is an orientational *and* directional reference point.[6] Caller's question, "is it marked?" produces an inserted question–answer sequence which requests and obtains clarification before the direction-giver proceeds any further with the sequence of operations. The clarification is provided in line 19 and contains two items oriented to the issue of recognizability: one, a street sign mentioned with a qualifying uncertainty ("I think") and the second, "an *in*tersection with *l*ights" mentioned without any qualifier. These are accepted by the caller (line 20, "okay") and A then proceeds with the rest of the set from that point.

This suspension is produced here at a turn transition point (end of line 15) where recipient could produce an understanding marker or continuer. Instead, a question with regard to the location mentioned before is produced (line 16). This indicates that C has been listening, understanding the set of directions up to this point, and now produces a question which is hearable as relevant to the ongoing activity. Caller's question displays an orientation to the unfolding character of the operations and to the orientational reference point which has just been mentioned, in fact, a recognition of its significance as also a possible directional reference point.

The direction-giver resumes the direction set in line 21 without any repetition of the last part of the operations produced prior to C's question. The resumption is with an operation which is to be done at just the point where the last operation ended, some six turns before. If we were to eliminate the inserted questions and answers, the directions would read as follows:

15 **A:**   u:m (0.4) Two A will take ya right *across* Mass
            avenoo an ya just stay on two A (0.6) uh until
            ya get to *Lowell* Street. (1.4)

21 A: An ya turn *right* on *Lowell Street* (1.2) an its about
          (.) quarter to a half a mile (0.4) um (.) take another
          right on *Bartlett avenoo*. (1.0)

The repeated element, "Lowell Street," establishes the connection
between the utterances in lines 15 and 21. Lowell Street was the *point* that
had been reached (that is, an orientational reference point). The "an,"
operating syntactically as a conjunction, connects the prior point to the
next part of the sequence of operations, "ya turn . . ." Lowell Street thus
becomes both a directional reference point, a point at which direction will
change, and an orientational reference point, the point *at which* one is to
arrive before any next step.

The pattern of directions is one that direction sets commonly contain,
namely, a sequence of named points connected by operations performed
in relation to these named points. The pattern is:

move *to*   a   *named point*
at which   a   *change* of direction is to be made.

As reference points which have both orientational and directional
significances, such named points are recognized as critical by both
direction-givers and recipients since failure to locate or identify the
named point at just that part of the sequence of operations could result in
"missing the turn" or "turning at the wrong place." The request for
clarification can be heard as a recognition by the caller of the significance
of that point for an impending change of direction.

8.15   (SBL 1)

14 **B:**   Go to Elmhurst, pass the courthouse and go to
                   Elmhurst and then to Elmhurst, uh north.
15 **A:**   mm hum.
16 **B:**   Towards Riverton, till you come to that Avilla Hall
17 **A:**   Oh yes
18 **A:**   //uh huh
19 **B:**   →   //Dju know where that//is?
20 **A:**   →   Oh, surely
21 **B:**   →   Avilla Hall on the corner of Bor//don
22 **A:**   →   //uh huh
23 **B:**   Well there, on Bordon you turn back to town, left.

In 8.15, just after the direction-giver has provided the name of a
landmark as an orientational reference point at which a change of

direction will be made (line 16), a question is asked with regard to the recipient's knowledge of Avilla Hall (line 19). This insertion sequence consists of four turns, two question–answer sequences, with the second question a repeated expansion of the first (lines 19–22) and both being responded to affirmatively by recipient. After the confirmation of knowledge of this particular landmark, direction-giver resumes the route.

Here it is the direction-giver who suspends the route construction in order to receive repeated confirmations that recipient knows the orientational reference point (landmark) "Avilla Hall" before the next operation will be produced. The direction-giver is marking the impending significance of this landmark as one at which a change of direction will be proposed.

We can thus see that suspension may be done by either direction-recipient or direction-giver and that resumption of the sequence of operations is easily accomplished. "Suspension" is not an exit into some other activity or topic but a "suspension-of-operations-production" such that the next turn or turns do not continue the sequences of operations relevant to route construction. To suspend that sequenced production is to "delay" the introduction of the next operation but the set is recognized as "still underway" by virtue of the fact that the destination has not yet been "reached."

Closings

There are two parts to closings of direction-giving. The first is the ending of the operations or route construction marked by "arrival" at the destination. Since directions have an ending in view which is already known in common, that is, *arrival* at the place to which the directions are being provided, both parties are able to hear that the set of operations designed to bring the recipient to the destination is concluded when the destination is "reached" or "arrived at." The named place or its pronominal referent ("we," "it"), coming at that place in the set where all of the preceding operations presumably have led, is hearable as marking the "end of the set" or "arrival."

The second part of closings is acceptance of the arrival point by the recipient in next turn. If acceptance occurs, the parties may then move to a next topic in the conversation or to a closing of the entire conversation. In calls where the "reason for call" is to obtain directions, the closing of the direction-giving activity may lead next into pre-closing for the entire conversation followed by terminal exchanges.

First part of closing

"Arrival" may be presented by the direction-giver as follows:

8.16

(Topsfield)

>   **A:**   . . . an you go down two blocks an you see the hotel
> (SBL 1)
>   **B:**   . . . and that's my house.
> (Insight)
>   **A:**   an that takes ya *right* to the Academy

Direction-givers may also provide an assessment at: the point of "arrival" hearable as an invitation to recipient to provide the second part of a close. The assessment, in the form of such expressions as "its very easy to find" or "you won't miss it,"[7] proposes that no additional information is necessary for the recipient. For example:

> *8.17*   (Cherry Orchard)
>
>   **A:**   Big farm big red barn says Mellow Lane all over it
>   you won't miss it.
>   **C:**   Ok(h)ay good.

Such assessments are related to the immediately prior part of the set of directions and also to the entire set. That is, the last operation and the descriptors of the features of the place which would be seeable/ recognizable at just that point are assessed as adequate to the task of locating the place. In addition, the assessment is hearable as a retrospective assessment of the adequacy of the set as a whole. That is, to say "you won't miss it" just after the entire set of directions has been completed is to provide, for the recipient, a hearable claim that all of the steps and sequences of the direction set which led up to the "arrival" are, when considered *as a set*, adequate to the task.

Second part of closing

In next turn, recipient may then produce an understanding or acceptance and a positive assessment as in 8.17 above ("ok(h)ay good"). It is also possible for recipient to not accept the offered closing and continue with another turn or additional turns on the topic of directions. Two such instances appear in 8.18 and 8.19, both of which deal with the issue of recognizing/locating the destination at the point of arrival.

8.18   (Crestview Plaza)

13	**A:**	Yer on Markdale avenoo an we're down about two miles on the right
14	**C:**	.hhh Two miles on the right an what are you a hotel or a-
15	**A:**	No- a function room
16	**C:**	Oh I see just-
17	**A:**	Functions facility
18	**C:**	An there's a big sign out there saying what-
19	**A:**	Yeah
20	**C:**	Yuh .hh okay fine
21	**A:**	Okay?
22	**C:**	Thank you
23	**A:**	You welcome
24	**C:**	Righ-⌈bye
25	**A:**	⌊bye

8.19   (Insight Workshop)

23	**A:**	→an that takes ya *right* to the Academy. (1.0)
24	**C:**	°Okay° an its one building? (0.2)
25	**A:**	*Yeah*, um (0.4) Bartlett avenue sortsuv- sort of curves around and (0.2) its a great big *sch*ool. (0.4)
26	**C:**	°uh°
27	**A:**	An they'll be somebody (0.2) near the *door* taking registrations
		(0.2)
28	**C:**	°uh°
29	**A:**	Saying=hello=tellin=people=where=to=go. (0.4)
30	**C:**	°Okay° (0.4) good. (.) tk⌈ .hh ⌉
31	**A:**	⌊ok*ay*? ⌋
32	**C:**	*Th*ank=you. (.)
33	**A:**	*Yur* welcome.=
34	**C:**	=°bye°=
35	**A:**	=bye=
36	**C:**	=*by*e=

In both of these instances, recipient produces an understanding of the prior utterance either by a repeat or an understanding token but immediately in same turn produces a question concerning the features of the destination that would make it recognizable. In 8.18, the ambiguity of what kind of place "Crestview Plaza" is (the name provided earlier by the answerer in first turn of the call) is then resolved by C's proposing a hotel and A's saying "no a function room," repaired in his next turn to "a functions facility." Caller also provides another possible recognition marker "an there's a big sign out there . . ." in the form of a question addressed to the direction-giver who confirms it (line 19). It is then that recipient produces an upgraded understanding and acceptance with a positive assessment ("yuh .hh okay fine").

Similarly, in 8.19, caller's turn after the direction-giver's "arrival" (in line 23) is an "okay" immediately followed by a question. The understanding token ("okay") is directly connected to the prior turn but acceptance of the conclusion of the direction-giving is withheld. The absence of an upgraded acceptance with a positive assessment may be indicative of recipient's having difficulty at just this point. When the issue raised by the question is resolved by the direction-giver providing additional information (lines 25 and 27), recipient accepts with an assessment "okay, (0.4) good" (line 30).

In contrast, we can compare the following instances where an acceptance plus positive assessment occurs just after the point of arrival is reached by the direction-giver.

8.20

(Cherry Orchard)
   32 **A:** Big farm big red barn says Mellow Lane all over it
             you won't miss it.
   33 **C:** Ok(h)ay good

(Apple Orchard)
   22 **A:** An then we'll be on your first left
   23 **C:** Oh, oh that sounds easy (0. 5) okay: y-. . .

(Lexicon)
   66 **A:** . . . building that- the brick building that calls out
             Lexicon.
   67 **C:** Okay good.

Each of these responses by recipient indicate acceptance without any question appended in same turn, plus a positive assessment. For the direction-asker/recipient to provide a positive assessment at this point can be heard as retrospectively tying back to the entire direction set and as achieving closure.

What may follow in the same turn by same speaker (recipient) or in next turn by direction-giver is either a move to close the conversation or a move to a next topic.

8.21   (Apple Orchard)

23   **C:**   Oh, oh that sounds easy (0.5) okay:
→   y- um do you have boxes or should we bring something?

In 8.21, the transition by same speaker into a next topic is also marked by a post-assessment pause, 0.5 of a second, and disjunct marker ("okay:") before next topic is mentioned and a question asked. In the following example, direction-*giver* takes up the conversation after recipient's acceptance plus positive assessment and a post-acceptance pause.

8.22   (Lexicon)

67   **C:**   Okay good (0.2)
68   **A:** →   An the individual there is Harry. (.) H-A-R-R-Y?
69   **X:** →   mm hmm,

The move to next topic is positioned just after the closing of the direction-giving activity and marks the completion for now of that activity. Where the direction set was the "reason for the call" we find that when the direction-giving section is closed the parties may then move to close the conversation.

It appears then that questions about operations in the sequence of the route construction are produced by recipients, or clarifications, repetitions and elaborations are provided by direction-givers, and occur in the main body of the direction-giving sequence. Once the operations are concluded and "arrival" at the destination is achieved, questions that are raised concern the recognition/locatability of the destination and not the operational sequences. Once closing is achieved, the parties move to next topic or to conversational closure. Moves to conversational closure are similar to those already studied and reported in the literature.

At this time, it appears that the production of a move to close the direction set by direction-giver with the utterance indicating arrival at the destination (with or without an assessment) operates as a first pair part of an adjacency pair (similar to a pre-closing first pair part) for which a relevant second part is acceptance plus positive assessment by the recipient. If acceptance plus positive assessment does not occur, the absence is a noticeable one. Talk may continue on the topic of directions, generally with regard to the details of arrival, but other questions may also be raised.[8] When recipient produces acceptance plus positive assessment, the direction-giving activity ends and the parties move to other topics or conversational closure.

Conclusion

Our studies of direction-giving have thus far shown that direction-giving in conversation is a multi-faceted structure, organized sequentially in a turn-by-turn fashion. Aspects of this structure which we have analyzed are (1) the entry into direction-giving; (2) the sequence of operations; (3) suspensions and resumptions of operation sequences; and (4) the ending or closing of the direction-giving activity.

As a structured activity, direction-giving/receiving, produced interactionally in conversation, is socially structured, that is, it involves the collaborative efforts of both parties in accomplishing its recognizable features. As a social structure, it is occasioned, sequentially organized, and responsive to the particulars of the parties (their knowledge, assumed knowledge, displayed understandings, etc.) that is, it is context sensitive. And yet, as a structure, it can be shown to have an organization that is recurrent, orderly and patterned with organized modes of suspension and restorability and with recognizable beginnings and endings, that is, it is context-free. It holds across any number of direction sets and direction-givers/recipients.

Notes

This paper was originally presented at the Talk and Social Structure Conference. I am grateful to Graham Button and Jay Meehan for their helpful discussions and to Darlene Douglas-Steele, B. J. Fehr and Jeff Stetson for their detailed comments.

1 Harvey Sacks in his lectures of March–April 1970 (see Sacks 1964–72 and Sacks, forthcoming) examined stories as "routinely tak[ing] more than one utterance to tell." Since they take more than one utterance to produce, it is relevant that recipient learns (hears) that a story is to be produced. Otherwise, because of the turn-taking system of conversation, a speaker at a turn completion point may find that another person begins to speak. How is the other to know that it is not a place to speak since any next possible completion point is a place to speak. One way would be to produce an utterance which says that what I plan to say will take more than one utterance and that the number of utterances cannot be specified in advance. If this is accepted by the others, then the speaker may retain the right to speak over a series of

utterances. A story preface, Sacks proposes, is a way to do this. The "story preface" is an "utterance that asks for the right to produce extended talk and says that the talk will be interesting . . . At the completion of that 'interest arouser' . . . one stops, and it's the business of others to indicate that it's okay and maybe also that they're interested, or it's not okay or they're not interested."

Another problem is how to tell when the story is over. The story preface may contain information which reveals what it will take for the story to be over. The hearer can then attend to the telling to find the point at which this information occurs. If missed, the teller can point out that that point has now been reached.

With regard to the organization of the story, "hearer's business is not to be listening to a series of independent utterances, but to a series of sentences that have their connectedness built in so that their connectedness has [to be understood to understand any one of them]. Coherence of the story [depends on] requiring that if you're going to understand it at the end, you've got to keep in mind what's been told earlier" (lectures of 9 April and 16 April 1970).

2   While "repair" initiated by the recipient can result in "repair" being achieved in the next turn, more than repair is involved here. "Repair" is the technical term introduced and studied by Schegloff, Jefferson and Sacks (1977) and refers to the "self-righting mechanisms for the organization of language use in social interaction." "Repair" is addressed to the "troubles" that emerge in interaction whether these be word replacement, person references, next-speaker selection, mishearings, misstatements, or whatever. We are not interested in examining these data to study the phenomenon of "repair" but rather wish to find how the parties address the troubles that develop in their interaction with regard to their relevance for the activity of direction-giving itself.

3   The first study and description of insertion sequences is by Schegloff (1972) and also involved a study of the activity of direction-giving.

4   All data were obtained either through audio tape recordings of telephone calls or audio tape or videotape recordings of face-to-face interaction. Identifying names have been changed in most instances.

5   In examining the internal features of the set of directions, we can also note the following constitutive elements: (a) a *named* (or implied) and understood-in-common *destination*; (b) *toward* which movement is presumed possible; (c) and which is presumed to be *recognizable-locatable*. Also (d) named sets of *operations* implying or describing movements; (e) to be performed in *relation* to particular reference *points* or *places* which are understandable as orientational and/or directional reference points; (f) which appear or are named *sequentially*; and (g) the *sequence of operations* (in relation to named orientational or directional reference points) is presented through *sequences of utterances* (or within a single utterance or turn at talk).

6   In Psathas and Kozloff (1976:122–3) we have noted that: "The directional reference point signals the point at which a *change* in directions is to be made. Some feature of the setting is noted as the point at which the change is to be

made, e.g., signs, street names, traffic lights, buildings, blocks (which are counted) or cross streets which are named. Each of these, because they are used in the context of D[irection-giver] giving directions to an R[ecipient] who is driving, tend to occur at points where streets intersect. A change in directions from one pathway to another is generally a move from one street to another . . ."

7 One meaning of "you can't miss it" may be "you can't miss finding your goal if you follow my instructions." Such an expression may convey to R(ecipient) that D(irection-giver) considers his instructions valid and complete and regards himself as a competent Director. This may also mean that, as far as he is concerned, he has fulfilled the request made of him and that the responsibility now rests with the Recipient to follow the set (see also Psathas and Kozloff 1976).

8 We also have the following case where, at the arrival section, recipient produces a second request for an alternative set of directions.

(Ski School)

```
 7   A:   An that brings ya onto one thirty eight going=no:rth.
 8   C:   Uh huh (0.5)
 9   A:   An we're half a mile from the exit at the most=its very easy
          ta find (0.4)
10   C:   What about=uh: is there another way comin
          out of the- uh vee ef double you ((VFW)) parkway or
          somethin? ⌈ah
11   A:              ⌊oh gee ah I come from the south
          shore, ⌈uh
12   C:           ⌊yeah
```

This request comes just after the direction-giver has produced the last operation of the set "an we're half a mile from the exit at the most . . ." (line 9), i.e., a presupposed "taking" of that road mentioned in the just prior utterance ("one thirty eight going=no:rth", line 7) and "arrived" at the destination ("we're half a mile from the exit", line 9) i.e., a description of *where* "we" (the ski school) is. In the immediate next utterance (line 10) caller asks "what about uh: is there another way comin out of the- uh vee ef double you ((VFW)) parkway or somethin?", which is now responded to with a self-categorization proposed as one that should be recognized as "not knowledgeable enough to provide directions" from the starting point proposed by caller (i.e., VFW parkway). Nevertheless, answerer proceeds to provide a possible alternative route and, over a series of turns, discusses with the caller alternative routes.

9

Hold the Phone

Robert Hopper

The telephone provides the principal electronic medium for interpersonal communication. Certain recurrent moments in telephone talk display interactions of technology, social structure and speech communication. This chapter describes some moments at which people say to each other: "hold on."

Telephone talk is constrained by the medium's channel capacities in at least three ways. First, *telephone talk highlights dyadic exchange.* The phone is a medium built for two. Since the invention of the telephone, dyadic speech has joined the oration and the sentence as a central exemplar of human speech communication (see Shannon 1948).

Second, *telephone talk restricts conversation to sounds.* The world of phone talk displays a rich conversation ecology performed in audio only. The telephone provides for speech split off from visual co-presence. This limit to sound provides one empirical basis for the study of speech: an audio tape recording of a telephone conversation displays precisely what an encounter's participants can make available to one another (Schegloff 1986c:112).

Third, *telephone encounters display definite beginnings.* Co-present speech routinely grows from non speech pre-beginnings, such as visual recognition displays. It is difficult to pinpoint a moment when such encounters begin. But a telephone encounter opens at a definite moment (Schegloff 1979a:26; see also Houtkoop, chapter 10 below). A telephone encounter begins at a summons, usually a repetitive ringing sound. Callers who dial a phone number are blind to the current activities of the summoned party. To allow a telephone in one's home or office is to make oneself accessible to such intrusive summoning. Most of us routinely interrupt a variety of ongoing activities, including speech events in progress, in order to answer the telephone.

There are also occasions when telephone speakers interrupt phone interaction, often by saying "hold on." When participants in telephone talk say "hold on," they usually stop talking to each other for a while without hanging up the phone. They stop taking turns without closing the encounter. The present essay describes some uses of "hold on."

We begin by examining one environment that routinely elicits "hold on": the *call-waiting preface*. A second section of this essay displays other instances of "hold on" in telephone talk. In both sets of instances "hold on" is like a referee's whistle, calling "time out" (Jefferson 1972) from the game of conversational turn-taking.

The Call-waiting Preface

When you dial someone's phone number in the USA, you often fail to reach that party because the phone is busy. The channel capacity for most telephone conversations is two participants, one dyad. The purpose of one recent innovation, telephone "call waiting" is to allow its subscriber to waffle between two dyads, in a primitive way, one at a time.

The call-waiting subscriber pays a monthly fee for a device to signal an incoming call during an ongoing phone encounter. Subscribers to call waiting buy into this situation: at any time during a phone encounter there may occur a distinctive "beep" signifying that an unknown caller seeks access to the line. In order to speak to this caller, subscriber must suspend or terminate ongoing talk with the current partner. There are three parties to a call-waiting transaction.[1]

- *Subscriber* with phone equipped with call waiting. Subscriber hears a beep of 1.5 seconds that begins and ends with electronic noise (transcribed as #-##).
- *Partner* is talking to subscriber at the time of the call-waiting summons. When subscriber hears the beep, partner (usually) hears only the electronic noise.
- *Caller* has placed a phone call to subscriber's phone such that the summons occurs in overlap with the subscriber–partner telephone encounter. Caller does not know that there is an encounter already in progress.

Participants carry unequal knowledge into the call-waiting preface. Subscriber hears the distinctive "beep" that signals an incoming call.

Partner usually hears electronic noises, but these could be taken for any line disturbance. Caller is least informed and rings up subscriber hoping to initiate an ordinary phone call.

The call-waiting preface has no pre-beginning. It begins at the "beep" which cannot be locally managed by subscriber or partner. Each call-waiting summons, then, provides a case study in how parties to conversation adapt to a surprising new stimulus that invites situational change. Consider 9.1:[2]

9.1   Family Phone 2

40	**Partner:**		But y'know what?=
41	*Summons:*		=#-##
42	**Subscriber:**	→	*Ha*ng on I got a call on the other line.
43	**Partner:**		Kay
44	*Switch:*		#-##

In 9.1 a call-waiting *summons* triggers an immediate, brief set of turns in which the parties interact to put partner on hold so that subscriber may switch partners. This activity occurs within a sequential environment bounded by two electronic noises (transcribed as lines 41 and 44).

A first observation: the call-waiting preface unfolds quite quickly. From the caller's standpoint the summons at 41 is just an ordinary phone call. Presumably caller would allow at least 20 seconds for an answer. Yet subscriber shows immediate orientation to the summons and completes the preface within three seconds.

A second observation: when the summons occurs, there is already sequential business on the floor. At line 40, partner says "Y'know what?" which is hearable as a first part of a sequence at least three turns long (Sacks 1972b:342; Nofsinger 1975:2). Items like partner's line 40 ("y'know what?") ordinarily elicit responses like "what?" followed by some telling from the first speaker. Subscriber's problem is that just as line 40 ends, the summons sounds. Subscriber is therefore presented in one moment with constraints to respond to two pieces of sequential business.

Subscriber displays orientation only to the summons, abandoning ongoing sequential business.[3] Subscriber orients to the summons but does not answer it. Rather, subscriber says to partner: "*Ha*ng on I got a call on the other line." With this turn, placed immediately after an electronic noise, subscriber offers partner evidence for identifying that noise as having provided a summons to subscriber: (a) the turn displays no relevance tie to ongoing sequential business in the talk; (b) the turn is hearable as in reference to the electronic noise due to its sequential placement contiguous to it; and (c) the turn mentions "I got a call on the other line."

The speaker of line 42 accomplishes a request. Evidence that partner understands line 42 this way emerges as partner assents in next turn (line 43).

| 42 | **Subscriber:** | → | *Ha*ng on I got a call on the other line. |
| 43 | **Partner:** | | Kay |

As soon as partner says "Kay" at 43, subscriber switches away, completing the call-waiting preface.

To summarize: the turn at line 42 displays to partner an orientation to the "noise" in the immediate past, and gives grounds for identifying the noise as a summons. In the same turn, the speaker establishes a request that is granted in next turn.

Subscriber initiation of the call-waiting preface

Initiation of the call-waiting preface differs depending on whether subscriber or partner speaks next after the summons. Most often subscriber initiates the preface, as in 9.1 above and 9.2 and 9.3 below.

9.2   UTCL A9

80	**Subscriber:**		What do they do: exa⌈ctly
79	*Summons:*		⌊#-##
80	**Subscriber:**		Bobbie?
81	**Partner:**		Yeah.
82	**Subscriber:**	→	Hold on I have a call=
83	**Partner:**		O::kay-

9.3   UTCL A10

40	**Subscriber:**		U:h we're ⌈two-
41	*Summons:*		⌊#-##
42	**Subscriber:**	→	Can you hold o:n
43	**Partner:**		Yeah.

In these examples, subscriber initiates orientation to the summons noise, and does so in a pivotal hold-on turn.

The timing of the summons is not managed by partner or subscriber. In 9.1 and 9.2 an expectable second-pair part, due at the moment of the summons, never takes place. In each instance ongoing talk comes to a halt. Subsequent utterances display orientation to the noise as possibly a summons.

The turns that display orientation to the summons are marked with arrows in 9.1–3. These hold-on turns by subscriber are produced after the noise, without gap, in instances 9.1 and 9.3. In instance 9.2 only an insertion sequence intervenes. This contiguous placement of the hold-on turn is one way in which subscribers display orientation to the noise. This placement co-occurring with discontinuation of ongoing business suggests a sudden shift in the encounter's direction.

Only a small number of elements get formulated with "hold on" in those turns.

9.1: *Hang* on I got a call on the other line.
9.2: Hold on I have a call
9.3: Can you hold o:n

In addition to "hang on/hold on," only four other elements occur. Two of these supplemental elements are exemplified above: "I have another call" (9.1 and 9.2), and "Can you" 9.3. "I have a call" mentions the kind of event that is intruding and may be heard as accounting for the request; "Can you" asks about a condition felicitous to posing a request, the ability or willingness to perform the action (Austin 1962:12–18; Searle 1975; Heritage 1984a:265–79).

Instances not shown here include mention of an unrealistically brief period of time, and/or a questioning "okay?": for instance, "hold on one second okay?" No other elements appear in these hold-on turns. Further, no instance uses more than two of these supplemental elements, indicating possible constraint to minimize or elide. The turns in question appear to be relatively unmarked in emphasis, fluency, pause and pitch.

In sum, hold-on turns are delivered quickly in deadpan, displaying minimized detail beyond what can be taken as recognition that the noise has been heard and is being framed up as a summons competing with ongoing conversation. The hold-on turn is constructed to suspend ongoing business, to display orientation to a competing summons, to project subscriber's answering the summons, and to request that partner suspend turn-taking to allow this to occur.

How does next speaker respond to "hold on?"

Next speaker after the hold-on turn is partner, who quickly says "okay" or "yes." These seconds are fitted to the firsts: "Yes" is done in response to "can you hold on" (9.3), while "okay" is returned when "hold on" begins the first turn (9.1 and 9.2). The choice between "yes" and "okay" seems dictated by surface grammar of the hold-on turn.

The sequential second to "hold on" (yes/okay) is produced without gap, providing a grant to the request. This "yes/okay" turn is the last speaking in the call-waiting preface. In conjunction with the switching noise that follows it, this turn finalizes the suspension of turn-taking. Partner takes this turn. Then *there is no next speaker* for a while. This silence displays the accomplishment of suspending turn-taking in the subscriber–partner encounter.

The paired turns "hold on – okay" occur quite quickly following the "beep." However, subscriber may choose to abort call-waiting business at almost any time. Example 9.4 shows that the call-waiting preface may be aborted even after its completion. Subscriber is reading a draft of a speech.

9.4   UTCL A18r

59	**Subscriber:**		((reads)) . . . This slow development in popula=
60	*Summons:*		=#-##=
61	**Subscriber:**		=ud after-
62	**Subscriber:**		Can you hold on?=
63	**Partner:**		=Yeh.
64			(0.7)
65	**Subscriber:**	→	Naw *f*– it (0.5) This slow development ((continues reading))

At 63, the call-waiting preface stands completed. But after a pause subscriber says, "Naw *f*– it." Then subscriber resumes at the last sentence-beginning before the summons. Line 65 brackets lines 60–3, the call-waiting preface, and sequentially deletes it. Continuing from the repetition of "This slow development," subscriber resumes business-as-before.

The ease with which this call-waiting preface is aborted suggests that the decision to put the other on hold is primarily subscriber's. Perhaps that is why subscriber ordinarily speaks next after a summons.

To summarize: subscriber is usually next speaker after a call-waiting summons. Subscriber initiates a hold-on turn that: (1) stops ongoing sequential business; (2) displays orientation to the incoming summons; and (3) begins a sequence that leads toward suspension of turn-taking. Partner immediately responds with "okay" or "yes," and subscriber switches away. We have not shown why this switching episode happens so fast, but we have shown something about *how* it is so speedily accomplished.

Partner's initiations to the call-waiting preface

In 9.5 it is not subscriber (Cara), but partner (Pete) who initiates orientation to the summons. Partner does this only after subscriber has had ample opportunities to do so.

9.5   UTCL A10

```
123  Pete:      I did all right (0.2) coulda=
124  Summons:   #-##
125             (0.6)
126  Cara:      Hello?
127  Pete:      Is that your phone?
128             (.)
129  Cara:      U:h Yeah hang on.
130  Pete:      Okay
131  Summons:   #-##
```

Here there is a six-tenths of a second gap (line 125) between the summons noise and any further speech. Subscriber's next turn appears oriented toward rechecking contact. Partner then initiates orientation to the summons by asking "Is that your phone?" Partner's initiation occurs only after subscriber has been given ample opportunity to do so. Further, partner uses a different call-waiting preface initiation than subscriber. In 9.1–4 subscriber moves directly to "hold on". In 9.5 partner displays orientation to the occurrence of the electronic noise, but leaves subscriber to speak the crucial request. Subscriber seemingly owns decision rights at this moment. The call-waiting summons is "subscriber's problem." Subscriber pays for the service, and reaps its social costs with its channel capacity benefits.

To summarize: call-waiting prefaces are triggered by a summons signal to which subscriber responds in ways that suspend other sequential constraints and initiate a hold-on request. Partner responds with a grant-turn and the episode ends. This brief episode effects a suspension of turn-taking. The episode is played out as a fast-paced turn pair. Subscriber and partner have differential initiation privileges in call-waiting prefaces. Subscriber has first rights to speak, and usually speaks a hold-on request immediately following the summons.

Some of these features of hold-on sequencing recur in other environments.

Hold On

"Hold on"/"okay" sequencing is brought into strong relief in the call-waiting preface. But to thicken description of how hold-on turns initiate suspension of turn-taking without closing a call, we turn to some instances of "hold on" in other telephone conversation environments. Consider 9.6:

9.6　　A & M

```
40   Sal:   See we never get any sleep-
41          (0.2) h- hold on ju' sec
42   Pat:   Okay
```

At line 40 Sal is completing a clause, perhaps a turn, but the final syllable is cut off ("sleep-"). A short pause is followed by a stammering beginning of a "hold on" request. The two cut-offs with a pause between them can be heard as possible disjunct markers (Jefferson 1978:220–1), or markers that what is to follow is not a direct continuation of what has gone before. By the time "hold on" is spoken, there has already been some warning.

In Examples 9.6 and 9.7 speakers of "hold on" and its precursors initiate these signals amid displays of orientation to boundaries of "turn constructional units" (Sacks, Schegloff and Jefferson 1974). (By contrast "hold on" in the call-waiting preface is spoken by subscriber immediately adjacent to and following the summons noise, apparently overriding turn-taking constraints.) Consider 9.7:

9.7　　UTCL A9

```
90   Jane:        Who ca:res if we a:re
91                y'⌈know ⌉ big dea⌈:1.
92   Robin:  →       ⌊ Yeah.⌋        ⌊Hold- on. Hold on-
```

The placement of "hold on" at line 92 shows orientation to current speaker's probable turn completion. As Jane stretches "de:al" at 91, the "hold on" (line 92) is spoken partially in overlap with the turn's ending, but beginning at a probable completion point.

"Hold on" also displays orientation to sequential entities larger than a turn.

9.8   UTCL A10a ((simplified))

Joan:	Seth says that the bro:wnies were wonderful and he's eaten a whole lot of them
Skeet:	Are you serious? They're *aw*ful
Joan:	Robert too he *lo*ves them.
Skeet:	Oh hoh my God they're some of the *wor*st brownies I've ever tasted
Joan:	Well that=
Skeet:	=And they weren't supposed to be brownies anyway they were supposed to be chocolate chip *cookies*
Joan:	Hah well they turned out to be good brownies
	(0.2)
Skeet:	Hah *they*'re hah
	(0.3)
Joan: →	Okay would you hold on a second?
Skeet:	Okay

In 9.8 Joan compliments Skeet's brownies, and Skeet deflects the compliment amid laughter and joking. The after-compliment episode runs its course before being diplomatically ended with a hold-on turn. Joan times the "hold on" to both conform to and accomplish this episode boundary.

In sum, hold-on turns orient to "turn and sequence boundaries," and often preannounce themselves. Besides disjunct markers and "hold on," the turns described in instances 9.6–8 display components noted above in descriptions of call-waiting prefaces, especially mention of units of time (such as "a sec"). These features may assist marking these hold-on turns as triggers for suspension of turn-taking. Recipients respond to "hold on" in immediate subsequent turns, either with "okay," "yes," "alright," or by providing no responding next. This not taking a next turn is the strongest evidence that speakers have accomplished turn suspension.

Problem cases

Additional evidence that hold-on turns request suspension of turn-taking is displayed in instances in which that outcome is not immediately achieved. Participants orient to such non-achievement by recycling elements of the sequence. Example 9.9 shows a first "hold on" that does not initiate suspension of turn-taking:

9.9   UTCL F1 ((simplified))

281	**M:**		But it's not like you all can't get along on
282			a small salary for awhile if you're gonna get
283			(0.6) promotions=
284	**M:**	→	Hold on a minute=
285	**D:**		=Is there any colleges in (1.1)
286	**M:**		Llano?=
287	**D:**		=Llano?=
288	**M:**	→	=No. Hold on

In line 284 M rushes to take an additional turn constructional unit at the end of her utterance to say "hold on." D responds quickly with line 285, latching to M's "hold on" a turn that (does not grant a request, but) seems to be a previously relevant question-in-progress when suddenly D pauses (at end of 285). Why the pause? Is D word-searching for the place identification "Llano?" She packages the turn as if that is what she is doing, but leaving her utterance to be completed by M is also a way of checking that M has not already left the phone following her "hold on." M does complete D's turn, supplying a candidate place term, try-marked, in next turn, line 286. D confirms this selection at 287, and by doing "Llano?" also completes the question begun at 285. M provides an immediate (if rushed and minimal) answer at 288 ("No").
Immediately after saying "no" M self-selects to redo "hold on." This recycled "hold on" effects suspension of turn-talking.

Example 9.9 shows a "recycling" of "hold on" as M pursues a suspension of turn-taking. In effect, D's question about colleges gets treated as an insertion sequence. As soon as M provides an answer, she redoes "hold on" in same turn. This redoing displays M's analysis of her prior turn and indicates her continued orientation to the request.

Example 9.10 displays recycled "okay" following "hold on."

9.10   UTCL D8

42	**Cara:**	→	Hold o:n (0.2) kay (0.8) kay?
43			(0.4)
44	**Rick:**		Okay

At line 42 Cara issues a "hold on," then pauses. Recall the contiguity of "okay"-seconds in instances reported above. The pause in line 42 may be enough to suggest there is a problem in eliciting "okay." The next verbalization, following a short pause and spoken by Cara, is "kay" which appears to be an elided "okay." If "okay" is an expectable response in this situation, could Cara be prompting her partner by supplying tokens of an expected second? This speculation receives some support in the rest of line 42, which consists of a longer pause followed by a try-marked "kay?" that elicits Rick's responding "Okay." Immediately on receipt of Rick's "Okay," speakers suspend turn-taking.

To summarize: hold-on turns much like those in the call-waiting preface recur in phone talk. The production of these turns begins a two-part sequence that suspends turn-taking without ending the phone call. Evidence supporting this analysis is displayed in the production of "hold on," in the production of agreeing second turns following "hold on," and in the subsequent display of not-taking-turns while remaining on the phone. If "hold on" fails to elicit these outcomes, its user may recycle signals to pursue these outcomes.

The call-waiting preface, then, seems to have been developed through the application of these general-use telephone talk resources to a new situation. An innovation affecting possibilities of telephone channel capacity has apparently stimulated a novel application of a previously used speech technology.

Discussion

The sequential relevance of "hold on" operates both prospectively and retrospectively. In the description of call-waiting prefaces, the first-pair-part relevancies of "hold-on" show most clearly. "Hold on" appears in request turns and usually receives an assenting second such as "okay." Hold-on turns initiate suspension of turn-taking in telephone talk without closing a call.[4]

However, the retrospective relevance of "hold on" merits attention when we consider the full range of its uses. Hold-on turns are designed to be heard as consequent to some *absent* (to the recipient) sequential first. "Hold on" displays to an interaction partner an orientation to respond to something outside the present encounter, and also outside the probable perception-attention field of the partner. This intrusion may be some "co-present event" (cases 9.6–10) or a call-waiting summons (cases 9.1–5).

Schegloff (1968) provides some warrant for description of a sequential second to an absent first:

> not only does conditional relevance operate "forwards" . . . but it works in "reverse" as well. If, after a period of conversational lapse, one person . . .

should produce an item that may function as an A to an S, such as "What?" or "Yes?," then another person in that environment may hear in that utterance that an unspoken summons was heard. The connection between a summons and an answer provides both prospective and retrospective inferences.

"Hold on" seems to be a speech object designed to be heard as sequentially consequent to some stimulus of which the recipient of "hold on" is presumed to be unaware.

However, "hold on" is not a sequential second in the sense that it addresses the speaker of the first. The function of "hold on" is to switch interactive focus from the party to which it is addressed.

"Hold on" and telephone history

Conversation participants must use interaction-ordering principles that are already at hand in adapting to new technologies. However, in adapting to new technologies, speakers may transform the interactive practices so employed. The current materials may illuminate one such adaptive transformation.

The description of "hold on" in the present chapter unfolds in an order suited to descriptive purchase, but *backwards* in history. Call-waiting prefaces are recent phenomena. Hold-on turns are older forms that may have recurred since telephone dyads became routine. Hence, to contrast properties of "hold on" in the call-waiting preface (9.1–5) with other uses (9.6–10) may identify transformations adaptive to call-waiting.

One difference between call-waiting "hold on" and pre-call-waiting uses: call-waiting "hold on" routinely directly intrudes into ongoing turns and sequences, whereas previous uses respect turn and sequence boundaries. Hence, call-waiting technology not only increases the range of telephone summons intrusiveness (into ongoing phone encounters) but also creates a recurrent situation in which intrusion into turn constructional units is normal. This constitutes interaction of talk and social structure in that an institutional-technological innovation (the offering of call-waiting to consumers by the phone company) affects speaking practices.

I speculate that the widespread introduction of phone technology (just a century ago) elevated the dyad's importance and thereby increased the range and scope of practices like "hold on." A telephone dyad is a form of life achieved by the putting by participants of potential others into nonparticipant status: "on hold." Telephone talk, in principle, performs a social-structuring operation of segregating one dyad from the rest of a speech community. Telephone speakers, blind to the visual contingencies in which they encounter each other, recurrently experience disruptive or "interruptive" stimuli at one end of the call.[5] Dyad members respond to intrusions by perfecting and extending a speech technology including "hold on." The lexicon of "hold on" provides apt description for the activity of a phone partner left waiting, as that party literally is left in the absurd posture of holding the unused phone at the side of the head.

Today, "hold on" has developed into a ready resource at hand, one applicable to new problems such as those of the telephone call-waiting subscriber. The call-waiting subscriber adapts hold-on technology for new uses, and some of these adaptations touch turn-taking. That is, call-waiting provides a new environment in which "hold on" is an appropriate response to a recurrent problem. In the praxis surrounding such use, the nature of the device is altered.

Talk and social structure

Scholars sometimes write as though communication is stuff that comes packaged in pre-established sets of social structures or contexts (being male; working for the phone company). This view proposes that contextual features are in place at moments of talk and that they constrain talk. This view bypasses participants' achievements of contextual features. A contrasting approach, exemplified by this chapter, examines recorded talk to discover and specify the accomplishments of speaking. Call-waiting prefaces provide an illustration.

At the moment of the call-waiting summons, subscriber falls victim to an institutional bind, a difficult choice emerging in direct consequence of a commercial arrangement with the telephone company. It is the *display of orientation* to this arrangement which does the social-structuring work of the call-waiting preface.

Subscriber takes immediate decisive action consequent to an unexpected stimulus. That Janus-faced action, "hold on," simultaneously orients to the unforeseen intrusion and invites consequences in subsequent action. It is tempting to see subscriber as in the grip of some external institutional vice. But what is being done and how?

To subscribe to call waiting is to make oneself accessible to intrusion. Like the professor who leaves an office door ajar, subscriber has self-positioned to receive summonings. When these occur, subscriber may enact the role of a self who is institutionally obligated to speak with any individual who happens along. That's easy in the abstract, but as any open-door professor admits, actual concrete cases frequently bring interaction problems.

At the moment of the call-waiting "hold on," subscriber pays the interactional price of accessibility. That price is to be presented with an opportunity to ask partner to accept second-banana status. What happens at the call-waiting summons may be compared to the TV show *Let's Make a Deal* in which contestants are offered opportunities to trade items they've won for something unknown – something "behind the curtain." The call-waiting subscriber is offered a trade of the current conversation partner for whomever is behind the curtain. TV contestants who already possess something of value may bypass the suggested "deal." So may an authentic subscriber who displays orientation to the present encounter by ignoring the beep. But at the point of the summons a "deal" has been proposed (albeit by an offstage *unknowing* caller) and *either* its acceptance or rejection has been made specifically relevant. That manufacture of relevance seems (to subscriber) to arrive "out of the blue." Subscriber may then experience the beep as an inescapable, or institutional constraint.

When institutional constraints emerge, their clout mystifies us. In the call-waiting preface, participants react quickly; they get swept along in a collective Leviathan that seems to offer only bifurcated choices in response to preconstructed dilemmas. Some scholars explain speech as caused by exogenous "contexts" (Heritage 1984a:282). These explanations might invoke "social-structural" variables for explanation: the phone company's institutional power, or that of males, or something else big, like a "culture." Such claims ignore the ethnomethodological practices by which we accomplish these constraints. Hence regardless of their truth value, claims about exogenous context fail to describe messages. In my own discipline of communication studies, this becomes a critical weakness of those approaches. The work of interaction is accomplished in messages. At call-waiting, as on other occasions, we invoke social structuring through speaking. Without speech, wrote Hobbes, "there had been amongst men, neither commonwealth, nor society" (1962:33).

To describe social structure, describe its accomplishment in speech. In the present case, we find a reflexive relationship between a speaker's use of "hold on" to intrude into speaker turns and the institutional arrangement allowing a summons to boldly go where none had gone before – while actors may disclaim responsibility for this intrusion. Call waiting's intrusion is that of the telephone itself, writ small.

Notes

1 These roles of subscriber, partner and caller are not preassigned, but rather achieved during the emergent course of call-waiting prefaces.

2 Instances in this chapter are drawn from a collection of 60 hours of telephone talk. Instances marked UTCL are in the University of Texas Conversation Library, in care of the author. This chapter describes 36 call-waiting prefaces tape recorded on 16 different telephones.

3 Rarely in the present data do parties reorient to sequential business truncated by the call-waiting summons. Resumptions are all of lengthy tellings. See instance 9.4 below.

4 An earlier version of the present chapter also described some hold-on turns produced in response to switchboard requests. These now seem to be different sorts of objects:

> **M:** Hello?
> (.)
> **H:** H:h may I speak to Robert?
> **M:** Sure hold on a second please.

These "hold on" turns, like those in call-waiting prefaces, initiate a switch of telephone partners. However, (1) the sequential second to "hold on" is usually "thanks"; (2) these turns occur at call beginnings and hence do not stop ongoing business; (3) the hold-on turns show relevance to the prior turn rather than disjunction; and (4) hold-on tokens occur in a minority of these instances.

5 Alternatively one might conceptualize the segregated dyad as the problem.

10

Opening Sequences in Dutch Telephone Conversations

Hanneke Houtkoop-Steenstra

Introduction

A central concern of conversation analytic research is that of sequential organization. In an early and pivotal study, Schegloff (1968; see also 1986c) focused on the sequential structure of the opening section of telephone conversations, using American calls and pointing to certain systematic features that stand in strong contrast to observable features of telephone conversation in at least one other culture, namely Dutch society. Dutch people who watch American films or go to the United States often report that "Americans do not mention their own names in a telephone conversation." The fact that so many Dutchmen say this highlights an "observable absence" in the organization of self-identification in American telephone calls. The fact that this is remarkable to the Dutch not only addresses their reaction to American talk, but also underlines a systematic feature of Dutch telephone talk. In this chapter a comparison will be made of American and Dutch telephone openings to see if this apparent difference is real, and if so, how it affects, and is managed in, the respective opening sequences.

The American Way

Schegloff proposes that the opening section of American telephone conversations consists of four distinct and staged sequences (see Schegloff 1968, 1979a, 1986c). Each sequence addresses a different organizational task, although there is no neat "one-to-one" relationship between them. Firstly there is the *summons–answer sequence*. The summons is the ringing[1] of the telephone at someone's home, which is acknowledged by "answerer", usually with a "hello" (Schegloff 1986c), for instance:

> **summons:** ((ringing))
> **answer:**   Hello:

In case of a call to a business or an office, however, answerer will add a self-identification or a self-formulation, for instance:

> **summons:** ((ringing))
> **answer:**   Good *evening*, W.N.B.C.

The summons–answer sequence is "overtly addressed to opening, and confirming the openness of, a channel of communication, and the availability of an attentive ear and a mouth ready to speak" (Schegloff 1986c:117). Apart from that, the answer also plays a role in the identification work. By saying "Hello" answerer provides a voice sample to be recognized by caller. This voice sample is not necessarily the start of the sequence which is overtly addressed to identification, that is, the identification sequence. "If caller recognizes answerer from the voice sample in the answering turn, then caller should show (or claim) such recognition in next turn, the second in the call" (Schegloff 1986c:126). He goes on to note the variety and range of forms used.

> **summons**   → ((ringing))
> **answer**   → **A:** H'*llo:*?
> **recognition** → **B:** hHi:,
>
> **summons**   → ((ringing))
> **answer**   → **A:** Hel*lo*:.
> **recognition** → **B:** Miz Parsons?

After caller's recognition of answerer, answerer displays his or her recognition of caller by doing a sequentially appropriate second part for the type of sequence initiated by the caller:

```
                   ((ringing))
     Feldman:      (Hell)o,
     Bonnie:       Hello Missiz Feldman,
  →  Feldman:      Hi Bonnie.
```

This then is the *Identification (and/or recognition) sequence* (Schegloff 1986c:117), which for this American data displays a preference to be recognized through voice token alone, rather than through self-identification. Briefly, this preference appears to depend on the caller: (a) being "recognizable"; and (b) being a "potential caller" for this answerer (see especially Schegloff 1986c:126). Subsequent exchanges, in the American data reported by Schegloff (1968), include the greeting sequence and the "howareyou sequence," neither of which will be discussed in this paper.

To summarize, in case of informal telephone calls, American conversationalists exhibit a preference for recognition of other party, rather than for self-identification. Answerer produces a first Hello-like utterance, in which s/he provides a voice sample, which in its own turn is preferably responded to by caller claiming or displaying recognition of answerer, upon which answerer claims or displays recognition of caller, on the basis of caller's voice sample. In effect, the organization of American telephone call openings is highly indexical and informal. In the following sections, I will demonstrate that this primary preference for voice recognition is not to be found in Dutch telephone conversations.

The Dutch Way

Whereas American calls start off with answerer answering the telephone by means of a single answer to the summons ("Hello"), Dutch calls do not. Secondly, and related to this, although American calls have a preference for using a voice sample for recognition of other speaker, Dutch calls have a preference for speaker's self-identification through name mention.[2] In order to make this claim, I went through a collection of Dutch telephone openings my colleague, Paul ten Have, and I made some years ago. With all obvious business calls omitted, the collection contained 87 calls, with four distinct categories of opening types, and one small collection of somewhat different openings.

The following fragments have been categorized on two axes: (1) answerer and caller; (2) the use of either self-identification or a voice sample. This yields to four possibilities, and a residual category of specifically "strange" cases. It should be noted that these "categories" of types of openings do not coincide with very many Dutch standard procedures for initiating a telephone conversation, and are thus used here as contrastive cases with the American data studied by Schegloff. When I refer to "voice sample," I mean an utterance without a self-identification in it. By "self-identification" I mean the proffering of one's own name. Following is a list of the categories and the number of cases in each:

1 Answerer: *self-identification*
   Caller: *self-identification*   74 cases

2 Answerer: *self-identification*
   Caller: *voice sample*   4 cases

3 Answerer: *voice sample*
   Caller: *self-identification*   4 cases

4 Answerer: *voice sample*
   Caller: *voice sample*   1 case

5 Variant cases   4 cases

I will give some examples of the majority of the cases in which both speakers self-identify in first and second turns. I will then give all the other cases and discuss each of them. In providing both English and Dutch versions of the examples, I have used the following translation:

Dutch	*English*
Hallo	Hello
Dag	Hi
(u spreekt) met X	{ (You're speaking) with X
	This is X
	This is X speaking

Answerer and caller both self-identifying

First we look at some instances from category 1:

10.1

HH:18:245 ((sisters))

| **A:** | It's Reina de Wind?, | **A:** | Met Reina de Wind?, |
| **C:** | Hello:, it's Bren. | **C:** | Hallo:, met Bren. |

HH:12:98 ((acquaintances))

A:	It's Catrien,?	A:	Met Catrien,?
	(0.7)		(0.7)
C:	It's Maarten.	C:	Met Maarten.

HH:1:2 ((friends))

| A: | It's Mies Habots.= | A: | Met Mies Habots.= |
| C: | =Hi:, it's Anneke de Groot. | C: | =Da:g, met Anneke de Groot. |

HH:2:1 ((strangers))

A:	Konnie Stabosch.=	A:	Konnie Stabosch.=
C:	=Hi:, it's Anneke de Groot.	C:	=Da:g, met Anneke de
	In Rotterdam.		Groot. In Rotterdam.

As noted, in 74 out of the 87 cases we find answerer self-identifying in first turn, with caller self-identifying in second turn. There is no simple summons–answer sequence of the type that Schegloff found in American calls, that is, there is no first turn utterance which has as its single function opening the channel of communication. In contrast to American practice in personal telephone calls, then, Dutch call openings accomplish a dual activity, namely opening the communication channel *and* moving to the next interactional problem of providing for identification/recognition by name. The fact that so many parties self-identify is an indicator of a very strong preference in Dutch calls for self-identification over voice recognition alone.

In the next section, fragments will be discussed in which answerers, rather than self-identifying, only say "Hello." And as we will come to see, all of these voice samples of answerers in first turn cause puzzlement on the part of the callers, thereby demonstrating rather effectively normative orientation to answerers self-identifying.

Answerer self-identifying, caller providing a voice sample

This category 2 contains three conversations between spouses and between close relatives. As in the first category, answerer self-identifies, whereas caller provides a voice sample only, which is (claimed to be) recognized by answerer.

10.2

HH:6:1:2 ((spouses))
A:	Walloord.	**A:**	Walloord.
C:	Hello.	**C:**	Hallo.
A:	Hello.	**A:**	Hallo.

PtH:40 ((spouses))
A:	*Annelies* Kr*au:*wel?,=	**A:**	*Annelies* Kr*au:*wel?,=
C:	=*HI*:!=	**C:**	=*DA*:g!=
A:	=Hell*o*!	**A:**	=Hall*o*!

PtH:8 ((spouses))
A:	Annelies Kr*au*:wel?=	**A:**	Annelies Kr*au*:wel?=
C:	=Hi:i, it's m*e*.=	**C:**	=D*a*:g, met m*ij*.=
A:	=Hell*o*!	**A:**	=Hall*o*!

HH:5:5 ((Man and daughter-in-law))
A:	Anneke de Vries.	**A:**	Anneke de Vries.
C:	Hi: Anneke.	**C:**	D*a*:g Anneke.
A:	Hi:.	**A:**	D*a*:g.

Thus occasionally in this Dutch corpus we find callers not self-identifying in return to answerers' self-identification, and in so doing, callers may be seen as doing special intimacy work.[3] Several points can be made about this category of answerer self-identifying and caller providing a voice sample. First, if we add these four answerers who self-identify in first turn to the preceding set of 74 cases, we find 78 out of 87 answerers self-identifying in first turn.

A second point is that for Dutch telephone conversationalists the class of callers who may use a voice sample only to be recognized by answerer, in response to answerer's self-identification, is very small: spouses and other close relatives, and, as we will come to see later, callers who are calling for a second or third time in a series.

There is therefore a preference for self-identification over recognition, and only a very restricted class of potential callers who occasionally use voice sample. I say "occasionally" because the spouses in this category 2 use self-identification on other occasions, that is, the very same speakers are also to be found in category 1. To which extent there is a preference here for the one or the other option is not clear. In order to be able to say more about this, we need more elaborate statistics as well as a more differentiated and elaborated database.[4]

Answerer saying "Hello," caller (doing recognition) and self-identifying

Although Dutch answerers overwhelmingly self-identify in first turn, they sometimes do not, in which case they may say "Hello" or some version of this. Callers may then self-identify in second turn. They also may, or may not, precede their self-identification with a recognition of the answerer. Category 3 consists of four fragments of which the first is:

10.3   HH:18:310 ((woman and child))

    A: Hello:? ((child's voice))
    C: Hi David Halendonk.
             (0.7)
    C: It's Reina de Wind. Is your mother home?

    A: Hallo:?
    C: Dag David Halendonk.
             (0.7)
    C: Met Reina de Wind. Is jouw moeder thuis?

When answerer just says "Hello:?," caller shows that she has recognized answerer ("Hi David Halendonk"), and in so doing also provides a voice sample. After a silence of 0.7 of a second, caller self-identifies. Now the problem is the following. Should this 0.7-second pause be seen as a place for answerer to do recognition if he is able to do so, as is the case with American calls, or does such a pause show the reverse, that is, an appeal to caller to self-identify?

Phrased differently, whose pause is this? Is it the pause of the answerer, who does not provide a recognition, or is it the pause of the caller, who does not self-identify right away? Since 10.3 is a Dutch opening, and since Dutch callers overwhelmingly self-identify, this pause may be seen as caller's pause, that is, as an inter-utterance silence, rather than as answerer's pause, that is, an intra-utterance silence. This is especially so because this caller does not belong to the restricted class of callers who may expect to be recognized on the basis of a voice sample only.

In fact, this fragment seems to be a little more complicated. By using this stressed "Hi David Halendonk", after David has only said "Hello:?", caller seems to be indicating "I know who you are, even when you don't mention your name." In that respect, caller's voice sample may be seen as setting up a similar puzzle for answerer, who may now try to guess who caller is. And when answerer does not respond to this puzzle, caller proceeds according to the general Dutch rule of caller self-identifying in second turn.

Now we come to the few Dutch fragments in which answerers only say "Hello" in first turn, and in which callers only respond to that after a pause.

10.4   PtH:6 ((call to a colleague's home))

    A: He-llo.
    C: .hhh=Hello: this is Peet de Veer, is::- (.) Tom
         Lansink to be reached here?

    A: Ha-llo.
    C: .hhh =Hallo: met Peet de Veer, is::-(.) Tom
         Lansink ook bereikbaar hier?

10.5   HH:31:236

A:	Hello:.	**A:**	Hallo:.
	(0.9)		(0.9)
C:	Rene:?=	**C:**	Rene:?=
A:	=Yah.=	**A:**	=Ja.=
C:	=Karl Ko:nings.=	**C:**	=Karl Ko:nings.=
A:	=Hi.=	**A:**	=Hai.=
C:	=Hello.	**C:**	=Hallo.

Both answerers give just a "Hello", and in both cases this "Hello" is followed by a pause. In 10.4 caller waits a short time after answerer's "He-llo", then self-identifies and goes on to treat answerer as a possible operator in saying "is::- (.) Tom Lansink to be reached here?", by which he shows that he has recognized answerer as not the one he called. The formulation seems to imply that caller is also signalling that he may be mistaken.

In 10.5 it becomes much clearer that answerer's "Hello:" as the entire first turn utterance causes puzzlement for caller. Caller waits for 0.9 second before he takes a next turn. Since 10.5 is a Dutch opening, and since Dutch answerers overwhelmingly self-identify, this pause constitutes a place for answerer to self-identify. And it is only when this does not happen that caller takes the initiative. One might reason that these fragments show that in Dutch calls a "Hello" in first turn position is the answer to the summons, after which caller is expected to show or claim recognition of answerer, using this "Hello" as a voice sample to be recognized, as in the US data. The arguments against this are, first of all, that whereas openings tend to run off quickly and fluently,[5] we tend to find pauses after these hellos, rather than caller producing his turn right away. Moreover, as I will discuss shortly, such a "Hello" is also to be found right before answerer's self-identification ("Hello, it's so-and-so"). This suggests that a caller hearing a "Hello" may wait for answerer to continue his first turn utterance to self-identify, and may start speaking himself only when nothing more is said.

In the last fragment of this category we find caller eventually soliciting answerer to self-identify.

10.6   HH:21:034

A:	Y*a*h hell*o:*?,
	(0.6)
C: →	Hello:, it's *u:*h Ro:nny. R*oo*dmans.
	(1.0)
C:	From St*aa*lstreet number 47.
	(1.0)
C:	Who is this? Is this u::h
	(0.3)
A:	‹U:h it's Patr*i*cia:.
	(0.3)
A:	Jan and u:h Ricky aren't th*e*re.
C:	O::h I see:. Because (. . .)
A:	J*a* h*a*ll*o:*?,
	(0.6)
C: →	Hallo:, m*e*t e:h Ro:nny. R*oo*dmans.
	(1.0)
C:	Van St*aa*lstraat nummer 47.
	(1.0)
C:	Met wie spreek ik? Met e::h
A:	‹E:h met Patr*i*cia:.
	(0.3)
A:	Jan en e:h Ro:nald *zij*n er niet.
C:	O::h ja:. Want (. . .)

When after a pause of 0.6 second, answerer has not self-identified, caller mentions his own name. After caller's self-identification, answerer gets the opportunity to do the same. When she has not done so after a silence of 1 second, caller extends his self-identification by providing further details of his identity. This extension post-completes (Sacks 1971:13) his initial self-identification and it provides a new opportunity for answerer to mention her name. When she still has not done so after a 1-second pause (cf. Jefferson 1989 on the plus or minus 1-second pause), caller becomes more explicit: "Who is this? Is this u::h," and now Patricia hurries to fill out this unfinished utterance with her name.

These fragments show that after an answerer just says "Hello," caller may wait some time before initiating identification work. Since about 90 per cent of these 87 fragments turn out to begin with self-identification by answerer, who typically does so by saying "Hello, it's so-and-so" instead of "it's so-and-so" (see next subsection), this pause after answerer's "hello" may be seen as a place for answerer to self-identify, rather than a place for caller to start speaking.

These four cases of "answerers not self-identifying, callers self-identifying," have been taken as one type of opening. However, since all four of these answerers cause problems for the callers, we may wonder whether these fragments really constitute a distinct "opening type" in Dutch telephone repertoire. In fact, it may well be the case that these instances should instead be treated as demonstrations of the normative orientation of Dutch telephone conversationalists to answerers self-identifying in first turn, that is, as variants of category 1.

"Hello" plus self-identification

There are cases in this collection of 87 openings in which the first word uttered by answerer is "Hello":

10.7   HH:21:049

A:	→	Hello:, it's Ro:nny:.	A:	Hallo:, met Ro:nny:.
C:		Hello: it's Br*i*git.	C:	Hallo: met Br*i*git.

We might argue that this first "Hello:" of Ronny's is an answer to the summons and a voice sample only, which may be followed by a caller's action. However there are two arguments against this, the first one being that this "Hello:" is followed by answerer self-identifying.[6] The second argument is that we also find such a succession of "Hello:" plus self-identification in the caller's turn: "Hello: it's Br*i*git."

In this collection of data it turns out that some speakers, and among them Ronny, tend to start their first turns in this way, "Hello, it's so-and-so"; not only in first sequence position, but also in second position.

10.8   HH:21:044

A:		This is W*i*m,?=	A:	Met W*i*m,?=
C:	→	=Ya hello:,	C:	=Ja hallo:,
		this is Ro:nny:.		met Ro:nny:.

Whereas Ronny tends to start his first turn (either in first or in second position) with a "Hello" or "Ya hello", speaker Peter van der Broeck will start with:

10.9   HH:22:2

A:	→	Ya: This is Pe:te:r.		A:	Ja: met Pe:te:r.
C:		Yea:h, Peter.		C:	Ja:, Peter.
		This is Jennie Ton.			Met Jennie Ton.

or in second position:

10.10   HH:22:1

A:		*This*'s Bonnie.
C:	→	Ya. Good afternoon this is van der Broeck speaking.
A:		Me:t Bonnie.
C:		Ja. Goedemiddag u spreekt met van der Broeck.

Returning to the category 3 openings, in which answerers do not self-identify, we have found that in 10.3 caller recognizes answerer, and self-identifies after some silence. In 10.4 caller waits a very short time after answerer's "He-llo" and then self-identifies. In 10.5 caller produces a question-intoned recognition token after a silence: "Rene:?", which is responded to by answerer saying "Yah", after which caller self-identifies. In 10.6 answerer says "Yah Hello:?," upon which caller self-identifies after a silence and solicits a self-identification on answerer's part.

It is clear then that an answerer's "Hello" is the first part of the first turn self-identification utterance, rather than the answer to a summons (phone ringing, cf. Schegloff 1968) and a voice sample to be recognized by caller. When a caller hears a "Hello," he may wait for answerer to self-identify, and only when this does not follow, may caller speak himself. So, using a "Hello" as a voice sample to be recognized is clearly not the preferred activity in Dutch telephone conversations.

It may also be noted that if a "Hello" as an answer to the summons and a voice sample had been a likely Dutch option, we should have found several cases in this collection in which such a "Hello" was followed by a caller's return "Hello" right away. And although the next paragraph will show that there is one such case (that is, one out of 87) this is a very special case, which can hardly count as evidence that Dutch speakers tend to do it the American way.

Matching voice samples

Among the 87 fragments there is one case in which we find an instance of category 4, answerer's voice sample matched with caller's:

10.11   HH:25:020

> **A:** U:h goo:d mo:rni:ng.
> **C:** Hello:ho:.=
> **A:** =Y⌈ah.
> **C:**   ⌊I just talked to Louis (. . .)
>
> **A:** E:h goeie:mo:rge:.
> **C:** Hallo:ho:.=
> **A:** =J⌈a.
> **C:**   ⌊Ik heb net Louis gebeld (. . .)

These two speakers are not just a "potential and recognizable" answerer and caller; they are a special "potential and recognizable" answerer and caller, since they have spoken on the telephone a little earlier. Caller then promised to call Louis right away, to invite him to come along on a racing cycle tour the conversationalists have planned. And on that occasion caller promised to call right back to answerer. For that reason answerer's "Goo:d morni:ng" should signal his anticipation of being called by this very caller; it should also be noted that this answerer answered the preceding call by self-identifying.

Caller produces this specially pronounced "Hello:ho:". Since he does this in many other calls to and by friends, this pronunciation identifies him as the person, that is, Peter (cf. Schegloff on the "highly idiosyncratic recipient-designed utterance-forms," 1986c:126). Whereas some other fragments (10.3–6) have demonstrated that, when an answerer does not self-identify, caller still tends to do so himself, this does not occur here. Caller just signals who he is by using this idiosyncratic "Hello:ho:".

There are some fragments, not included in this collection because they lack the first turn on the tapes, which turn out to be very similar. These calls also occur very shortly after a prior telephone conversation by the same speakers. And again, callers do not self-identify, but they signal who they are by using a callback marking, that is, by indicating that they are the same caller as earlier. For example,

10.12   HH:18:148 ((friends))

     A: ((opening not taped))   **A:**   ((   ))
     C: → It's m*e* agai:n.=   **C:**   Met m*ij* nog e:ven.=
     A: =Y*ea:h* Reina:.   **A:**   =J*a:* Reina:.

10.13   HH:30:014

     A: ((opening not taped))   **A:**   ((   ))
     C: → M*e:* ag*ai*n.   **C:**   Ben ik w*ee:*r.
            (1.2)   (1.2)
     A: Yea:h.   **A:**   Ja:.

It becomes clearer and clearer that there is a very strong preference for both answerer and caller to self-identify in their first turns at talk. When callers do not mention their names, they still tend to give strong cues and clues as to who they are, for instance, by marking the callback. Moreover, this is only the case when callers belong to the very restricted class of "potential and recognizable callers," for example close relatives. Interestingly enough, however, the fact that one belongs to this restricted class does not mean that one will necessarily use a voice sample.

Variant cases

We now come to the remaining cases which do not fit into the suggested typology. First, we have:

10.14   PtH:32 ((call to a colleague, who expects this call))

     A: Jus'a m*o*:ment.   **A:** 'n O:genblikje.
        (.)   (.)
     C: Yeah,   **C:** Ja,
        (19.6)   (19.6)
     A: Yeah- P*ee*:t?   **A:** Ja- P*ee*:t?
     C: HHH(h)eh heh Ohw.   **C:** HHH(h)eh heh Ohw.
        HEh .Hh Eh: 'at   HEh .Hh Eh: 'om
        tw*e*lve o'clock.   twaluf uur.
     A: Tw*e*lve o'clock.   **A:** Tw*a*alf uur.

Opening up the call by saying "Jus'a m*o*:ment" indicates that answerer is not available yet. This first utterance is responded to by caller's "Yeah", offering answerer a voice sample only. And as it turns out later on, answerer has recognized Peet as the person who has produced this "Yeah."

To turn to another case:

10.15   PtH:41 ((the conversationalists had earlier arranged to call))

A:	*Broo:d?*		**A:**	*Broo:d?*
C:	*Hu:h?*		**C:**	*He:?*
	(.)			(.)
A:	*Yea:h, I just got in.*		**A:**	*Ja:, ik kom net binne.*
C:	⌈O:k ay		**C:**	⌈O:k ee
A:	⌊That-is (.) I was		**A:**	⌊Dat-is (.) ik stond
	was just gonna call you.			op 't punt je te belle.

It is not entirely clear what is really going on here. Possibly caller has not
heard the ringing of the telephone before answerer picks up the receiver.
This might be concluded from caller's surprised "*Hu:h?*" after hearing
answerer self-identifying. And answerer seems to give an account when
he replies: "*Yea:h, I just got in*", and "*That-is (.) I was just gonna call
you.*" But since it is not clear, we may simply note for present purposes
that caller has not self-identified, yet is nevertheless recognized by
answerer. In that respect, this fragment might have been looked on as
belonging to the category of expectable answerer self-identifying, caller
providing voice sample, which is recognized by answerer.

Finally I will examine two fragments together:

10.16   PtH:28 ((C is the telephone operator of the answerer's office))

A:	*Van Hoeve.*		**A:**	*Van Hoeve.*
	(.)			(.)
C:	*I've got uh Henk*		**C:**	*Ik heb hier-eh Henk Menken*
	Menken here on the			*voor je onder de witte phone*
	for y⌈*ou.*			*kn*⌈*op.*
A:	⌊*Th*anks.		**A:**	⌊*Bedankt.*

10.17   PtH:133 ((colleague, with whom answerer has worked all day))

A:	*Jelgersma?*		**A:**	*Jelgersma?*
	(.)			(.)
C:	*Your cOAt's here.*		**C:**	*Je jAs hangt hier.*
A:	*Ohw-. I'll come*		**A:**	*Ohw-. (Die) kom ik even*
	and get it.			*ha:le.*

In these two fragments, callers do not self-identify but start talking to the
topic right after answerers' self-identifications. This talk constitutes a
voice sample for the answerer, but, what is more, the talk itself gives a

clue to caller's identification. If at the beginning answerer does not know whom he is talking to, he should know by then. The caller of 10.16, who is the secretary of answerer's institute, has a typical "telephone operator message." Caller of 10.17 is well known to answerer since the two of them have been working together all day. And when answerer's coat is at some identifiable and shared "here," answerer has simply to locate "here" in order to identify caller.

Conclusion

The aim of this chapter has been to address the question of whether Dutch telephone calls have the same types of opening sequences as calls in American English. As noted, American calls begin with a summons–answer sequence, which is overtly addressed to the openness of the channel, confirming the availability of "an attentive ear and mouth ready to speak" as Schegloff has pointed out. The answer also constitutes a voice sample, to be recognized by caller, and there follows a sequence which addresses issues of identification for co-participants.

We have seen that Dutch callers proceed quite differently. Unlike American calls, Dutch openings display few instances of an answer to the summons as their first turn, which should be used for caller to recognize answerer as such. As we have seen, this happens in only 5 out of 87 cases. Of all these answerers, 78 say "This is so-and-so speaking" or "Hello, it's so-and-so" in first turn. They self-identify in first turn, and this utterance is the first part of the identification sequence, as is common in more formal American settings such as the police calls studied by Zimmerman (1984), in service calls more generally (Schegloff 1967, 1968), and in a wide range of telephone calls in business settings (Boden, forthcoming). This procedure explicitly informs the caller as to the person he or she has reached, and does so with just the methodic and efficient interaction consequences of these Dutch data. The result is that the second turn in the opening section of Dutch calls is then the caller's own self-identification. So what we get as the very first sequence is:

> ((ringing of the telephone))
> **answerer:** self-identification   "This is Jan."
> **caller:**   self-identification   "This is Tom."

The fact that Dutch calls do not start off with a single answer to the summons does not mean, of course, that the summons, that is, the ringing of the telephone is not answered. It is done by means of the first identification utterance which stands as a second pair part to the initial summons, whereas American calls start off with a simpler summons– answer sequence which initiates identification in a less rigorous manner (that is, through voice sample). Dutch calls start off with a self-identification component, which "additionally" does opening-work.

The second important difference is that whereas American personal calls exhibit a preference for recognition by voice sample alone, Dutch calls show a marked preference for explicit self-identification. The cross-cultural ramifications of this have yet to be analyzed; clearly, a number of European countries alone have similar, but not identical, identification formats.

Related to this, there is a third difference: whereas in the USA there is a large class of potential personal callers who make use of a voice sample only, this class is very restricted in domestic telephone calls in the Netherlands. This is notably shaped by call recipient's self-identification, but merits close consideration. In the Netherlands, only spouses and other close relatives use voice sample alone, and even they do not always do so.

In closing, it is worth noting that the suggestion that there are cultural differences with respect to conversational practices opens a number of interesting considerations for conversation analytic research. In particular, I wish to suggest that different cultures may have different solutions to solve the "unproblematic problem" of opening a telephone conversation and of making clear who is speaking. These cultural differences are, in turn, interesting in that while conversational mechanisms of talk apply, as Sacks, Schegloff and Jefferson (1974), most accurately predicted, to "any conversation" across both language and culture (cf. Moerman 1977; Boden 1983; Schegloff 1987a; Ren 1989), their particular and local production may also achieve interesting cultural differences that enhance our understanding of how the machinery of talk is *both* context-free and context sensitive. The enabling institution (see Schegloff, chapter 3 above) of talk can thus be seen to consequentially facilitate and even fashion achieved issues that are conventionally characterized as "social" or "cultural."

In Dutch society, for example, people who do not self-identify in answering their home telephones are considered to be generally impolite or uneducated. Dutch callers have the expectation, manifested throughout the foregoing data and discussion, to be unambiguously informed as to who they are talking to as they place a telephone call.[7] The American assumption of voice recognition is not played out in Holland, where people assume that they will not be so recognized. Lack of recognition, even between close family members, leads to embarrassment and we may thus have a striking Dutch example of some of Goffman's classic concerns, played out here in rich empirical detail (cf. Schegloff 1988a). Indeed, Dutch telephone interactants often provide more self-identification cues even than necessary. Thus, while the Dutch *over*-identify themselves, Americans offer *minimal* recognition cues. Similarly, Dutch openings have the added interactional consequence of providing a preferred level of address, by nickname, first name only, last name only, marital status, or full title, as, for instance, in: "This is Maggie," "Margaret here," "Friedman," "Ms Friedman," or "Dr Friedman." American openings leave such conversational matching ambiguous.

The larger question, then, is whether this difference in telephone openings suggests that it is a more general difference between American and Dutch culture which has shaped such delicate yet mundane issues as identification in everyday telephone interaction? The answer clearly lies outside this small study. Based on this data, we might speculate, however, that Dutch people are both less ambiguous and more formal about the local accomplishment of social position as a conversational matter, and that absence of such status information is problematic in the Netherlands in ways it is not in the United States.[8] While some variation of formality is clearly indicated in this study, it would be premature to conclude larger cultural and social-cultural differences between the Netherlands and the United States simply on the basis of telephone call openings. The complexity of such issues remains to be resolved. What is evident from this study is that the interactional resolution of an everyday technical problem such as telephone openings is a matter of both local and cultural variation, and that, in the final analysis, culture is, after all, a matter of members' achievement.

Notes

This paper was made possible by the Netherlands Organization for the Advancement of Pure Research (ZWO). An earlier version was presented at the Talk and Social Structure Conference. I wish to thank Gail Jefferson for her inspiration and helpful comments on earlier drafts. I also wish to thank Paul ten Have for his comments and suggestions.

1 Since the ringing of the telephone, i.e. the summons, plays a key part in the discussion that follows, I have added it to all my data fragments although it was not recorded on the tape.
2 As Berens (1981) shows, the same holds for West Germany.
3 Especially in telephone calls between friends and relatives, one often finds a

series of utterances which look like greetings, as in the following conversation
between sisters:

> **R:**   This is Reina de W*i*nd?
> **B:** → Hell*o:*, it's Bren.
> **R:** → Hey hell*o:*=
> **B:** → =IIi:.=
> **R:** → =Hi:.

In fact these utterances are rather complicated in terms of what work they are
doing in these openings. Although they have not been analyzed yet, it may be
suggested that the two hello's are treated by the co-participants as objects of
recognition, rather than as greeting-objects. Since a "hello" or a "Hi" may be
treated both as a recognition object and as a greeting object, we may find a
different number of such utterances:

> **A:**   De Vr*ie*s.
> **C:** → Hi:, it's Anneke.
> **A:** → Hello Anneke.
> **C:** → Hi:. ((reason for calling))

> **A:**   W*aloo:*rd
> **C:** → Hi Dad. It's Wilfred.=
> **A:** → =Hi: son.=
> **C:**   Have you got a day off today?

4   Another way to show such a preference would be to show a normative
    orientation to one or the other option on the part of the participants
    themselves. Such an analysis may be carried out on another occasion.
5   We may provisionally say that openings do not run off quickly and fluently:
    (a) when the answerer is not the person called, e.g. as in the second fragment in
    10.1, where there is a silence of 0.7 of a second; (b) when answerer provides a
    business name, and caller recognizes answerer's personal identity from voice,
    for example:

> **A:**   Medical Committee Netherlands Ang*o*la:.
>   (0.5)
> **C:**   Hi Ge:rard, it's Fr*a:*ns.

(c) when answerer provides voice sample only, as in fragments 10.5–6 and
10.13. In 10.13 the silence is 1.2 of a second. See also Schegloff, chapter 3
above, and the introduction, chapter 1.)

6   If we take fragments of the following kind

> **A:**   This is Reina de W*i*nd?
> **C:**   Hell*o:*, it's Bren.

it is not always clear whether or not there is a tiny silence (i.e. shorter than 0.3 second as indicated by a " (.)" in these fragments) between caller's "Hell*o:*" and "it's Bren." If there is a micro-pause, this may be caused by the fact that the two parts of the turn have different intonation contours, which together constitute such a pause, which can then be looked upon as a syntactic pause. The question is whether one should see such a pause as doing interactional work, i.e. as a place for answerer to do recognition on the basis of the "Hello" voice sample. One might say that there are things which have been identified by some researchers as micro-pauses, and analyzed as possible opportunities for co-participant activities, which in fact are an integral part of a standard intonation contour. Successive utterances like "Hell*o:*, it's Bren." may therefore be seen as a single action, in which the phenomenon identified as a "pause" constitutes part of the proper intonation contour for that action.

7   My brother, who has lived in Australia now for two years, still complains that Australians are impolite in not self-identifying.

8   It is my impression, for instance, that Americans meeting face-to-face proceed more informally than do Dutch interactants. Even in face-to-face settings, Americans do not self-identify, while Dutch people routinely provide their names as they also shake hands.

11

Conversation-in-a-Series

Graham Button

Introduction

This chapter is concerned with how aspects of the organization of talk-in-interaction have a bearing on the organization of one domain of social structure: social relationships. It examines a way in which a current conversation is organized as one in a series of conversations and how, through this specific mechanism, a relationship is achieved or reachieved between the participants that they may use to structure some parts of their conduct. The relationship is described as a "standing relationship,"[1] and the conduct it is relevant for is the initiation of closings in conversation.

In their consideration of the closing section of conversation, Schegloff and Sacks (1973) indicated how, in "bounding off" some topic for conversation, a co-participant might be presented with a "free turn" in which he or she could initiate closings. This chapter will explicate how the organization of junctures within a topic-in-progress can provide a sequential environment that can facilitate *either* the initiation of closings or of a new topic. It will describe how *arrangements* may be oriented to as a "special status topic" that is specifically used to place the conversation on a closing track, in contrast to other ways of providing for closing initiation. Using arrangements as a method for placing conversation on a closing track constitutes a sense of social relationship between the speakers that they, in turn, orient to in the organization of closing their exchange. Thus, an aspect of social structure – social relations – can be seen, in part, to be the local achievement of the organization of talk-in-interaction.

Topic Organization and Closing Initiation

Over the course of a number of analyses, reference has been made to activities which are closing implicative.[2] It appears that these activities have a common organizational feature in that all, in accomplishing some local task, may also organize a "juncture" within a topic-in-progress. That is to say, conversationalists may accomplish a local activity such as, for example, an assessment, but in doing so they may also attend to the organization of a topic "as a whole." This can be seen for the following five types of activities.

1   Holding over prior activities

The first activity to be considered is where the participants "hold over and preserve," in subsequent turns, some prior activity.

11.1   (NB:III:1:15)

```
1   Fran:       Ah-ee- Well that's why I said I'm
2               not making any commen⌈ts about anybu:ddy
3   Ted:                              ⌊mkhm
4   Ted:        deh Ye::a::h ⌈hhh
5   Fran:   →                ⌊Y:::⌈:a:::h.
6   Ted:                          ⌊Yea::h.
```

11.2   (Lerner:SF:II:26:26–27)

```
1   Mark:       .hhhhh We:ll ah:::nm (.) yihkno:w
2               maybe:: uh:, hh maybe something'll come
3               up.=
4   Bob:    →   =Yeh maybe something'll develop,
5   Mark:   →   .hhh Yes. hh
```

11.3   (NB)

```
1   Portia:     Becuz they would really be the spring.
2               Lets ⌈see that's twunny fi dollars, that's
3   Agnes:           ⌊Yeah
4   Portia:  →  uh eight dollars, cheap
```

5	**Agnes:**	→	.hhh *Darn* cheap.
6	**Portia:**	→	( ), sixteen *do*llars.
7	**Agnes:**	→	((soft)) 's Wonderful.

In all three extracts some activity or set of activities are preserved in subsequent turns. In 11.1 Fran's formulation of her talk (lines 1–2) receives affirmation from Ted (line 3). The affirmation is held over by both Fran and Ted for two subsequent turns. In 11.2 Mark's optimistic conclusion (lines 1–2) is agreed to by Bob and then affirmed in his recycling part of Mark's utterance. Mark subsequently agrees to and affirms this. In 11.3 Agnes's second assessment to Portia's assessment (line 4) is held over in Portia's correction of eight dollars to sixteen dollars; Agnes still affirms her previous assessment even in the light of the corrected price.

By holding over and preserving some prior activities, participants may orient to talk on that topic as being possibly exhausted. They may display this orientation through the possible *initiation of closings*. Thus the extracts 11.1, 11.2 and 11.3 continue like this:[3]

(NB:III:1:15)

Ted:		Yea::h.
Fran:		.hhh A::lrighty.
Fran:	→	Well ah'll give yih call before we decide
		tih come down. Ok:⌈y?
Ted:		⌊Oka:y
Fran:		*Aw::*righty::.
Ted:		Oka⌈y
Fran:		⌊Wil- see y'then,
Ted:		Oka⌈y
Fran:		⌊*Bye* b⌈ye
Ted:		⌊Bye

(Lerner: SF:II:26–27)

Mark:		.hhh Yes. hh
		(0.4)
( ):		.hhh
Mark:		⌈( )⌉
Bob:	→	⌊A*l*ri ⌋ght Mark.

(NB)

| **Agnes:** | | ((soft)) 's Wonderful. |
| | | (0.6) |

Agnes: →   .hhh ALRIGHT HONEY, I JUS' THOUGHT I CALL
               YOU ONE more time,

2 Formulating summaries

Notice that extract 11.1 involves "formulating"[4] part of the prior
conversation: "*th*at's why I *s*aid I'm not making any comments about
anybu:ddy" (see p. 252). Formulations may also be used to manage the
topic "as a whole." For instance, in formulating what has been said, a
participant may be oriented-to as providing some sort of "summary" of
what has been said:

11.4   (WPH:5)

Jack: He doesn't like you very much.
Phil: →   We::ll what I've been saying to *you* for
              the last ten minutes is that *I* don't like
              him. Yeah?
Jack: →   Uh-huh.

Phil's formulation of part of the prior conversation targets his run of talk
and thereby offers a summary of that talk "as a whole."

This sequential possibility can also be observed with respect to an
activity that was also involved in 11.2: providing an "optimistic
conclusion"[5] to the topic-in-progress. This can be seen in 11.5, which
follows. Here A projects a possible conclusion to some troubles – the
topic-in-progress – in the form of an optimistic conclusion offered as a
possible outcome of the troubles.

11.5   (SBL:2:6:11)

B: You know, its just like bringin the blood up.
A: →   Yeah well, things uh always work out for the best
B: Oh, certainly

Assessments, as in 11.3 above, can also provide a summary of, or
conclusion to, a topic-in-progress. In fragment 11.6 below, B's assessment
that the weather is too hot offers a conclusion to the prior talk by trying
to settle the matter of whether or not to play tennis.

11.6   (SBL:2:1:8:11)

> A: I'll see what I c'n *do*.
> B: →   I think its too hot to work anyhow.
> A: Yeah. Well I just feel pokey too.

Co-participants may orient to the possible offer (contained in the summary or conclusion) that talk on the topic-in-progress could be concluded, by at least agreeing, or receipting it, or in the case of assessments, by providing a second assessment that may broadly concur with the first assessment.[6] Notice that Jack in 11.4 marks the receipt of the formulation; that B in 11.5 agrees to the optimistic conclusion; and that in 11.6 A agrees and offers a second assessment that affirms B's prior assessment. Thus, in formulating, providing an optimistic conclusion, and in providing an assessment, one speaker may engage in an activity that summarizes or concludes, and thus offers a possible conclusion to the topic-in-progress. Next speaker may orient to the summarizing or concluding character of these activities. Over the course of two turns at talk, participants may display to one another that talk on the topic-in-progress may possibly be complete and consequentially initiate closings. Here are the continuations of 11.4, 11.5 and 11.6:

(WPH:5)

> Phil: →   We::ll what I've been saying to *you* for the
>   →   last ten minutes is that *I* don't like him.
>   →   Yeah?
> Jack: →   Uh-huh
> Phil: →   Okay Jack
> Jack: Okay
> Phil: By⌈e
> Jack: ⌊Goodbye.

(SBL:2:6:11)

> A: →   Yeah well, things uh always work out for
>   →   the best
> B: →   Oh, certainly
> B: →   Alright, ⌈Bea
> A: ⌊Uh huh, okay,
> B: G'bye
> A: Goodnight

(SBL·2:1:8:11)

A:		I'll see what I c'n *do*.
B:	→	I think its too hot to work anyhow.
A:	→	Yeah. Well I just feel pokey too.
B:	→	Okay, fine
A:		Alright, I'll uh I'll letch know.
B:		Well, alright, i- i- don't uh if you don't
		get a quorum, why don't worry,
A:		Okay,
B:		A(h)righty
A:		⌈⌈Alrighty
B:		⌊⌊Bye
A:		Bye

3 Projecting future activities

Co-participants may also conclude some topic-in-progress by projecting
that some future activity is relevant:

11.7   (SBL:3:7)

A:		She works in the after⌈noon, so that- that's out=
B:		⌊In the afternoon.
A:		=I guess,
B:		Mmhm, Yeah,
A:		⌈⌈Uh huh,
B:		⌊⌊(Well that lets me out)
B:	→	Well uh, I'll try an' get ahold of Dorothy,
A:		Okay honey you uhm uh I'll- I'll call 'er
		anyway so I c'n check 'er off, but I just
		thought maybe that if you had time you
		might ask 'er.
B:		Yeah. uh-uh huh,

11.8   (JG:I:6:2)

P:	→	hI .hh Well anyway I'll tell uh *A*ce then
		that ou uh you, if you ken make it you'll
		be down.
M:		Yeah.=

11.9   (MC:II:2:13–14)

Reg: Well thank you very much ⌈(fer whatcher doing)
Lila: →   ⌊We'll go ahead,
        →   en I'm sure she'll get in touch with you
        →   about the ti:me.
Reg: Yah.

In these instances, the participants have been involved in making
arrangements (involving a third, nonpresent person). By providing for
some activity to be undertaken in the future, a speaker may offer a
possible resolution to the arrangements and thereby furnish a resource for
finding that talk on arrangement-making could possibly be concluded.
Next speakers may orient to this possibility by agreeing to the resolution.
Thus, again, over the course of two turns[7] at talk, participants may also
display to one another that the topic-in-progress could be possibly
concluded. The next speaker may orient to this by possibly initiating a
closing section, see these continuations of 11.7, 11.8 and 11.9:

(SBL:3:7)

B: →   Yeah. Uh-uh huh,
A: →   O⌈kay,
B: ⌊Okay, okay well I will we'll see you,
A: Okay ⌈dear
B: ⌊Bye
A: Bye.

(JG:I:6:2)

M: →   Yeah.=
P: =Okay yuh Mark

(MC:II:2:14]

Reg: →   Yah.
Lila: →   ⌈⌈Okay,
Reg: ⌊⌊Okey doke.
Lila: Thank you ⌈Reg
Reg: ⌊Thankyou ⌈Lila
Lila: ⌊Bye- bye

4 Announcement of closure

The next activity to be considered that involves the organization of a topic-in-progress and the initiation of closings may operate as a pivot between on-topic talk and closing initiation. It is where one participant may "announce closure" by marking it explicitly:

11.10 (SBL:3:5:10)

<pre>
G: (Well I'll think about that.)
M: An' then Marcia call; me about another
     →   meeting but I'll haftuh letche go.
G: →   hhh .hh! O:: ⌈kay,
M: ⌊Okay thanks ⌈Ginny,
G: ⌊Alright,
M: By::e
G: Bye.
</pre>

11.11 (JG:Reel 3:15:10–11)

<pre>
A: . . . an god damn she got the cigaretts an
             (⌈   )that's
B: ⌊oh:::.
A: murder Pat.
B: →   I know it. I know it. Well listen Jim
     →   I'll let you go an I'll talk to you later.
A: →   Okay Pat.
B: Take it easy.
A: Yeah ⌈Bye.
B: ⌊Okay.
</pre>

In extracts 11.10 and 11.11 participants begin their utterances on the topic-in-progress, (in 11.10 this is marked by "and," and in 11.11 through an agreement to a prior assessment). The speaker then moves on, within the same turn, to propose that the conversation could possibly be complete by providing an announcement of closure. By announcing closure, a participant may possibly suspend the topic-in-progress, and next speaker may orient to this possibility by initiating a closing section.

5 Arrangement reintroduction

Finally, an arrangement item or component may be "reintroduced." This may be done where an arrangement has been marked as having been made previously in the conversation (for example, by using a component such as "anyway" to position and tie an utterance into a prior, though not immediately prior, utterance) but where that arrangement has not been the immediately prior topic for the conversation. In 11.12 and 11.13 below, the arrangement item that is reintroduced restates the time of the proposed meeting:

11.12   (Rahman:A:2:JA(9):5)

```
J:          I mean there wz only Su:s'n who wz et the
            age sohrt of h .hh who'd of been left in
            the house ⌈et (.) on 'er ow:n.
A:                    ⌊Ye:s.
                 (0.3)
A:          Mm:,
                 (0.4)
A:          ⌈⌈Yes,
J:    →     ⌊⌊A:nyway. .hh:
A:    →     ⌈⌈(Ah'll seh-)
J:    →     ⌊⌊I'll see you inna few min⌈utes then.
A:                                     ⌊See you inna
            few min⌈utes.
J:               ⌊.hh
J:          O⌈kay Ann⌉ B ⌈uh bye,
A:           ⌊'ka:y  ⌋   ⌊Bye:.
```

11.13   (JG:II:2:36)

```
M:          's a nice luxury ye:s I can't remember its
            been so long ag(hhh)o hn-uh-uh.
G:          (      )
M:          .kh ⌈hhhh
G:              ⌊But!t- I'll give yih ca::ll? en nuh:::::=
M:    →     =hhh Okay Gene well then gimme a call in
      →     the nex' couple oh weeks en the:n:: uh::
      →     .hh yih know we'll see wuh we c'n work
      →     ou:t.
G:    →     Grea:t.
M:    →     .t Awri:ght⌈y?
G:                    ⌊Okay Maggi⌈e
M:                               ⌊O ⌈kay  love⌉
G:                                  ⌊wil see yuh⌋ then
            yeah.
M:          Right. Bye ⌈bye
G:                     ⌊Bye.
```

Reintroducing arrangements may, thus, be used to move from talk on some topic into closings. But notice that the arrangement items that are reintroduced have the same status as the items that were previously seen in 11.7, 11.8 and 11.9 to be the outcome or resolution of arrangement making. Through reiteration, arrangement items achieve their "closure" character.

All of the sequences and activities considered above operate to organize the course of a topic-in-progress "as a whole" by providing for the topic to be understood to be either exhausted, concluded or suspended. They operate in such a way that over the course of a number of turns at talk participants may display to one another that they are not elaborating or continuing a topic-in-progress. In this respect, participants may collaboratively organize talk on a topic as being possibly "shut down," or "capped-off" and may thereby organize a juncture in a topic-in-progress. Thus it would appear that over the course of a sequence of talk (where one participant engaged in one of the activities described, and next speaker returns in an affiliating, agreeing or affirmative fashion, or where some elaboration or expansion of that might take place) speakers may, as a collaborative matter, organize a topic-in-progress as being possibly complete. Next speakers to affiliative, agreeing or affirmative activities may, intelligibly, initiate a closing section. The organization of a juncture within a topic in progress, thus, also provides the sequential opportunity for the intelligible initiation of the suspension of the conversation.

Topic Organization and Conversation Continuation

These junctures, however, may also provide the sequential opportunity for the intelligible production of activities other than closing initiation. In marked contrast to closing initiations, these activities seem to provide instead for conversation continuation. Two specific activities are relevant in this regard: (1) collaboratively organizing the initiation of a further topic for the conversation, and (2) initiating the particular topic of arrangements in a seemingly unilateral fashion. Both implicate conversation continuation.

Initiating further topics

Sacks has described how a methodic way in which topics in conversation are organized provides for some subsequent topics to a first topic to flow from one to another.[8] However, as described elsewhere (Button and Casey, 1984, 1985), at certain places in conversation the mechanisms that organize a flow of topics may not be used. Rather, the initiation of a new topic may, in these places, be done using certain sequence structures that provide for the collaborative initiation of a new topic over the course of a number of turns at talk.[9] One of these places is organized through bounding off or capping off a topic in progress, and one of the sequences that may be used to collaboratively initiate a possible new topic is a "topic initial elicitor sequence" (Button and Casey 1984). So, for some of the sequences that have been examined above, it is possible to find that not only may they be followed by activities that may initiate a closing section, they may also be followed by turns at talk that provide for the possible initiation of a new topic.[10] This can be seen in the extracts below.

11.14　　(WPH:17)

　　E:　　. . . . and I don't think block board would wo::rk
　　　　　there.
　　P:　　No::
　　E:　　→No:::
　　　　　　　　　　(0.5)
　　E:　　→Uhm:::. So, anything new with you.

11.15　　(NB:IV:13:2)

　　A:　　.hh Oh the kids cried, they wan' duh stay
　　　　　on she *did* have liddle stuff *pa:*cked. But,
　　　　　uh, .hhh *I*: s:uh we got up at five thirdy
　　　　　en left her et six yesterday so uh Guy ⌈had tuh=
　　P:　　　　　　　　　　　　　　　　　　　⌊Yuh
　　A:　　→=work, I guess I told yuh that.
　　P:　　→Yea:th uh ⌈huh
　　A:　　→　　　　⌊What's new with *you*

11.16　　(WPH:21)

　　E:　　.hhh it seem we jus can't sell it.
　　L:　　But its in goo::d *cond*ition isn't it?
　　E:　　Oh:: yes its *first* class.
　　L:　　→Well I'm sure it'll all work out ⌈then,
　　E:　　→　　　　　　　　　　　　　　⌊Mhm. Lets
　　　　　→hope so.
　　　　　　　　　　(0.5)
　　E:　　→Anything new for *you* to report?

11.17   (NB:II:1:4)

A: →(Ih) was too depre⌈ssing
B: →   ⌊Oh::::: it is
      →te::rruhble-=
B: →=What's *new*

In 11.14 P's agreement with E's assessment is *held over* in the two subsequent turns. Neither participant takes up the opportunity to develop on the topic-in-progress that this holding over may provide for, and they may thus display to one another that talk on the topic is exhausted. At this juncture, as previously noted (for 11.1), a participant may initiate a closing section for the conversation. Here, however, P provides for the possibility of initiating a new topic, instead of initiating a closing.

In 11.15 A's *formulation* (of her prior talk as being something which she has told P before) receives confirmation from P. Following this sequence of formulation and confirmation, where again the topic-in-progress may be orientable to as being possibly concluded, A attempts to elicit a possible topic initial from P, rather than initiating a closing. In 11.16 L's *optimistic conclusion* is followed by E's affirmation, again providing a reciprocal display that the topic-in-progress is possibly concluded. But, following this, E provides for a possible topic initial utterance, instead of initiating closing. In 11.17 A's *assessment* of some troubles and B's confirming second assessment also provides a possible summary of the troubles. However, rather than this being an occasion to initiate closing, it is used to elicit a possible new topic in the subsequent turn.

The sequential organization of a juncture within a topic-in-progress may thus be used by a speaker possibly to elicit the initiation of a new topic. Consequently, sequences that organize a juncture in a topic-in-progress provide the occasion to either: (1) initiate closings, or (2) collaboratively initiate some new topic.

Unilaterally initiating the topic of arrangements

There is a further possibility. A *particular* topic may be initiated in an apparently unilateral manner, as in the case of arrangements:[11]

11.18   (WPH:18)

     E: Life's a bitch.
     B: Yeah isn't.
     E: →   Yeah,
     B: →   Uhm
     E: →   So, are you goin Thursday?
     B: Natch.

11.19   (WPH:14)

     E: PROUST IN HIS FIRST ⌈BOOK. ((singing))
     J: ⌊Heh heh(hh)heh, I kn(h)ow,
                    I know.
     E: PROUST I(h)N 'IS FIRST BOOK!
     J: →   You know what we've been talkin 'bout. HUMOUR.
     E: →   You bet.
                        (0.5)
     J: →   So::: you all set for Thursday?
                        (0.2)
     E: I've ironed my fli(h)ghts.

11.20   (JG:I(S):X15:6)

     P: →   .hhh But *I* think it'll *i*ron itself out,
     M: →   *I* sure hope ⌈so.
     P: →   ⌊I'll *see* you *Tues*day.

In 11.18 E's description of "life's course" is agreed to by B, and is *held over* in the two subsequent turns. With the topic-in-progress possibly exhausted, E initiates a new topic that pertains to their meeting for an event they are both going to. In 11.19 J's *formulation* that the talk has been about humour is agreed to by E and following this sequence of formulation and agreement that may provide a conclusion to the topic-in-progress, J initiates talk on making arrangements to meet, for, as it happens, just the same event that B and E in the previous example are going to. P's optimistic conclusion in 11.20 receives confirmation from M, and again the summary or concluding character of this sequence for the topic-in-progress is followed by an arrangement item.

In sum, a juncture in a topic-in-progress may also provide for an opportunity for participants to move into the specific topic of making personal arrangements. It appears that three organizational structures can be identified which provide, in turn, for three alternative activities: (1) the initiation of a closing sequence, (2) the initiation of the collaborative development of a new topic, and (3) the unilateral initiation of the particular topic of arrangements.

Conversation Continuation and Conversation Closure

Each of the activities are *methodic* possibilities in the sequential environment that is occasioned for next turns by the organization of a topic-in-progress. This is due to the sequential implications each has in relation to the general activity of initiating closings in conversation. This relationship has already been explicated with respect to actual closing initiation in the section on "topic organization and closing initiation" above, but it can also be explicated with respect to the collaborative provision of a new topic, as well as for unilateral initiation of the particular topic of arrangements, even though, on the face of it, these activities may involve conversation continuation, rather than closing.

The collaborative production of a new topic

As noted, one way a topic may be collaboratively initiated in the sequential environment of the shutting down or capping off of a topic-in-progress is through the use of a "topic initial eliciting" sequence (Button and Casey 1984). A feature of this sequence is that participants may initiate a new topic so as to display that the production of on-topic talk is a vehicle through which they may stay in conversation with one another. Topic initial elicitors may include components that mark out that any newsworthy event which is offered as a positive response to the enquiry may be a *further* topic for the conversation (Button and Casey 1984). Thus, notice that in extracts 11.14–17 examined above, speakers include components such as "news for you". In so doing, a speaker may mark out that any resulting talk on this newsworthy event may continue the conversation by now turning to co-participant's possible news. A feature of this orientation to co-participant's possible news is that closings may be initiated should co-participant decline to present a "newsworthy-event-report." This can be seen in the following extract, where C's negative response which declines to provide a possible topic initial is used by M as an occasion to possibly initiate a closing section.

11.21 (SB:6)

M:		Crust bread's the tops.
C:		I luv it.
		(0.5)
M:	→	Anything new for *you*
C:	→	Uhm (0.5) Nope.
M:	→	Uhm .hh Okay::y.
C:		Alwr::ght and thanks fer ringin,
M:		Glad I gottcha.
C:		'Kay by:⌈e,
M:		⌊Bye Colin.

Initiating arrangements

Arrangements in conversation may also be observed to be organizationally related to the possibility of closing initiation. This is because participants display an orientation to arrangements as a "special status topic" for conversation. This status derives from the fact that arrangements are used in the *overall organization* of their interaction together.

Two activities are relevant here. First, arrangement initiating turns routinely include components that position them in relation to other topics, thus providing for them as having a "known-in-advance" status. Second, again routinely, arrangements occupy a particular place in conversation as *the last topic* (Schegloff and Sacks 1973). More cogently, they are organized *so as to be* the last topic in the conversation.

First, arrangements may be initiated so as to place them with respect to other topics for conversation. This may be done by placing (as described by Schegloff and Sacks 1973) positioning markers in the turn initial position of the arrangement initial turn. Common components are "so," "well," and varieties of "wells" such as "well now," or "well listen":

11.22 (RAH:C:2:JSA918):9)

J:		No I've gotta *pimple* on my chin en *one* on my eyebrow so ah ha⌈h ha
A:		⌊O*h*:::: deeuh.
J:	→	.hheh *Nevuh* mind. .h So ah'll c- ah'll *come* et u- well (.) yih know it. I'm *easy* you- you come round

11.23   (TG:27–28)

B: They were (0.2) t: dec:ding,
A: Y⌈eh.
B: →   ⌊Mmmn. Tch: .hh *WE*:ll, hmfhtch=
B: →   ⌈⌈*Al*wright so,
A: →   ⌊⌊Well if you *wan'* me tu give you a ring
             tomorrow morning.
B: →   Tch: .hh *we*:ll y- y know, ...

11.24   (JG:I:10:6–7)

R: Oh my ⌈heaven's on earth.
S: ⌊Yeah.
S: →   ⌈⌈Yeah
R: →   ⌊⌊.hhh Well now whadabout *Thurs*day. You
       →   think they'be open on Thurs⌈dee
S: ⌊(W') I think
             so. I think so.

11.25   (SBL)

D: I'm sure he does.
B: Mm hm
D: →   Well listen Bea, I'll probably see you
             Sunday then.
B: ⌈(Alright)
D: ⌊But I was *so* anxious . . . .

Of interest here is that, in initiating a topic as a general class of
conversational activity, participants may bring a particular topic to their
conversation which is constituted as *business* between them (Button and
Casey 1989). A methodic way in which its initiation may be provided for,
and on-topic talk organized, is to constitute the topic as having a known-
in-advance status between the participants and to then trade upon that
status as a warrant for its initiation "now." There are a number of ways in
which this may be done and which in their various forms accomplish
different, though related, activities. One way that is pertinent for the
present consideration is to use the opening section to *schedule* a topic for
later in the conversation (see 11.26). The opening section announces the
reason for call: J wants help in running his program. J, however, then
changes the shape of his turn by providing for E to orient her next turn to
what might be the matter with Colin, rather than the program problem.

11.26   (SB:4)

E:		Ha'lo.
J:		Hi Elsie, John here.
E:		Ah:: (0.2) so how are you.
J:	→	Fine, thanks=LOOK I rang to see if you
	→	could tell me how to run that fuckin
	→	progra::me, =but furst do you know what's
	→	the matter with Colin.
E:		Why?

Later, J is able to organize the initiation of the topic he has scheduled by invoking its known-in-advance status. That is, he is able to organize the initiation of the topic by displaying that he is turning to an item that both participants know in advance was upcoming. Notice that he uses a turn position marker "well" to locate the scheduled item in relation to prior talk:

(SB:4)

J:		Well he's stopped talkin tuh me and- we::ll
		he's just being off hand.
		. . .
E:		You know what he's like,
J:		Yeah. Ah PRICK.
E:		Hmhm
		(0.5)
J:	→	Well now lets get te(h)nic- technic⌈al.
E:		⌊Have
		you typed LOAD

Returning to the initiation of arrangements in conversation, note that conversationalists may organize the initiation of arrangements in a similar way. The turn position marker "well" in the example above displays an orientation to the known-in-advance character of the arrangement. Initiating arrangements in this way provides an account for their initiation. Thus, although participants may not schedule an arrangement as a topic for the conversation in the opening section, nevertheless, in the way in which it is initiated, they provide for that arrangement initiation *as if* it were scheduled. They thereby mark out the topic as if it were a *possibly known* topic for the conversation.

Initiating arrangements in this way displays an orientation to them as having a particular status for the conversation. Consequently, although arrangements between the participants may not be proposed as the reason for call, and although there may have been other topics for the conversation, initiating them thus marks them as if they had a known-in-advance status and provides for them as a topic that "this" conversation may take. Conversationalists may thus constitute any "this" conversation as one that can become one in which arrangements may be made.

The second observation was that arrangements are routinely organized *so as to be* the last topic for conversation. This may be done in several ways. First, by positioning arrangements as a topic that participants orient to, arrangements may possibly be the last topic for the conversation. Second, they may also give way to further topics for the conversation;[12] on these occasions, arrangements may be subsequently and systematically returned to in such a way that they become "the last thing talked to." Thus, it can be observed that the arrangement, or arrangement components, may be reintroduced as a method for moving off some other topic and into closing initiation. In extracts 11.13–15 it is just this activity that was being described.

Third, arrangements may figure in the actual closing section, once initiated. Previous discussions of closings (Button 1986, 1990) detailed how arrangement reintroduction (post a first close component) could be used retrospectively to account for a closing initiation. Hence, where the reintroduction of an arrangement component has not been used as a method for moving off a topic in progress and into closings (and where arrangements have been a prior, but not immediately prior, topic for the conversation), conversationalists are able to preserve arrangements, again as the last thing talked to.[13]

Finally, even where arrangements have not been a topic for the conversation, participants may introduce *arrangement tokens* that operate to display an orientation to the possibility of a further encounter. In the following extracts one participant moves off the topic-in-progress and possibly provides for closing initiation by referencing the possibility of a further encounter.

11.27   (OCS)

N:	He's paran*oid*.=
D:	=He's *definitely* paranoid.
N:	Yeah well- hhh
D:	Hm::::.
	(0.5)
N:	We::ll, look, I'll talk tuh y'later.
D:	Yeah, see yuh.
N: →	Okay, bye.

D: Okay,
N: Bye.

11.28   (WPH:7)

E: Its uh n*a*sty business, but it'll clear up,
            they always do.
H: Yeah, its the waiting though but I suppose
            yer r'ght.
                     (0.5)
E: → Oh we::ll (0.2), I'll no doubt bump into
     → yer' next we::k.
H: → Yeah. I'll see yuh sometime.
E: → Alrigh::t?
H: Alrighty::⌈:
E: ⌊Bye Henry
H: Take care, bye.

11.29   (SB:6)

B: Luv's labours lost.
E: → Aren't they always, well:: I'll be seein
            yeah.
B: → Okey doke.
E: Anything better to end on?
                     (0.5)
B: Uh::: hm, can't think of anything.

These arrangement tokens may be used in much the same way as arrangement components. They can pivot from on-topic talk into closings. In this respect, although arrangements may not have figured in the talk, nevertheless an orientation which arrangements display to a future encounter may also be displayed by an arrangement token which is used to provide for possible closing initiation.

This suggests that there are a number of arrangement-related activities that may be used to provide for the methodic initiation of a closing section. These are: (1) to provide for the resolution of an arrangement that has been a topic for the conversation; (2) to reintroduce an arrangement item where arrangements have not been the prior topic for the conversation; and (3) to introduce arrangement tokens. Furthermore, arrangements may attend to the overall management of conversation, for arrangements are, in effect, used to place the conversation on a *closing track*.

This latter point has to do with an orientation speakers may display towards "this" conversation as but one in a number of possible conversations or encounters between the participants: *conversation-in-a-series*. That is to say, the use of arrangement-related items to organize a "next" encounter provides for "this" conversation to be one in a series. This may be an obvious point with respect to talk that is designed to coordinate participants meeting one another, and for the reiteration of an arrangement to meet, but it can also be seen to be a feature of the use of arrangement tokens. As noticed above, the production of an arrangement token also displays an orientation to "this" present conversation being but one of others that the participants may possibly have. Consequently, if arrangements display and provide for this conversation as a conversation-in-a-series and for the organization of some future encounter, they may also provide for "this" conversation to relevantly close.

Thus far we have seen that following the relevant sequences initially described, a speaker may display an orientation to conversation continuation or closure. Closure may be provided for by placing the conversation on a closing track by introducing arrangement-related activities either in the form of initiating the topic of arrangements which, upon their resolution, provide a methodical occasion for the initiation of closings, or by reintroducing arrangement items, or by introducing arrangement tokens. Continuation may, instead, be done by attempting to provide for the possible initiation of a new topic, done in such a manner as to provide for its initiation to be a collaborative matter, and thus drawing a co-participant along with the speaker. So, should a co-participant decline, closing initiation may be legitimately done. The organization of a juncture in a topic-in-progress provides an occasion whereby conversationalists may collaborate in conversation continuation or place the conversation on a closing track. Arrangement-related activities initiated at this juncture then, seem to be a method for providing for the intelligible, warranted, and collaborative initiation of a closing section for the conversation.

A Method for Providing for Closing Initiation

The above description emphasizes how closing initiation may be organized with respect to arrangements, but, as noted earlier, participants may also organize the initiation of a closing section without using arrangements. This, too, may be done following activities that provide for a topic-in-progress to be recognizably complete. Thus, in examples 11.4–6 above, possible completion of the topic-in-progress is achieved by one conversationalist being able to intelligibly initiate a closing section without producing activities that place the conversation on a closing track. This observation can be strengthened by providing some more instances, which are drawn from a series of calls to the police:

11.30   (NP:I–2:4)

C: . . . I think I (0.5) checked at the department but
          I didn'tteh (0.5) ⌈say (I said) they were=
P: ⌊You (   )
C: ⌈⌈A big
P: → ⌊⌊No well I'll fill in a report Miss
    → Thompson and er thank you so much for
    → phoning.
C: → Okay, ⌈thanks⌉
P: ⌊Bye,   ⌋ now.
C: Bye.

11.31   (NP:XVI–23:28)

L: → Well I'm sure it'll all work out ⌈then,
A: .hh Oh the kids cried, they wan' ⌊duh stay
C: You'll be on the look out then, eh?
P: Yes we sure will.
C: (   ) I'll be lookin myself too.
P: → Thankyou, Mister Kottam.
C: → Thankyou very much sir.
P: → Bye now

In these instances the officer receiving the call specifies an activity to be undertaken and offers it as the outcome of the call. The officer then provides an appreciation of the call, following which closings are initiated or terminals produced. That is to say, in these extracts closings may be methodically provided for by displaying that the business of the call may be possibly complete. This may be done through offering an outcome of the call, or appreciating the call. Note that the initiation of closings is *not* provided for by the use of arrangement-related activities in order to place the conversation on a closing track.

This suggests that there may be different methods that participants may use to provide for the intelligible initiation of a closing section of their talk together. In noticing this it becomes possible to ask the following question: what are participants doing in providing for the initiation of closings in one way over another? In particular: what are participants doing in providing for the initiation of closings by posing arrangements to place the conversation on a closing track?

A number of answers to this question can be discounted. An answer does not reside in merely saying that for "this" interaction it was possible to make an arrangement because the participants had to meet, while for "that" interaction it was not. The reason for this is because, as has been noted on a number of occasions throughout this examination, even when arrangements have not been a topic for the conversation, participants may use arrangement tokens.

Also, an answer does not reside in merely proposing that what they say is organized in terms of assignable relationships between them. For example, friends use arrangements to close a conversation, strangers do not. The reason for this is that persons who may, in other ways, display themselves to be what could be called, for example, intimates, may not use arrangements to place the conversation on closing track (see 11.5 on p. 254 and its continuation on p. 255).

Rather, an answer to this question can be located in how participants display an orientation to one another in the use of arrangements to place the conversation on a closing track; how they constitute as relevant for their interaction achieved social relational categories. It is in using arrangements to place conversation on a closing track that participants may, as a collaborative matter over the course of their unfolding talk, or in the context of a single utterance, invoke as relevant, just then, and for just "whatever" contingent reasons, a particular relationship that may be used to organize their conversation as being possibly complete.

In using arrangements to place conversation on a closing track, participants may, in providing for some future conversation, and thereby providing for the present conversation as a conversation-in-a-series, testify to, elaborate upon and invoke as relevant a relationship between them that is "*standing*." This is not to say that conversationalists might be abstractly thought of as having a "standing" relationship, as if that were omnirelevant for their conversation, and as if that interactionally disembodied and attributed relationship itself structured and organized how they interacted with one another. Nor is it to say that conversationalists who might have this relationship attributed to them use arrangements to place conversation on a closing track. Rather, it is to say that in using arrangements to place conversation on a closing track they constitute at that juncture of their interaction a sense of what a "standing" relationship might be for them; they elaborate upon it and constitute it as relevant for their talk and conduct, *in* their talk and conduct.

A "standing" relationship becomes relevant for participants in that they may provide for the initiation of a closing section for their conversation by placing conversation on a closing track in such a way as to display an orientation to this relationship. Conversationalists may, thus, employ a method for providing for the initiation of a closing section which is to place conversation on a closing track. Using this method at the organized junctures in a topic-in-progress contrasts with moving straight into closing initiation. The use of this method to provide for closing initiation displays participants' orientation to a relationship that they invoke as being part of their now beginning to leave one another.

It is possible to see this understanding being displayed and made relevant at other places in conversation. For example, Sacks (in his 1972 lectures) has described how the opening section of conversation can be used by participants to "refind" one another. They may thus provide for the possibility of bringing one another up to date with respect to anything that could be news between them and which might have occurred since they last spoke. Here the interactants are making relevant for the organization of their conduct together a relationship which involves conversation-in-a-series.

Now, if examples 11.4–6 are returned to (pp. 254–5), then it might be possible to observe that participants are not using an understanding of their relationship as involving conversation-in-a-series to place the conversation on a closing track. Instead, they move straight into the initiation of a closing section. In 11.4 Jack and Phil have got into a wrangle with each other over a mutual acquaintance:

(WPH:5)

Jack:	He doesn't like you very much.
Phil:	We::ll what I've been saying to *you* for the last ten minutes is that *I* don't like him. Yeah?
Jack:	Uh-huh.
Phil:	Okay Jack
Jack:	Okay
Phil:	By⌈e
Jack:	⌊Goodbye

Initiating closings on the receipt of the formulation testifies to that wrangle being part of Phil's initiating the closing section "now."

In 11.5 the participants have been talking to the topic of B's current troubles.

(SBL:2:6:11)

B:	You know, its just like bringin th blood up.
A:	Yeah well, things uh always work out for the best
B:	Oh, certainly

Jefferson (1984b) has described how participants may get off a troubles telling through the organization of conversation termination. That is, she describes how participants may orient to a troubles telling in such a way that it constrains the introduction of other matters. Thus, initiating a closing section at the organized juncture in the topic-in-progress becomes a way of moving out of the troubles talk without first placing the conversation on a closing track or introducing or reintroducing other matters. If further troubles talk may be curtailed by initiating a closing section which provides for termination, as Jefferson describes, the very topic of a troubles telling may be oriented to by participants as possibly placing the conversation on a closing track. And, as with arrangements, a juncture within the topic-in-progress may be used to methodically initiate a closing section.

In this continuation of 11.6 an arrangement item that has previously figured in the talk is reintroduced in the second turn of the closing section.

(SBL:2:1:8:11)

```
A:   I'll see what I c'n do.
B:   I think its too hot to work anyhow.
A:   Yeah. Well I just feel pokey too.
B:   Okay, fine
A:   Alright, I'll uh I'll letch know.
B:   Well, alright, i- i- don't uh if you don't
     get a quorum, why don't worry,
A:   Okay,
B:   A(h)righty
A:   ⎡⎡Alrighty
B:   ⎣⎣Bye
A:   Bye
```

Arrangements in closings (Button 1986, 1990) organize a minimal movement out of those closings to produce a "longer-than-archetype" closing sequence. Although not terminal elicitive, an arrangement item is closing implicative, so that initiating a closing section at a juncture in the topic-in-progress is itself another method which provides for the systematic and warrantable production of a closing. In this case, an orientation to conversation-in-a-series also provides for an account of initiating closure. Due to the design of arrangements in closings, however, the reintroduction of any material (even arrangement items) may make possible the suspension of possible contingent organizations for continuing the conversation.

There may thus be a number of methods through which conversation-alists provide for the intelligible and warranted initiation of a closing section that may be coordinated at the organization of a juncture within a topic-in-progress. This discussion has focused on one where an orientation to conversation-in-a-series may invoke an "orientable to" category of relationship, as relevant for the conversation and for participants' conduct with one another. The chapter has also described how participants' understanding of relationships may be displayed and constituted in the actual details of talk and as relevant for the organization of conduct.

With respect to an understanding of the relationship between talk and social structure, it becomes possible to see that it is in the details of actual talk and conduct that participants constitute and achieve a relevant understanding of social structure for their talk and conduct. It is in the oriented-to methods that conversationalists use to bring off some activities that an understanding of what social structure could possibly consist of may, as an empirical and inspectable matter in persons' talk and conduct, reside. This can be seen with respect to an orientation to relation-ships as they are made relevant by participants in their conversation.

Notes

This research was funded by a grant from the ESRC, no. G00230092. A version of this paper was given to the Talk and Social Structure Conference. I am indebted to Deirdre Boden and Don Zimmerman for their comments and assistance on previous drafts.

1 This phrase is not being used as a general and abstract category of relationship. To propose this usage would be to make "standing" interaction-ally disembodied. Rather, it gains a technical sense in conversationalists' actual orientation to one another in the details of their talk as displaying an orientation to conversation-in-a-series. That is, it is in displaying an orientation to conversation-in-a-series that participants build into their talk an understanding of a category of relationship as relevant for their conduct. Thus "standing" as a relational category has only that definitive sense which is displayed on actual occasions of participants' orientations to conversation-in-a-series. For some clear similarities, though some dissimilarities, of interest, see Maynard and Zimmerman (1984).

2 Schegloff and Sacks (1973), Pomerantz (1975), Davidson (1978), and Jefferson (1984b) make reference to activities that may be closing implicative.

3 Some of the extracts that will be presented involve closings in which the interactants organize a movement out of closings. Although this issue will not be elaborated here (see Button 1987 for a comprehensive examination), it can be noted, however, that the organization of a movement out of closings is

done in the actual closing section and thus, although talk may develop, and on some occasions substantially develop post the initiation of closings, its organization is accountable for in terms of the "sequence types" that may figure in closings once initiated.

4 See Garfinkel and Sacks (1970) and Heritage and Watson (1980) for systematic examinations of "formulating."

5 Schegloff and Sacks (1973) describe the general class of activities of which an "optimistic conclusion" is one, as "aphoristic conclusions." It is the proposal that the topic-in-progress may possibly be concluded which is the decisive feature of their organization.

6 See Pomerantz (1975) for a detailed description of the organization of assessments and second assessments.

7 The sequences examined take an "archetype" form of two turns in which first speaker produces the particular activity that is being considered, and second speaker either receipts or agrees, or in the case of assessments, offers a second assessment. However, expansions on this may take place which affect the possibility for conversation continuation or conversation closure. A full examination of this is not possible here. However, to indicate the sorts of concerns that may be at issue, consider 11.7 above. Here A does not just mark the receipt of, or just agree to the projected activity. Rather (as described in Button 1987), she possibly initiates a closing section with her "Okay honey," then changes the shape of her turn by introducing arrangement-related material. This organizes a minimal movement out of closings and provides for a minimal return, following which closings may be reinitiated. The continuation of the extract on page 257 shows this. Thus, A is able to elaborate upon the projected activity whilst still orienting to the possibility of conversation closure.

8 Sacks elaborates upon this in his lecture of February 19, 1971 and describes how topic flow is a product of conversationalists preserving understanding in the design of their utterances.

9 See Button and Casey (1984, 1985) for a detailed description of these sequences of conversation.

10 The exceptions are "announcements of closure," "reintroducing arrangement items," and "arrangement resolution." The second and third sequences will figure in this examination. A reason why they do not methodically provide for the possibility of a new topic initiation has to do with their organization, used as a method for providing for the initiation of a closing section by placing conversation on a closing track (see below). The announcement of closure also operates to provide for the initiation of a closing section by its very announcement of a warrant (Schegloff and Sacks 1973) for closing initiation. It, however, will not be considered in the following text. Thus from now on attention will be focused on the relevant sequence types.

11 The phrase "apparently unilateral" is being used to mark out a difference with the way in which topic may be introduced when a warrant for talking on-topic is established through the collaborative production of a sequence of talk designed to provide for on-topic talk. The apparently unilateral initiation of a

topic is where one participant provides for on-topic talk in a next turn. For example, as with reason-for-call initiation. For a detailed examination of these issues see Button and Casey 1989.

12 Arrangements may give way to other topics through at least two ways in which any topic for conversation may methodically result in a further topic. In the first, a topic may be organized to coincide with reason for call; conversationalists may, however, provide for their conversation as having more than one topic, and consequently may organize a further topic beyond the reason for call. The second is where a topic may be organized to flow from out of the topic of arrangements. For example, where something may "trigger off" a further topic.

13 There are "good interactional reasons" for this: should arrangements that involve meeting, or coming together, or activities to be undertaken in the future be at issue, then checking them out, or having them be the last thing talked to, may maximize the possibility of productive expenditure of resources involved in meeting people.

Transcription Appendix

The conversational materials in this book are transcribed according to a detailed method of notation developed by Gail Jefferson. Based on audio and video materials, the transcription conventions are an evolving set of symbols designed to capture for the reader the interactional nuances of the talk. Those presented here are a subset of the large and growing system of symbols used to document the material of conversation analysts, standardized to facilitate scholarly exchange of materials, and used by researchers in conjunction with audio or video recordings. This appendix borrows heavily from two excellent and more extended discussions of transcription notation in Atkinson and Heritage (1984) and Button and Lee (1987).

The transcription notations presented here are grouped in terms of the type of feature represented.

Simultaneity and Silence

Simultaneity
Speakers may start to speak simultaneously, indicated by double left-hand brackets:

A: → [[(Ah'll seh-)
J: → [[I'll see you inna few minutes then.

Utterances in progress may be overlapped by the utterance of another speaker; the onset of overlap is indicated by a left-hand bracket:

I came from the south *shore*,[uh
　　　　　　　　　　　　　　[yeah

The end of overlapping may also be indicated by a right-hand bracket:

'Ka:y, ⎡an' ho:w ⎤
⎣I worked⎦ with Chris on bo:th=

An alternative symbol for the phenomenon of simultaneity is the double slash(//):

A: ohh (0.4) coming from Boston oh//kay
C: // on the Expressway?

Continuous talk

Utterances may follow each other without perceptible silence or overlap. Where there is no audible gap or overlap between one utterance and the next, the "latching" is represented by equal signs:

A: Do you want us in.=
B: =That's a decision that *you* have to make

Equal signs may link continuous talk by a single speaker that has distributed across two lines of transcript in order to show an intervening overlap:

J: An⎡yway=
V: ⎣Yes
J: =.hh I'm jus . . .

Single right-handed brackets and equal signs are used when overlapping utterances end at the same time and are latched to a following utterance:

Tom: I used to smoke ⎡a lot⎤
Bob: ⎣I see⎦=
Ann: =So did I.

Gaps, pauses and silences in the course of talk

Intervals in talk are timed in tenths of a second and indicated in a parentheses either within turns:

I'm uh (0.4) looking fer Peter Lorenzes

or between turns:

A: So: when dja get i::n?
   (0.4)
B: 'Bout ten twenny,

with (.) denoting a very brief untimed pause:

Yes uh (.) I'm uh (0.4) looking fer Peter Lorenzes

Characteristics of Speech Delivery

Conventional punctuation symbols are used throughout these transcripts to indicate pacing and inflection of speech delivery, rather than as grammatical markers.

A colon indicates sustained sound of either vowel or consonant, or whole syllable:

Hello: this is Peet de Veer

more colons indicate more sustained "stretch":

A::::nd sort of recommendations of:- of what

Other standard punctuation markers are used as follows:

. A period denotes a falling intonation, not necessarily the end of a grammatical unit.
, A comma indicates a continuing intonation which may or may not occur at a grammatical phrase.
? A question mark indicates a rising intonation on a word or utterance, but not necessarily a question.
¿ A combined question mark and comma indicates a milder rising intonation on a word or utterance.
! An exclamation mark indicates an emphatic and animated tone but not necessarily an exclamation.

Emphasis is indicated in italics:

Becuz *they* would really be the *spring*.

Loudness is noted by sections of utterances in capital letters:

PLE*A::SE* DON'T *t*ell me we're travelling Thurs?da:::y!

Softness or delivery that is markedly quieter than surrounding talk is indicated with a degree sign at each end of the passage:

Oh. °I see,°

A single dash at the end of a word or word particle marks a "cut-off" or abruptly arrested utterance, which may be brief:

What do you see? as- as his difficulty.

or entail more extended cuts:

.hhhh I- I- I was living a life o- o- of a *fam*ily man

Laughter and other audible breathy sounds such as inhalations (.hhh or 'hh) and aspirations (hhh) are inserted where they occur in the speech stream:

Yeah, well- well, I'll ju(h)s*t* ski::p that pa(hhh)rt!
(.hhh) Heh-heh (.) *HE::H*!

Transcribers' Notations and Presentation Devices

Transcription doubts and difficulties:
Passages involving poor recording quality, competing sounds, or other features which impair intelligibility are transcribed either within parenthesis or, in even more doubtful cases, with parentheses enclosing blank space:

D: Nothing at all (.) ⎡Well *do*ne
P: ⎣(   )

Transcriber's descriptive comments:
Transcripts occasionally include brief descriptive remarks, enclosed in double parentheses and designed to characterize such issues as manner of delivery:

Sue: ((softly)) Thanks.

or relevant activity description:

Subs: ((reads)) . . . This slow development in . . .

or notable features of the interactional setting:

((ring-ring))

or related local sounds, for example, the clicking of a computer keyboard in parallel with talk:

C: Yhes I'd like to um: tst I'm at thirty one
seventeen uh tenth avenue sou:th?
kb[-------------------

CT: Mnhm
          -------]
 C: .hh Uh there's uh . . .

Presentation symbols:
Arrows are used in front of key lines of transcription to alert readers' attention to aspects of the analysis being developed in the text:

   →   *Ha*ng on I got a call on the other line.

In chapter 9 of this volume, the following symbol is used to denote the special "beep" on American phone calls that indicates that a second call is incoming on a subscriber's line:

   #-##

References

Alexander, J., Giesen, B., Munch, R., and Smelser, N.J. (eds) 1987: *The Micro–Macro Link*. Berkeley: University of California Press.

Atkinson, J.M. 1979a: Postscript: notes on practical implications and possibilities. In J.M. Atkinson and P. Drew, *Order in Court: The Organisation of Verbal Interaction in Judicial Settings*, London: Macmillan, 217–32.

—— 1979b: Sequencing and shared attentiveness to court proceedings. In G. Psathas (ed.), *Everyday Language*, New York: Irvington.

—— 1982: Understanding formality: notes on the categorisation and production of "formal" interaction. *British Journal of Sociology*, 33, 86–117.

—— 1983: Two devices for generating audience approval: a comparative study of public discourse and texts. In K. Ehlich and H. van Riemsdijk (eds), *Connectedness in Sentence, Discourse and Text*, Tilburg: Katholieke Hogeschool Tilburg (Tilburg Studies in Language and Literature 4).

—— 1984: *Our Masters' Voices: The Language and Body Language of Politics*. London: Methuen.

Atkinson, J.M. and Drew, P. 1979: *Order in Court: The Organisation of Verbal Interaction in Judicial Settings*. London: Macmillan.

Atkinson, J.M. and Heritage, J. (eds) 1984: *Structures of Social Action: Studies in Conversation Analysis*, Cambridge: Cambridge University Press.

Au, K.H. 1980: On participation structures in reading lessons. *Anthropology and Education Quarterly* 11, 91–115.

Austin, J.L. 1962: *How to Do Things with Words*. Cambridge, Mass.: Harvard University Press.

Berens, J.F. 1981: Dialogeröffnung in Telephongesprächen: Handlungen und Handlungsschemata der herstellung sozialer und kommunikativer Beziehungen. In P. Shroeder and H. Steger (eds), *Dialogforschung*, Düsseldorf: Schwann, 402–18.

Bittner, E. 1967a: Police discretion in emergency apprehension of mentally ill persons. *Social Problems*, 14, 278–92.
—— 1967b: The police on skid-row: a study of peace keeping. *American Sociological Review* 32, 699–715.
Blau, P.M. 1977: *Inequality and Heterogeneity: A Primitive Theory of Social Structure*. New York: Free Press/Macmillan.
—— 1987: Contrasting theoretical perspectives. In Alexander et al. (eds), *The Micro-Macro Link*, Berkeley: University of California Press, 71–85.
Boden, D. 1983: Talk international: an examination of turn-taking in seven Indo-European languages. Paper presented at the American Sociological Association meetings, Detroit.
—— 1989: Everyday life as history: President Kennedy and the Mississippi Crisis. Keynote paper presented at the First Annual International Conference on Language Use in Everyday Life, Calgary, Canada.
—— 1990: The world as it happens: ethnomethodology and conversation analysis. In G. Ritzer (ed.), *Frontiers of Social Theory: The New Synthesis*, New York: Columbia University Press, 185–213.
—— forthcoming: *The Business of Talk: Organizations in Action*. Cambridge: Polity Press.
Booth, T.A. 1978: From normal baby to handicapped child: unravelling the idea of subnormality in families of handicapped children. *Sociology*, 12, 203–21.
Bourdieu, P. 1981: Men and machines. In K. Knorr-Cetina and A.V. Cicourel (eds), *Advances in Social Theory and Methodology: Toward an Integration of Micro- and Macro-sociologies*, London: Routledge and Kegan Paul: 304–17.
Burt, R.S. 1982: *Toward a Social Theory of Action*. New York: Academic Press.
Button, G. 1986: Moving out of closings. In G. Button and J.R.E. Lee (eds), *Talk and Social Organisation*, Avon: Multilingual Matters, 101–51.
—— 1987: Answers as interactional products: two sequential practices used in interviews. *Social Psychology Quarterly*, 50, 160–71.
—— 1990: On varieties of closings. In G. Psathas (ed.), *Interaction Competence*, Washington, DC.: University Press of America, 93–147.
Button, G. and Casey, N.J. 1984: Generating topic: the use of topic initial elicitors. In J.M. Atkinson and J.C. Heritage (eds), *Structures of Social Action: Studies in Conversation Analysis*, Cambridge: Cambridge University Press, 167–90.
—— 1985: Topic nomination and topic pursuit. *Human Studies* 8, 3–55.
—— 1989: Topic initiation: business-at-hand *Research on Language and Social Interaction*, 22, 61–92.
Button, G. and Lee, J.R.E. (eds) 1986: *Talk and Social Organisation*, Avon: Multilingual Matters.
Cicourel, A.V. 1964: *Method and Measurement in Sociology*. New York: The Free Press.
—— 1967: *The Social Organization of Juvenile Justice*. New York: Wiley.
—— 1974: *Cognitive Sociology*. New York: Free Press.
—— 1975: *Theory and Method in a Study of Argentine Fertility*. New York: Wiley-Interscience.

—— 1981a: Notes on the integration of micro- and macro-levels of analysis. In K. Knorr-Cetina and A. Cicourel (eds), *Advances in Social Theory and Methodology: Toward an Integration of Micro- and Macro-Sociology*, London: Routledge and Kegan Paul, 51–80.

—— 1981b: Language and medicine. In C.A. Ferguson and S.B. Heath (eds), *Language in the USA*. Cambridge: Cambridge University Press.

—— 1981c: The role of cognitive-linguistic concepts in understanding everyday social interactions. *Annual Review of Sociology*, 7, 87–106.

—— 1987: The interpenetration of communicative contexts: examples from medical encounters. *Social Psychology Quarterly*, 50, 217–26.

Cicourel, A.V. and Mehan, H. 1985: Universal development, stratifying practices and status attainment. *Research in Social Stratification and Mobility*, 4, 3–27.

Clayman, S. 1987: *Generating News: The Interactional Organization of News Interviews*. Unpublished PhD dissertation, University of California, Santa Barbara.

—— 1988: Displaying neutrality in television news interviews. *Social Problems*, 35, 474–92.

—— 1989: The production of punctuality: social interaction and temporal organization. *American Journal of Sociology* 95, 659–91.

—— forthcoming: Footing in the achievement of neutrality: the case of news interview discourse. In P. Drew and J. C. Heritage (eds), *Talk at Work*. Cambridge: Cambridge University Press.

Clayman, S. and Whalen, J. 1989: When the medium becomes the message: the case of the Rather–Bush encounter. *Research on Language and Social Interaction*, 22, 241–72.

Cole, M., and Traupmann, K. 1980: *Comparative Cognitive Research: Learning From a Learning Disabled Child*. Minnesota Symposium on Child Development. Minneapolis: University of Minnesota Press.

Coleman, J.S. 1987: Microfoundations and macrosocial behavior. In Alexander et al. (eds), *The Micro–Macro Link*, Berkeley: University of California Press, 153–73.

Collins, J. 1986: Differential treatment in reading instruction. In J. Cook-Gumperz (ed.), *The Social Construction of Literacy*, New York: Cambridge University Press.

Collins, R. 1981: Micro-translation as a theory-building strategy. In K. Knorr-Cetina and A. Cicourel (eds), *Advances in Social Theory and Methodology: Toward an Integration of Micro- and Macro-Sociology*, London: Routledge and Kegan Paul, 81–108.

—— 1987: Interaction ritual chains, power and property: the micro–macro connection as an empirically based theoretical problem. In Alexander et al. (eds), *The Micro–Macro Link*, Berkeley: University of California Press, 193–206.

—— 1988: The micro contribution to macro sociology. *Sociological Theory*, 6, 242–53.

Cook-Gumperz, J. 1986: *The Social Construction of Literacy*. New York: Cambridge University Press.

Coser, L. 1975a: Two methods in search of a substance. *American Sociological Review*, 40, 691–700.

—— 1975b: Structure and conflict. In P.M. Blau (ed.), *Approaches to the Study of Social Structure*, New York: Free Press, 210–19.

Coulter, J. 1979: *The Social Construction of Mind*. Totowa, NJ: Rowman and Littlefield.

—— 1989: *Mind in Action*. Cambridge: Polity Press.

Davidson, J.A. 1978: An instance of negotiation in a call closing. *Sociology*, 12, 123–33.

Davies, P. 1978: *Assessing Others: An Interactional Study of the Discourse and Text of Juvenile Assessments*. Unpublished PhD Dissertation, University of California, San Diego.

Davis, A.G. 1982: *Children in Clinics: A Sociological Analysis of Medical Work With Children*. London: Tavistock.

van Dijk, T. (ed.) 1985: *Handbook of Discourse Analysis*, vol. 3: *Discourse and Dialogue*. London: Academic Press.

Dore, J. and McDermott, R.P. 1982: Linguistic indeterminancy and social context in utterance interpretation. *Language*, 58, 374–98.

Dunstan, R. 1980: Context for coercion: analyzing properties of courtroom questions. *British Journal of Law and Society*, 6, 61–77.

Durkheim, E. 1937 [1895]: *Les Règles de la Méthode Sociologique*. Paris: Quadrige/Presses Universitaires de France.

—— 1938 [1895]: *Rules of Sociological Method*, trans. George Kaplin. New York: Free Press.

—— 1952: *Suicide*. New York: Free Press.

Edgerton, R. 1967: *The Cloak of Competence*. Berkeley: University of California Press.

Emerson, J.P. 1969: Negotiating the serious import of humour. *Sociometry*, 32, 169–81.

Emerson, R. 1969: *Judging Delinquents*. Chicago: Aldine.

Epstein, E.J. 1973: *News from Nowhere*. New York: Viking.

Erickson, F. 1975: Gatekeeping and the melting pot. *Harvard Educational Review*, 45, 40–70.

—— 1986: Qualitative Research on Teaching. In M.D. Wittrock (ed.), *Handbook on Teaching*. New York: Macmillan.

Erickson, F. and Schultz, J. 1982: *The Counselor as Gatekeeper*. New York: Academic Press.

Fisher, S. 1983: Doctor talk/patient talk: how treatment decisions are negotiated in doctor–patient communication. In S. Fisher and A.D. Todd (eds), *The Social Organization of Doctor–Patient Communication*, Washington, DC: Center for Applied Linguistics.

—— 1984: Institutional authority and the structure of discourse. *Discourse Processes*, 7, 201–24.

Fisher, S. and Todd, A.D. (eds) 1983: *The Social Organization of Doctor–Patient Communication*. Washington, DC: Center for Applied Linguistics.

Frake, C.O. 1983: Plying frames can be dangerous. *Quarterly Newsletter of the*

Laboratory of Comparative Human Cognition, San Diego.

Frankel, R.M. 1983: The laying on of hands: aspects of the organization of gaze, touch, and talk in a medical encounter. In S. Fisher and A.D. Todd (eds), *The Social Organization of Doctor–Patient Communication*, Washington, D.C.: Center for Applied Linguistics.

—— 1984: From sentence to sequence: understanding the medical encounter through micro-interactional analysis. *Discourse Processes*, 7, 135–70.

—— 1990: Talking in interviews: a dispreference for patient-initiated questions in physician–patient encounters. In G. Psathas (ed.), *Interaction Competence*, Washington, DC: University Press of America, 231–62.

Garfinkel, H. 1967: *Studies in Ethnomethodology*. Englewood Cliffs, NJ: Prentice-Hall (also Cambridge: Polity Press, 1984).

—— 1987: Studies in ethnomethodology: a reflection. *DARG Newsletter*, 3, 5–9.

—— 1988: Evidence for locally produced, naturally accountable phenomena of order: an announcement of studies. *Sociological Theory*, 6, 103–9.

Garfinkel, H. and Sacks, H. 1970: On formal structures of practical actions. In C. McKinney and E.A. Tiryakian (eds), *Theoretical Sociology*, New York: Appleton-Century-Crofts, 338–66.

Garfinkel, H., Lynch, M. and Livingston, E. 1981: The work of a discovering science construed from materials from the optically discovered pulsar. *Philosophy of the Social Sciences*, 11, 131–58.

Garfinkel, H., Lynch, M., Livingston, E. and MacBeth, D. 1986: Respecifying the natural sciences as discovering sciences of practical action. Keynote paper presented at the International Conference on Talk and Social Structure, University of California, Santa Barbara.

Giddens, A. 1971: *Capitalism and Modern Social Theory*. Cambridge: Cambridge University Press.

—— 1976: *New Rules of the Sociological Method*. New York: Basic Books.

—— 1979: *Central Problems in Social Theory*. Berkeley: University of California Press.

—— 1984: *The Constitution of Society: Outline of the Theory of Structuration*. Cambridge: Polity Press.

Givon, T. (ed.) 1979: *Syntax and Semantics 12: Discourse and Syntax*. New York: Academic Press.

Goffman, E. 1959: *The Presentation of Self in Everyday Life*. New York: Doubleday.

—— 1961: *Encounters*. Indianapolis: Bobbs-Merrill Educational.

—— 1971: *Relations in Public*. New York: Basic Books.

—— 1981: *Forms of Talk*. Philadelphia: University of Pennsylvania Press.

—— 1983a: The interaction order. *American Sociological Review* 48, 1–17.

—— 1983b: Felicity's condition. *American Journal of Sociology*, 89, 1–53.

Goodwin, C. 1981: *Conversational Organization: Interaction between Speakers and Hearers*. New York: Academic Press.

Goodwin, C. and Heritage, J. 1990: Conversation analysis. *Annual Review of Anthropology*, 19, 283–307.

Greatbatch, D. 1985: *The Social Organisation of News Interview Interaction*. Unpublished PhD dissertation, University of Warwick, England.

—— 1986a: Aspects of topical organisation in news interviews: the use of agenda shifting procedures by interviewees. *Media, Culture and Society*, 8, 441–55.

—— 1986b: Some standard uses of supplementary questions in news interviews. *Belfast Working Papers in Language and Linguistics*, vol. 8, University of Ulster, 86–123.

—— 1988: A turn taking system for British news interviews. *Language in Society*, 17, 401–30.

—— forthcoming: The management of disagreement between news interviewees. In P. Drew and J. Heritage (eds), *Talk at Work*. Cambridge: Cambridge University Press.

Greatbatch, D. and Heritage, J. in preparation: *The News Interview: Studies in the History and Dynamics of a Social Form*. London: Sage.

Grimshaw, A.D. 1981: *Language as Social Resource*. Stanford: Stanford University Press.

Gumperz, J. 1971: *Language in Social Groups*. Stanford: Stanford University Press.

—— 1982: *Discourse Strategies*. Cambridge: Cambridge University Press.

Gumperz J. and Herasimchuk, E. 1975: Sociocultural dimensions of language use. In M. Sanches and B.G. Blount (eds), *The Conversational Analysis of Meaning: A Study of Classroom Interaction*. New York: Academic Press.

Gumperz, J. and Hymes, D.H. 1972: *Directions in Sociolinguistics*. New York: Holt, Rinehart and Winston.

—— 1986: *New Directions in Sociolinguistics*. Oxford: Basil Blackwell.

Gurwitsch, A. 1966: *Studies in Phenomenology and Psychology*. Evanson, IL: Northwestern University Press.

Gusfield, J. 1981: *The Culture of Public Problems*. Chicago: University of Chicago Press.

Hall, S. 1973: A world at one with itself. In S. Cohen and J. Young (eds), *The Manufacture of News*, London: Constable, 85–94.

Harris, S. 1986: Interviewers' questions in broadcast interviews. In J. Wilson and B. Crow (eds), *Belfast Working Papers in Language and Linguistics*, vol. 8, University of Ulster, 50–85.

ten Have, P. 1987: *Sequenties en formuleringen: Aspekten van de interactionele organisatie van huisarts-spreekuurgesprekken* (Sequences and formulations: aspects of the interactional organization of medical consultations in General Practice). Dordrecht/Providence, R.I.: Foris.

—— 1989: The consultation as a genre. In B. Torode (ed.), *Text and Talk as Social Practice*, Dordrecht/Providence, R.I.: Foris, 115–35.

Heath, C. 1981: The opening sequence in doctor–patient interaction. In P. Atkinson and C. Heath (eds), *Medical Work: Realities and Routines*. Farnborough: Gower, 71–90.

—— 1982a: The display of recipiency: an instance of a sequential relationship in speech and body movement. *Semiotica*, 42, 147–67.

—— 1982b: Preserving the consultation: medical record cards and professional conduct. *Journal of the Sociology of Health and Illness*, 4, 56–74.

—— 1986: *Body Movement and Speech in Medical Interaction.* Cambridge: Cambridge University Press.

—— in press: The delivery and reception of diagnosis in the general practice consultation. In P. Drew and J. Heritage (eds), *Talk at Work.* Cambridge: Cambridge University Press.

Hechter, M. 1983: *The Microfoundations of Macrosociology.* Philadelphia: Temple University Press.

Heritage, J. 1984a: *Garfinkel and Ethnomethodology.* Cambridge: Polity Press.

—— 1984b: A Change of state token and aspects of its sequential placement. In J.M. Atkinson and J. Heritage (eds), *Structures of Social Action: Studies in Conversation Analysis,* Cambridge: Cambridge University Press, 299–345.

—— 1985a: Analyzing news interviews: aspects of the production of talk for an "overhearing" audience. In T. van Dijk (ed.), *Handbook of Discourse Analysis,* vol. 3: *Discourse and Dialogue.* London: Academic Press, 95–119.

—— 1985b: Recent developoments in conversation analysis. *Sociolinguistics,* 15, 1–19.

—— 1988: Explanations as accounts: a conversation analytic perspective. In C. Antaki (ed.), *Analyzing Lay Explanations: A Casebook of Methods,* London: Sage, 127–44.

—— 1989: Current developments in conversation analysis. In D. Roger and P. Bull (eds), *Conversation: An Interdisciplinary Perspective,* Clevedon: Multilingual Matters, 21–47.

Heritage, J. and Greatbatch, D. 1986: Generating applause: a study of rhetoric and response at political conferences. *American Journal of Sociology,* 92, 110–57.

Heritage, J. and Watson, D.R. 1979: Formulations as conversational objects. In G. Psathas (ed.), *Everyday Language: Studies in Ethnomethodology,* New York: Irvington, 123–62.

—— 1980: Aspects of the properties of formulations in natural conversation: some instances analyzed. *Semiotica,* 30, 245–62.

Heritage, J., Clayman, S. and Zimmerman, D.H. 1988: Discourse and message analysis: the micro structure of mass media messages. In R. Hawkins, J.M. Wiemann and S. Pingree (eds), *Advancing Communication Science: Merging Mass and Interpersonal Processes.* Sage Annual Reviews of Communication Research, vol. 16, Newboury Park: Sage, 77–109.

Hilbert, R.A. 1984: The acultural dimensions of chronic pain: flawed reality construction and the problem of meaning. *Social Problems,* 31, 365–78.

Hobbes, T. 1962: *Leviathan,* ed. M. Oakeshott. York: Collier.

Hood, L., McDermott, R.P. and Cole, M. 1980: Let's try to make it a good day – some not so simple ways. *Discourse Processes,* 3, 115–68.

Houtkoop, H. 1986: Summarizing in doctor–patient interaction. In Ensink, T. et al. (eds), *Discourse Analysis and Public Life,* Dordrecht/Providence, R.I.: Foris, 201–21.

Houtkoop, H. and Mazeland, H. 1985: Turns and discourse units in everyday conversation. *Journal of Pragmatics,* 9, 595–619.

Hudson, R.A. 1980: *Sociolinguistics*. Cambridge: Cambridge University Press.

Hymes, D. 1974: *Foundations in Sociolinguistics*. Philadelphia: University of Pennsylvania Press.

Jefferson, G. 1972: Side sequences. In D. Sudnow (ed.), *Studies in Social Interaction*, New York: Free Press, 294–338.

—— 1974: Error correction as an interactional resource. *Language in Society*, 2, 181–99.

—— 1978: Sequential aspects of storytelling in conversation. In J. Schenkein (ed.), *Studies in the Organization of Conversational Interaction*, New York: Academic Press, 219–48.

—— 1979: A technique for inviting laughter and its subsequent acceptance/declination. In G. Psathas (ed.), *Everyday Language: Studies in Ethnomethodology*, New York: Irvington, 79–96.

—— 1981a: The abominable "ne?": a working paper exploring the phenomenon of post-response pursuit of response. Occasional paper 6, University of Manchester, Department of Sociology.

—— 1981b: "Caveat speaker": a preliminary exploration of shift implicative recipiency in the articulation of topic. Final Report to the (British) SSRC.

—— 1984a: Notes on a systematic deployment of the acknowledgement tokens "yeah" and "mm hm." *Papers in Linguistics*, 17, 197–206.

—— 1984b: On stepwise transition from talk about a trouble to inappropriately next-positioned matters. In J.M. Atkinson and J. Heritage (eds), *Structures of Social Action: Studies in Conversation Analysis*, Cambridge: Cambridge University Press, 191–222.

—— 1989: Preliminary notes on a possible metric which provides for a "standard maximum" silence of approximately one second in conversation. In D. Roger and P. Bull (eds), *Conversation: An Interdisciplinary Perspective*, Clevedon: Multilingual Matters, 156–97.

—— 1990: List-construction as a task and a resource. In G. Psathas (ed.), *Interaction Competence*, Washington, DC: University Press of America, 63–92.

Jefferson, G. and Lee, J. 1980: The analysis of conversations in which "troubles" and "anxieties" are expressed. Final Report to the Social Science Research Council. Manchester, England: University of Manchester.

—— 1981: The rejection of advice: managing the problematic convergence of a "trouble-telling" and a "service encounter". *Journal of Pragmatics*, 55, 399–422.

Jefferson, G. and Schegloff, E.A. 1975: Sketch: some orderly aspects of overlap in natural conversation. Paper presented at the meeting of the American Anthropological Association, December 1975.

Jefferson, G., Sacks, H. and Schegloff, M. 1986: On laughter in the pursuit of intimacy. In G. Button and J. Lee (eds), *Talk and Social Organisation*. Avon: Multilingual Matters.

Jucker, A. 1986: *News Interviews: A Pragmalinguistic Analysis*. Philadelphia: John Benjamins.

Jules-Rosette, B. 1976: The conversion experience. *Journal of Religion in Africa*, 7, 132–64.

Kasanin, J. S. 1944: *Language and Thought in Schizophrenia.* Berkeley: University of California Press.

Kitsuse, J.I. and Cicourel, A.V. 1963: *Educational Decision Makers.* Indianapolis, IN: Bobbs-Merrill.

Knorr-Cetina, K. 1981: *The Manufacture of Knowledge: An Essay on the Constructivist and Contextualized Nature of Science.* Oxford: Pergamon.

Knorr-Cetina, K. and Cicourel, A.V. 1981: *Advances in Social Theory and Methodology.* London: Routledge and Kegan Paul.

Knorr-Cetina, K. and Mulkay, M. 1983: *Science Observed: Perspectives on the Social Study of Science.* London and Beverly Hills: Sage.

Kuhn, T. 1970: *The Structure of Scientific Revolutions.* Chicago: University of Chicago Press.

Labov, W. 1972: *Sociolinguistic Patterns.* Philadelphia: University of Pennsylvania Press.

Labov, W. and Fanshel, D. 1977: *Therapeutic Discourse.* New York: Academic Press.

Latour, B. and Woolgar, S. 1986: *Laboratory Life: The Construction of Scientific Facts.* Princeton: Princeton University Press.

Levelt, W.J.M. 1983: Monitoring and self-repair in speech. *Cognition,* 14, 41–104.

Levinson, S.C. 1979: Activity types and language. *Linguistics,* 17, 356–99.

—— 1983: *Pragmatics.* Cambridge: Cambridge University Press.

—— 1988: Putting linguistics on a proper footing: explorations in Goffman's concepts of participation. In P. Drew and A. Wootton (eds), *Erving Goffman: Exploring the Interaction Order.* Cambridge: Polity Press, 161–227.

Liberman, K. 1986: *Understanding Interaction in Central Australia: An Ethnomethodological Study of Australian Aboriginal People.* London: Routledge and Kegan Paul.

Livingston, Eric 1986: *The Ethnomethodological Foundations of Mathematics.* London: Routledge and Kegan Paul.

Lukes, S. 1972: *Emile Durkheim: His Life and Work.* New York: Harper and Row.

Lynch, M. 1982: Technical work and critical inquiry: investigations in a scientific laboratory. *Social Studies of Science,* 12, 499–534.

—— 1985: *Art and Artifact in Laboratory Science.* London: Routledge and Kegan Paul.

Lynch, M., Livingston, E. and Garfinkel, H. 1983: Temporal order in laboratory work. In K. Knorr-Cetina and M. Mulkay (eds), *Science Observed: Perspectives in the Social Study of Science.* Beverly Hills: Sage, 207–38.

McDermott, R.P., Gospodinoff, K. and Aron, J. 1978: Criteria for an ethnographically adequate description of concerted activities and their contexts. *Semiotica,* 24, 245–75.

McHoul, A. 1978: The organisation of turns at formal talk in the classroom. *Language in Society,* 7, 183–213.

Maroules, N. 1985: *The Social Organization of Sentencing.* Unpublished PhD dissertation, University of California, San Diego.

Mather, L.M. 1973: Some determinants of the method of case disposition: decision-making by public defenders in Los Angeles. *Law and Society*, Winter, 187–217.

Maynard, D.W. 1984: *Inside Plea Bargaining*. New York: Plenum.

—— 1985: How children start arguments. *Language in Society*, 14, 1–29.

—— 1987: Language and social interaction. *Social Psychology Quarterly*, 50, v–vi.

—— 1988: Language, interaction and social problems. *Social Problems*, 35, 311–34.

—— 1989a: Perspective-display sequences in conversation. *Western Journal of Speech Communication*, 53, 91–113.

—— 1989b: Notes on the delivery and reception of diagnostic news regarding mental disabilities. In D. Helm, T. Anderson, A.J. Meehan and A. Rawls (eds), *New Directions in Sociology*. New York: Irvington.

—— 1989c: On the ethnography and the analysis of talk in institutional settings. In J. Holstein and G. Miller (eds), *New Perspectives on Social Problems*, Greenwich, CT: JAI Press, 127–64.

—— 1991: On the interactional and institutional bases of asymmetry in clinical discourse. *American Journal of Sociology*.

—— in press: On co-implicating recipients in the delivery of diagnostic news. In P. Drew and J. Heritage (eds), *Talk at Work* Cambridge: Cambridge University Press.

Maynard, D.W. and Clayman, S. 1991: The diversity of ethnomethodology. *Annual Review of Sociology*, 17, 385–418.

Maynard, D.W. and Wilson, T.P. 1980: On the reification of social structure. In S.G. McNall and G.N. Howe (eds), *Current Perspectives in Social Theory*, vol. 1, Greenwich CT: JAI Press, 287–322.

Maynard, D.W. and Zimmerman, D.H. 1984: Topical talk, ritual and the social organisation of relationships. *Social Psychology Quarterly*, 47, 301–16.

Mehan, H. 1978: Structuring school structure. *Harvard Educational Review*, 48, 311–88.

—— 1979: *Learning Lessons*. Cambridge, MA: Harvard University Press.

—— 1983: Assessing Children's Language Using Abilities. In J.H. Armer and A.D. Grimshaw (eds), *Methodological issues in comparative sociological research*, New York: Wiley.

Mehan, H. and Wood, H. 1975: *The Reality of Ethnomethodology*. New York: Wiley.

Mehan, H., Hertweck, A. and Meihls, J.L. 1986: *Handicapping the Handicapped: Decision Making in Students' Educational Careers*. Stanford: Stanford University Press.

Mercer, J. 1974: *Labeling the Mentally Retarded*. Berkeley: University of California Press.

Merleau-Ponty, M. 1968 [1964]: *The Visible and the Invisible*, ed. C. Lefort, trans. A. Lingis, Evanston, IL: Northwestern University Press.

Michaels, S. 1981: Sharing time: children's narrative style and differential access to literacy. *Language in Society*, 11, 423–42.

Mishler, E. 1984: *The Discourse of Medicine: Dialectics of Medical Interviews*. Norwood, NJ: Ablex.

Moerman, M. 1977: The preference for self-correction in a Tai conversational corpus. *Language*, 52, 872–82.

Moll, L. and Diaz, E. 1986: Bilingual communication and reading. *Elementary Education Journal*, 21, 23–49.

Molotch, H. and Boden, D. 1985: Talking social structure: discourse, dominance and the Watergate Hearings. *American Sociological Review*, 50, 273–88.

Nofsinger, R. 1975: The demand ticket. *Speech Monographs*, 42, 1–9.

O'Barr, W.M. 1982: *Linguistic Evidence: Language, Power and Strategy in the Courtroom*. New York: Academic Press.

Paget, M.A. 1983: On the work of talk: studies in misunderstanding. In S. Fisher and A.D. Todd (eds), *The Social Organization of Doctor–Patient Communication*, Washington, DC: Center for Applied Linguistics.

Parsons, T. 1937: *The Structure of Social Action*. New York: McGraw-Hill.

Philips, S. 1982: *The Invisible Culture: Communication in Classroom and Community on the Warmsprings Indian Reservation*. New York: Longmans.

Pollner, M. 1975: The very coinage of your brain: reality disjunctures and their resolution. *Philosophy of the Social Sciences*, 5, 411–30.

—— 1988: *Mundane Reason*. Cambridge: Cambridge University Press.

Pollner, M. and McDonald-Wikler, L. 1985: The social construction of unreality. *Family Process*, 24, 241–54.

Pomerantz, A.M. 1975: Second assessments: a study of some features of agreements/disagreements. Unpublished Ph.D. dissertation, University of California, Irvine.

—— 1980: Telling my side: "limited access" as a "fishing" device. *Sociological Inquiry*, 50, 186–98.

—— 1984a: Agreeing and disagreeing with assessments: some features of preferred/dispreferred turn shapes. In J.M. Atkinson and J. Heritage (eds), *Structures of Social Action: Studies in Conversation Analysis*, Cambridge: Cambridge University Press, 57–101.

—— 1984b: Giving a source or basis: the practice in conversation of telling "how I know". *Journal of Pragmatics*, 8, 607–25.

Psathas, G. 1979: *Everyday Language: Studies in Ethnomethodology*. New York: Irvington.

—— 1986a: The organization of directions in interaction. *Word*, 37, 83–91.

—— 1986b: Some sequential structures in direction-giving. *Human Studies*, 9, 231–45.

Psathas, G. and Kozloff, M. 1976: The structure of directions. *Semiotica*, 17, 111–30.

Ren, Juan 1989: Turn-taking in Mandarin Chinese. Unpublished M.A. thesis, Department of Sociology, University of California, Santa Barbara.

Robinson, M. and Sheehan, M. 1983: *Over the Wire and on TV: CBS and UPI in Campaign '80*. New York: Russell Sage Foundation.

Sacks, H. 1963: Sociological description. *Berkeley Journal of Sociology*, 8, 1–16.

—— 1964–5: Harvey Sacks: Lectures 1964–1965, edited by Gail Jefferson, with an introduction/memoir by Emanuel A. Schegloff, *Human Studies* (1989), 12(3–4) 211–393.

—— 1964–72: Lectures, unpublished mimeos, edited by G. Jefferson, 1964–68,

University of California, Los Angeles, and 1968–72, University of California, Irvine; Index to Harvey Sacks' Lectures 1964–72, by G. Jefferson, 1986, unpublished ms. See also Sacks, forthcoming, below.

—— 1972a: An initial investigation of the usability of conversational data for doing sociology. In D. Sudnow (ed.), *Studies in Social Interaction*, New York: Free Press, 31–74.

—— 1972b: On the analyzability of stories by children. In J.J. Gumperz and D. Hymes (eds), *Directions in Sociolinguistics*, New York: Holt, Rinehart and Winston, 325–45.

—— 1974: An analysis of the course of a joke's telling in conversation. In R. Bauman and J. Sherzer (eds), *Explorations in the Ethnography of Speaking*, Cambridge: Cambridge University Press, 337–53.

—— 1975: Everyone has to lie. In B. Blout and M. Sanches (eds), *Sociocultural Dimensions of Language Use*, New York: Academic Press, 57–80.

—— 1978: Some technical considerations of a dirty joke. In J. Schenkein (ed.), *Studies in the Organization of Conversational Interaction*, New York: Academic Press.

—— 1984: Notes on methodology. In J.M. Atkinson and J. Heritage (eds), *Structures of Social Action*. Cambridge: Cambridge University Press, 21–7.

—— 1987: On the preference for agreement and contiguity in conversation. (Edited by E. Schegloff from a public lecture at the 1973 Linguistic Institute held at the University of Michigan.) In G. Button and J.R.E. Lee (eds), *Talk and Social Organisation*, Avon: Multilingual Matters, 54–69.

—— forthcoming: *Harvey Sacks Lectures on Conversation*, vols 1 and 2, ed. G. Jefferson, with introduction by E. Schegloff. (Lectures 1964–72.) Oxford: Basil Blackwell.

Sacks, H., Schegloff, E. and Jefferson, G. 1974: A simplest systematics for the organization of turn-taking for conversation. *Language*, 50, 696–735.

Scannell, P. 1988: The communicative ethos of broadcasting. Paper presented to the International Television Studies Conference, British Film Institute, London, July.

—— in preparation: *Broadcasting and Modern Life*. London: Sage.

Scheff, T.J. 1966: *Being Mentally Ill: A Sociological Theory*. Chicago: Aldine.

—— 1968: Negotiating reality: notes on power in the assessment of responsibility. *Social Problems*, 16, 3–17.

Schegloff, E. 1967: The first five seconds: the order of conversational openings. Unpublished Ph.D. dissertation, Department of Sociology, University of California, Berkeley.

—— 1968: Sequencing in conversational openings. *American Anthropologist*, 70, 1075–95; reprinted in J. Gumperz and D.H. Hymes (eds), *Directions in Sociolinguistics*, New York: Holt, Rinehart and Winston, 1972.

—— 1972: Notes on a conversational practice: formulating place. In D. Sudnow (ed.), *Studies in Social Interaction*, New York: Macmillan/Free Press, 75–119.

—— 1979a: Identification and recognition in telephone conversation openings. In

G. Psathas (ed.), *Everyday Language: Studies in Ethnomethodology*. New York: Irvington Press, 23–78.

—— 1979b: The relevance of repair to syntax-for-conversation. In T. Givon (ed.), *Syntax and Semantics 12: Discourse and Syntax*, New York: Academic Press, 261–88.

—— 1980: Preliminaries to preliminaries: "Can I ask you a question?" *Language and Social Interaction*, special double issue of *Sociological Inquiry*, ed. D.H. Zimmerman and C. West, 50, 104–52.

—— 1982: Discourse as an interactional achievement: some uses of "uh huh" and other things that come between sentences. In D. Tannen (ed.), *Analyzing Discourse, Text and Talk* (University Roundtable on Languages and Linguistics, Washington, DC) Washington, DC: Georgetown University Press.

—— 1986a: Language processing and talk in interaction. Paper delivered at a Science Forum on Language Processing in Social Context, 600th Anniversary of the Founding of Heidelberg University, September 1986.

—— 1986b: On the organization of sequences as a source of "coherence" in talk-in-interaction. Paper delivered at the SRCD Conference on Development of Conversational Coherence, New Orleans, May 1986.

—— 1986c: The routine as achievement. *Human Studies*, 9, 111–52.

—— 1987a: Between micro and macro: contexts and other connections. In J. Alexander et al. (eds), *The Micro–Macro Link*, Berkeley: University of California Press.

—— 1987b: Analyzing single episodes of interaction: an exercise in conversation analysis. *Social Psychological Quarterly* 50, 101–14.

—— 1987c: Some sources of misunderstanding in talk-in-interaction. *Linguistics*, 25, 201–18.

—— 1988a: Goffman and the analysis of conversation. In P. Drew and A. Wootton (eds), *Erving Goffman: Exploring the Interaction Order*, Cambridge: Polity Press, 89–135.

—— 1988b: On an actual virtual servo-mechanism for guessing bad news: a single-case conjecture. *Social Problems* 35, 442–57.

—— 1989: From interview to confrontation: observations on the Bush/Rather encounter. *Research on Language and Social Action*, 22, 215–40.

—— 1990: On the organization of sequences as a source of "coherence" in talk-in-interaction. In Bruce Dorval (ed.), *Conversational Organization and its Development*, vol. 38 in the series, Advances in Discourse Processes, Norwood, NJ: Ablex, 51–77.

Schegloff, E. A. and Sacks, H. 1973 (1974): Opening up closings. *Semiotica*, 7, 289–327. Reprinted 1974 in Roy Turner (ed.), *Ethnomethodology*, Harmondsworth: Penguin, 233–64.

Schegloff, E., Jefferson, G. and Sacks, H. 1977: The preference for self-correction in the organization of repair for conversation. *Language*, 53, 361–82.

Schlesinger, P., Murdock, G. and Elliott, P. 1983: *Televising "Terrorism": Political Violence in Popular Culture*. London: Comedia.

Schutz, A. 1962: *Collected Papers I: The Problem of Social Reality.* The Hague: Martinus Nijhoff.

Scott, M.B. and Lyman, S.M. 1968: Accounts. *American Sociological Review*, 33, 46–62.

Searle, J. 1969: *Speech Acts.* Cambridge: Cambridge University Press.

—— 1975: Indirect speech acts. In P. Cole and J.L. Morgan (eds), *Syntax and Semantics*, vol. 3: *Speech Acts*, New York: Academic Press, 59–82.

Shannon, C.E. 1948: A mathematical theory of communication. *The Bell System Technical Journal*, 27, 379–423.

Sharrock, W.W. 1979: Portraying the professional relationship. In D.C. Anderson (ed.), *Health Education in Practice*, London: Croom Helm.

Sharrock, W.W. and Anderson, R. 1986: *The Ethnomethodologists.* Chichester: Ellis Horwood.

—— 1987: The definition of alternatives: some sources of confusion in interdisciplinary discussion. In G. Button and J.R.E. Lee (eds), *Talk and Social Organization*, Avon: Multilingual Matters.

Sharrock, W.W. and Turner, R. 1978: On a conversational environment for equivocality. In J. Schenkein (ed.), *Studies in the Organization of Conversational Interaction*, New York: Academic Press, 173–98.

Silverman, D. 1981: The child as a social object: Down's syndrome children in a pediatric cardiology clinic. *Sociology of Health and Illness*, 3.

Smelser, N. 1988: Social structure. In N. Smelser (ed.), *Handbook of Sociology*, Beverly Hills: Sage.

Stevenson, Robert Louis 1947 (1881): Talk and the Talkers. In Saxe Commins (ed.), *Selected Writings of Robert Louis Stevenson*, New York: Random House.

Streeck, J. 1980: Speech acts in interaction: a critique of Searle. *Discourse Processes*, 3, 133–53.

Strong, P.M. 1979: *The Ceremonial Order of the Clinic.* London: Routledge and Kegan Paul.

Sudnow, D. 1967: *Passing On: The Social Organization of Dying.* Englewood Cliffs, NJ: Prentice-Hall.

Tannen, D. and Wallet, C. 1983: Doctor/mother/child communication: linguistic analysis of a pediatric interaction. In S. Fisher and A.D. Todd (eds), *The Social Organization of Doctor–Patient Communication*, Washington, DC: Center for Applied Linguistics.

Terasaki, A. 1976: Pre-announcement sequences in conversation. *Social Science Working Paper 99*, Irvine: University of California.

Tilly, Charles. 1984: *Big Structures, Large Processes and Huge Comparisons.* New York: Russell Sage Foundation.

Todd, A.D. 1983: A diagnosis of doctor–patient discourse in the prescription of contraception. In S. Fisher and A.D. Todd (eds), *The Social Organization of Doctor–Patient Communication*, Washington, DC: Center for Applied Linguistics.

—— 1984: The prescription of contraception: negotiations between doctors and patients. *Discourse Processes*, 7, 171–200.

Tracey, M. 1977: *The Production of Political Television*. London: Routledge.

Waitzkin, H. 1983: *The Second Sickness: Contradictions of Capitalist Health Care*. New York: Free Press.

West, C. 1979: Against our will: male interruptions of females in cross-sex conversations. *Annals of the New York Academy of Science*, 327, 81–97.

—— 1982: Why can't a woman be more like a man? *Work and Occupations*, 9, 5–29.

—— 1983: "Ask me no questions . . .": an analysis of queries and replies in physician–patient dialogues. In S. Fisher and A.D. Todd (eds), *The Social Organization of Doctor–Patient Communication*, Washington, DC: Center for Applied Linguistics: 75–106.

—— 1984: *Routine Complications: Troubles in Talk Between Doctors and Patients*. Bloomington, IN: Indiana University Press.

West, C. and Zimmerman, D.H. 1977: Women's place in everyday talk: reflections on parent–child interaction. *Social Problems*, 24, 521–29.

—— 1983: Small insults: a study of interruptions in conversations between unacquainted persons. In B. Thorne and N. Henley (eds), *Language, Gender, and Society*, Rowley, MA: Newbury House, 102–17.

—— 1987: Doing gender. *Gender and Society*, 1, 125–51.

Whalen, M.R. and Zimmerman, D.H. 1987: Sequential and institutional contexts in calls for help. *Social Psychology Quarterly*, 50, 172–85.

—— 1990: Describing trouble: epistemology in citizen calls to the police. *Language in Society*, 19, 465–92.

Whalen, J., Zimmerman, D.H. and Whalen, M.R. 1988: When words fail: a single case analysis. *Social Problems*, 35, 335–62.

Wilson, T.P. 1970: Conceptions of interaction and forms of sociological explanation. *American Sociological Review*, 35, 697–710.

—— 1982: Qualitative oder Quantitative Methoden in der Sozialforschung. *Kölner Zeitschrift fur Soziologie und Sozialpsychologie*, 34, 487–508.

—— 1985: Social structure and social interaction. Unpublished ms., Department of Sociology, University of California, Santa Barbara.

—— 1986: Talk and institutional context. Paper presented at the annual meetings of the American Sociological Association, New York.

—— 1987: Sociology and the mathematical method. In A. Giddens and J. Turner (eds), *Social Theory Today*. Cambridge: Polity Press, 383–404.

—— 1989: Agency, structure and the explanation of miracles. Paper presented at the Midwest Sociological Society meetings, St Louis, Missouri.

Wilson, T.P. and Zimmerman, D.H. 1980: Ethnomethodology, sociology, and theory. *Humboldt Journal of Social Relations*, 7, 52–88.

Wilson, T.P., Wiemann, J.M. and Zimmerman, D.H. 1984: Models of turn taking in conversational interaction. *Journal of Language and Social Psychology*, 3, 159–83.

Zimmerman, D.H. 1976: A reply to Professor Coser. *American Sociologist*, 11, 4–13.

—— 1984: Talk and its occasion: the case of calling the police. In D. Schiffrin (ed.), *Meaning, Form, and Use in Context: Linguistic Applications*, Georgetown University Roundtable on Language and Linguistics, Washington, DC: Georgetown University Press, 210–28.

—— 1988: On conversation: the conversation analytic perspective. *Communication Yearbook 11*, 406–32.

—— forthcoming: The interactional organization of calls for emergency assistance. In P. Drew and J. Heritage (eds), *Talk at Work*, Cambridge: Cambridge University Press.

Zimmerman, D. and West, C. 1975: Sex roles, interruptions and silences in conversations. In B. Thorne and N. Henley (eds), *Language and Sex: Difference and Dominance*, Rowley, MA: Newbury House, 105–29.

—— (eds) 1980: *Language and Social Interaction. Sociological Inquiry* (special double issue), 50 (3–4).

Index